Cybermarketing

The Chartered Institute of Marketing/Butterworth-Heinemann Marketing Series is the most comprehensive, widely used and important collection of books in marketing and sales currently available worldwide.

As the CIM's official publisher, Butterworth-Heinemann develops, produces and publishes the complete series in association with the CIM. We aim to provide definitive marketing books for students and practitioners that promote excellence in marketing education and practice.

The series titles are written by CIM senior examiners and leading marketing educators for professionals, students, and those studying the CIM's Certificate, Advanced Certificate and Postgraduate Diploma courses. Now firmly established, these titles provide practical study support to CIM and other marketing students and to practitioners at all levels.

The Chartered
Institute of Marketing

Formed in 1911, The Chartered Institute of Marketing is now the largest professional marketing management body in the world with over 60,000 members located worldwide. Its primary objectives are focused on the development of awareness and understanding of marketing throughout UK industry and commerce and in the raising of standards of professionalism in the education, training and practice of this key business discipline.

Books in the CIM series

Forthcoming

Cybermarketing

How to use the Internet to market your goods and services

Second edition

Pauline Bickerton, Matthew Bickerton and Upkar Pardesi

*Published in association with
the Chartered Institute of Marketing*

OXFORD AUCKLAND BOSTON JOHANNESBURG MELBOURNE NEW DELHI

Butterworth-Heinemann
Linacre House, Jordan Hill, Oxford OX2 8DP
225 Wildwood Avenue, Woburn, MA 01801–2041
A division of Reed Educational and Professional Publishing Ltd

 A member of the Reed Elsevier plc group

First published 1996
Reprinted 1997 (twice), 1998
Second edition 2000

© Pauline Bickerton, Matthew Bickerton and Upkar Pardesi 2000

British Library Cataloguing in Publication Data
Bickerton, Pauline
   Cybermarketing: how to use the Internet to market your
   goods and services. – 2nd ed.
   1. Internet marketing
   I. Title   II. Bickerton, Matthew   III. Pardesi, Upkar
   IV. Chartered Institute of Marketing   V. Chartered Institute
   of Marketing
   658.8'00285'4678

Library of Congress Cataloguing in Publication Data
Bickerton, Pauline
   Cybermarketing: how to use the Internet to market your goods and services/Pauline
   Bickerton, Matthew Bickerton, and Upkar Pardesi – 2nd ed.
   p. cm
   Published in association with the Chartered Institute of Marketing.
   Includes bibliographical references and index.
   ISBN 0-7506-4704-3 (alk. paper)
   1. Internet marketing. 2. Internet advertising. I. Bickerton, Matthew.
   II. Pardesi, Upkar. III. Chartered Institute of marketing. IV. Title.
   HF5415.1265.B53
   658.8'4 – dc21   00-044449

ISBN 0 7506 4704 3

Printed and bound in Great Britain by
Biddles Ltd, Guildford and King's Lynn

Contents

Acknowledgements

We would like to extend a huge thank you to David Haggie and Jonathan Glasspool who helped massively to revise this book.

You were both marvellous and we could not have done this without you.

Read this first!

The Internet is no longer new. Most firms use it as an indispensable communications tool. It is an established focus of advertising spending. It is the biggest growing channel for sales and investment in any marketplace. Internet start-ups have become established companies, and the big players from the 'real world' have moved online. The once unexplored land has been colonized, and the rules of this new territory have started to become defined.

Since the first edition of *Cybermarketing* set out the core principles that would guide marketers as they went online, we have been learning from hundreds of companies as they started to market using the Internet. We believe that the experiments and successes of these early users have yielded important lessons. In this new edition, we have incorporated a vast amount of experience to set out what we believe is the established framework for success in the increasingly important virtual world.

The core of our vision of successful Internet marketing is the customer. While some firms have been led astray by technology and IT, the truly successful have used the net to apply the core concepts of traditional marketing in a new and powerful way. The paradox is clear. 'Customer focus' is traditional thinking, but its application on the net involves new and non-traditional approaches. Combining the best of the old *and* the new is the key to success on the Internet. This book is full of stories of companies adopting exactly that approach. In your world, the same model can bring you professional and organizational success, and this book will show you how to achieve it.

Focus on the customer

Internet technology has developed in an extraordinary way over the past decade. The numbers of users has risen exponentially, their computers have become faster and faster, and the software and lines that determine speeds of connection are becoming more and more sophisticated. More users, even faster computers and still broader-band lines are all on the way. But, however impressive, this technology does not, in itself, matter. The key is to understand the customers who use the network. As the Internet matures, it's becoming increasingly clear that the successful firms are the ones that build their businesses around people. Understanding why people use the net, what they expect from it, and how they communicate across it is critical to successful Internet marketing. In the early days of the technology, IT programmers took the lead. Now it's all about marketing.

Why the net gives the consumer more power

Marketers know that consumers always come first. But on the Internet their behaviour and preferences matter *even more* than they do in the traditional marketing environments like shops, television commercials and newspapers. On TV you can broadcast an advert into someone's home, and unless they're quick with the remote, they'll see it whether or not they want to. They don't choose to watch the adverts, but see them by accident. When a customer answers a call from a telephone sales firm he/she picks up the receiver because he/she doesn't know who's calling. (Anyone who has ever done telephone sales knows that they would get few replies if customers could tell who was on the phone!) If you're driving a car, it's hard to avoid seeing the billboards. Marketers have a certain degree of power, therefore, which expresses itself even in the language of the profession. They talk about 'penetrating' corners of a market, and 'exploiting' niches.

Online, different rules apply. Set up a website, and your potential customers have to choose to visit it. They have to type in your web address (your 'URL') into the top line of their web browser, and you can't do it for them. The customer is in control. It's as if the phone at home rang flashing a message, 'Double glazing salesman calling', and offered the user the choice, 'Answer or disconnect?' Web advertising presents the same picture. Web-ads are small – they have to be to leave room for the information that attracts visitors to the site where they are hosted. As a result they can't carry much information. To find out what the product's really about, Internet users have to click on the advert to reveal more details. Once again, the Internet user has the choice. It's not hard to see why the 'customer first' principle of marketing matters so much more on the net.

For companies, this means creating Internet materials that will entice users to choose to look at them. The customer must get something out of the experience, and so 90 per cent of what you do on the Internet must add value, 10 per cent can sell – any other combination fails. If you don't do this, your expensive website will lie dormant, ignored and unvisited by the Internet millions who know that they are in control. But if you do provide value, and present your public with offers, information and material they want to look at, you will be rewarded by access to a market that now encompasses most of the developed world.

Why has the Internet been so successful?

Millions of words have now been written explaining the success of the Internet. For the marketer, the most useful perspective is the user's. The Internet offers the user a cheaper, quicker and easier route to achieving various goals than any other technology. If, for example, you want to find some information, you may have to choose between going to the library, or going online. Logging on will save you time and effort (and probably money – there's no bus fare or petrol costs to pay). Not surprising, then, that so much information is collected from the net. Perhaps you want to buy something? If you travel to your local shop, you don't know if what you want will be in stock, and you don't know that the price will be competitive. Indeed, you may have to visit – or telephone – several shops to get the best deal. Online you can find a supplier and compare prices much more easily. If you think of the trouble taken to find information or compare prices in the real world as a 'cost', then it's clear that these costs fall online. The Internet allows its users to save costs, and so millions of people use it.

It also allows the firms supplying goods on the net to save costs. It's cheaper to store goods in a remote warehouse than in an Oxford Street store, and there are no sales assistants to pay. It's easier to do market research and sector analysis using online technology. As a result the online traders can undercut high street rivals, and pass at least some of this saving on to the consumer. Once again, the Internet offers lower costs and greater value to its customers. The success of the Internet, therefore, can be understood in simple, customer-focused, economic terms. It offers value.

Who benefits?

We have already seen that customers can benefit and online firms can benefit from the net. But so too can individual professional staff: the Internet offers you something, too! It enables the individual to gain and sustain competitive advantage by providing a

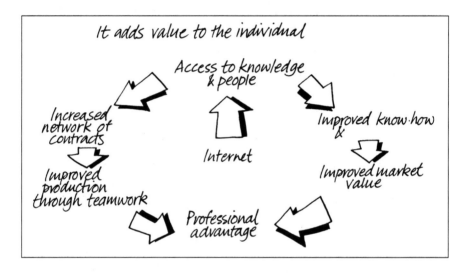

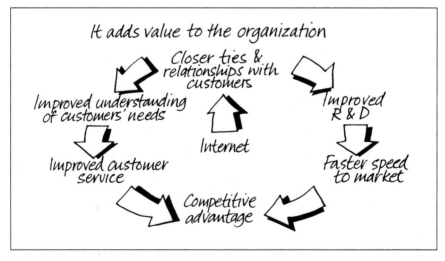

knowledge base and professional network of contacts. Successful people will be working smarter not harder; leveraging a network of contacts rather than re-inventing the wheel; relying on other people's knowledge bases rather than recreating one. Communicating will become critical to success and the Internet will be critical to communication. As Mary Cronin put it, 'Managed strategically, the Internet offers more than just a global lifeline to the future. It can become the key ingredient to leadership in the age of interconnectivity'.

Ongoing support – the *Cybermarketing* website

This book has been written to help you assess the Internet for yourself, and the book is accompanied by information on the Internet at:

http://www.marketingnet.com/cybermarketing

We have created an accompanying website for three reasons:

- to offer new users of the Internet a quick and easy way to get online and access relevant, professionally supportive information. The site also provides an easy one-stop shop to searching on the Internet, access to numerous sites which will excite and interest you, giving advice and reinforcing the messages in this book as you go.
- to strip out the Internet gobbledegook which appears in many of the Internet books, and enable you to look behind the hype and the mystique at some of the practical issues surrounding the Internet.
- to help you keep up to date. The principles in this book are now established, but the rapid pace of Internet evolution means points of fact will constantly change. The website allows us to present new and important developments which occur after publication.

The website works by displaying a summary of each chapter and linking references within it to the relevant companies' information on the Internet. Rather than giving the full Internet address, we include a link from the accompanying chapter online direct to these companies' websites.

So whenever you see a company name italicized in this book, it implies that there is a reference to it on the accompanying web chapter, e.g. *CD-Now* implies a web-page which you can visit by jumping from the accompanying web chapter.

Conclusion

This book will show you how to apply traditional marketing concepts for successful marketing using the Internet. It will also highlight challenges that a marketing person will face when confronted with this new medium and show in detail how successful companies have tackled these issues.

References

Business & Technology Magazine (Sept. 1995) published by Cromwell Media Ltd, London.

Mary Cronin (1995) *Doing More Business On The Internet*, Van Nostrand Reinhold, New York.

Chapter 1

Marketing with the Internet

Who is this book for?

This book has been written to help marketing professionals understand and use the Internet. It covers everything from market
research to delivering goods sold over the net. It is a practical book,
and is aimed at two groups.

- If you are new to the net, and have never written a website, set up
  an e-commerce facility or had to work out how the Internet fits in to
  your wider marketing strategy, this book will explain from first principles what you can do, and how you do it.
- If you do have some Internet experience, but feel you are not seeing the
  full benefits, this book will provide you with a set of powerful concepts
  which will help you improve your Internet results. We provide a series
  of models that explain, for example, how to analyse your market, prepare
  a marketing mix that works online and make judgements about online
  selling that will allow you to improve the results you get from the net.

We have also designed this book to help experienced marketers and
non-marketing professionals alike. Whenever we introduce a core
marketing concept (like 'segmentation', preparing a 'marketing
mix', or 'developing a marketing information system') we explain
from first principles what these ideas mean, why they are so
powerful, and how they can be used. Readers new to marketing as
well as seasoned professionals will be able to follow the advice and
guidance we have developed. You do not need to understand the
jargon of marketing and the Internet to use this book!

In this chapter we begin with a framework of the marketing planning process and we outline how the rest of the book has been structured.

Introduction to marketing

The term 'marketing' has become established in our everyday vocabulary, but unfortunately it is loosely used with many different interpretations. Many people associate marketing with, or confuse it to mean advertising, selling, packaging or public relations. It is not surprising therefore, to find that many proprietors, managers and employees in organizations invariably quote the words advertising and selling to mean marketing.

This misunderstanding can be explained by the fact that all of us, as employees, businesspeople or consumers are constantly exposed to media advertising and selling techniques by large multinational and retailing organizations. We have all been sold something: either in a store; on the doorstep; over the telephone; at work by a sales representative; through direct mail advertising or even via the Internet. So it is quite natural for employees and the general public to assume that marketing is something to do with advertising, selling or creating a company image.

The explosion in interest in the Internet as a new marketing medium has been accompanied by a plethora of articles, books, guides and online publications on 'How to market your business on the Internet'. Most of these publications have fallen into the classical trap of interpreting marketing to mean advertising, selling, online direct marketing and creating home pages to enhance the company's corporate image. Even some seasoned marketing professionals are seeing the Internet only as another means of promoting the company and its products around the globe. One possible reason for this narrow view is that much of the material published on the subject has been written by technocrats. Equally, many of the 'Internet marketing services agencies' that have mushroomed recently are managed by IT and computer specialists who have little understanding or experience of the marketing function.

In order to gain maximum benefit from the new communications medium, it is essential that marketing and non-marketing professionals are reminded of the essence of the marketing function prior to getting into detailed explanation of how to use the Internet as a marketing tool.

This chapter presents the 'big picture' and has two sections. We begin with the basic question: 'What is marketing?' by examining the purpose of any business organization and by explaining the marketing concept. Then we provide an overview of the marketing process, and highlight how the Internet can be used to provide access to valuable information and customers around the world.

Section I What is marketing?

The purpose of any business

When asked the question: 'What is the purpose of an organization?', the most common response is to make a profit. Obviously, firms must make profits in order to survive by reinvestment and by providing return to shareholder capital, but it is important to understand that profit comes from sales turnover. There is only one source of sales turnover, and that is from the firm's customers. Even in the non-profit-making and the public sector, the revenue generated is directly proportionate to the number of 'customers' served. The purpose of any business organization is much more than simply to make a profit by the manufacture and selling of goods or services.

Peter Drucker (1954) first proposed that the purpose of an organization is to create a customer or a customer base, and expressed it in the following terms:

*If we want to know what a business is, we have to start with its
purpose, and its purpose must be outside the business itself. In fact,
it must be in society, since a business enterprise is an organ of society.
There is one valid definition of business purpose: to create a customer.*

Levitt (1986) reinforced this message by emphasizing that 'the
purpose of business is to create and keep a customer'.

In reality, the ideal organizations are the market-orientated
businesses, large and small, that create and meet the needs of the
'customer'. The customer is created by means of identifying needs
in the marketplace, finding out which needs the organization can
profitably serve, and developing and offering to convert potential
buyers into customers of the firm. It is only through providing
customer satisfaction that organizations can achieve their goals,
such as survival, maximize profits or the attainment of other social
objectives. Drucker's definition of the purpose of the business in
society can be extended to provide an overall explanation of what
is meant by the term marketing.

What is marketing?

There are numerous formal definitions of marketing. In the UK, the
following definition, developed by the Chartered Institute of
Marketing, is accepted as one that encapsulates the essence of the
marketing function.

*Marketing is the management process responsible for identifying,
anticipating and satisfying customer requirements profitably.*

In addition to being an important business function, marketing is
an organizational philosophy – a concept, an approach or an
attitude to the way in which the organization is directed and
managed. The marketing concept is a business philosophy that
Kotler (1984) has expressed in the following terms:

*The marketing concept is a management orientation that holds that
the key task of an organization is to determine the needs, wants and
values of target markets and to adapt the organization to delivering
the desired satisfaction more effectively and efficiently than its
competitors, and to make a profit.*

This somewhat long definition can be broken down into four key components (those highlighted above) and explained more fully.

(a) Management orientation

The starting point of understanding the marketing concept is that it is a management orientation. This means that in order to successfully apply the marketing philosophy, an organization must be headed and managed by individuals who are themselves orientated towards meeting the needs of the customer. This attitude, or approach, to running the business must then permeate throughout the organization to ensure that it can survive and grow in a competitive environment.

Most organizations operate on the basis of one of the following three orientations:

- **Production orientation**: Making what the firm can or is best at and selling to whoever will buy it.
- **Selling orientation**: Placing major emphasis on advertising and selling to ensure sales.
- **Marketing orientation**: Place major emphasis on prior analysis of the needs of target markets and adapting products and services to meet those needs, if necessary.

Davidson (1987) has argued that in the UK, marketing orientation is an exception rather than the rule. This applies both in large and smaller firms. In smaller firms, the owners and/or partners represent the top layer of management and are agents for giving the organization its orientation and direction. But because most small firms are established by individuals with skills, crafts or ideas, the most common orientation and direction for the business operations is towards production and selling. Such production and sales-orientated businesses fail to create the necessary customer base to survive for very long in highly competitive markets.

The very successful businesses are those headed by entrepreneurial and marketing orientated chief executives. Alan Sugar (Amstrad), Richard Branson (Virgin) and Anita Roddick (Body Shop) are amongst the well known entrepreneurs who have built successful businesses by focusing their efforts on meeting the needs of their customers. Now, as larger organizations, these individuals still provide the management orientation and direction for the business operations, but have marketing directors and other marketing personnel to implement their corporate plans.

Management orientation is a starting-up point of implementing
the marketing concept and can be summarized as an attitude of
mind, and approach or a philosophy of running a business organization that regards the customer or the consumer as a focal point
around which all other decisions revolve.

Depending upon the size and nature of a business concern, a
typically marketing oriented organization has a marketing director,
and middle and junior marketing management personnel. The
appointment of marketing personnel is no longer confined to fast
moving consumer goods manufacturers such as chocolates,
cigarettes and beer. Local councils, hospitals, charities, bus companies and even political parties now employ marketing directors and
managers to market their products, services or ideas.

(b) Understand the needs, wants and values of target markets

The marketing concept is based on the principle that all the activities
of an organization should be geared to meeting the needs and wants
of its customers. This implies that the organization must allocate sufficient resources, attention and effort to constantly researching, monitoring and evaluating the needs, wants and changing values of those
customers. Organizational survival depends on the firm's ability to
secure repeat business amongst its customers. Repeat business or
purchase only occurs if and when customer satisfaction has been
achieved. An unsatisfied customer will, on the next occasion, buy a
competitor's product or service and may also spread unfavourable
word-of-mouth messages about a company or its products. Customer
satisfaction only results when the product, service or the organization
meets the exact needs, wants and values of its customers.

Needs

A need can be defined as a state of real or perceived deprivation.
It can also be thought of as a state of imbalance or dis-equilibrium.
For example, when an individual has gone without food for some
time, there is a feeling of deprivation, or imbalance between feeling
hungry and not feeling hungry. All human needs stem from our
basic physiological, social and individual needs for food, shelter,
warmth, safety, belonging, affection, knowledge and self-expres-
sion. A need can also be thought of as a problem. The recognition
of the problem prompts an individual towards problem-solving
behaviour. A hungry person therefore, will take action towards

correcting the imbalance or the problem, and buy or prepare something to eat. A need, or the recognition of a problem, is the starting point of all buying behaviour, including the buying behaviour in organizations for purchasing industrial products or services.

Wants

We translate our needs into wants that are heavily influenced by social and cultural norms or individual personality. For example, a need for clothing is not merely to serve the purpose of covering the body, but is translated into want of a fashionable pair of jeans that conforms to an individual's peer group behaviour and acceptance. The consumer in this case has not purchased a physical product but a number of benefits that may accrue from the label, manufacturer or design of the pair of jeans. Likewise, a manufacturer of chemical products may think that farmers need fertilizers and therefore place considerable effort in promoting and selling the features of his chemicals. What the farmers really need is greater yield of crops from their soil. Here, as customers for industrial products, the farmers would be buying benefits of a particular manufacturer's fertilizers and solving a common problem.

Whilst human needs remain constant – for example, we will always need clothing – our wants change in line with our age, fashion, economic conditions, technology culture and society.

Values

All customers have values made up of attitudes and beliefs that affect their perceptions and buying behaviour. Beliefs can also be thought of as knowledge, opinion or faith depending on whether they can be verified by personal experience or by research. An opinion is a belief which has not yet been verified, and faith is a belief that is unverifiable, but nevertheless adhered to.

For example, if customers believe that manufacturers of aerosol based products contribute to damaging the ozone layer, they may decide to stop using such products and look for alternatives. Manufacturers of deodorants and air fresheners have recently changed their products and emphasize their concern for the environment. In marketing terms therefore, we can see this as an example of how a customer's need for social acceptance and belonging has now been translated into a want of an 'ozone friendly' deodorant that would nevertheless ensure effective control of body odour.

An attitude can be defined as an individual's continuous favourable or unfavourable mental evaluation, emotional feelings, or tendency to act towards some object or idea. Attitudes influence beliefs and beliefs influence attitudes. Because attitudes involve thinking as well as emotional feeling and vary in intensity, they can be measured for use in marketing products and services. Although attitude measurement is difficult, there are many methods that can help marketers to change consumer attitudes or change their products to meet those attitudes.

The definition of marketing concept also specifies that organizations must determine the needs, wants and values of 'target markets'. This means that rather than making and promoting products and services to everybody in the hope that they might be bought (a shotgun approach), it is much more effective to target products to groups of customers with different needs or characteristics (targeting).

(c) Adapt to market demands

Adapt the organization to delivering the desired satisfaction more effectively and efficiently than competitors. An organization attempting to implement the marketing concept may fail to achieve sustained return from its marketing effort due to the lack of the required degree of change necessary to compete effectively in the marketplace. Adapting or changing the way in which an organization operates is probably the most difficult aspect of implementing marketing orientation in businesses that have a long history of being driven by production or sales considerations.

A pre-requisite of successful marketing orientation is the willingness and ability of an organization to use the market research data to design the required products and to change its methods of production, sales and customer relations.

(d) Make a profit

If we accept the fact that the purpose of an organization is to create customers, it follows that marketing is the sole revenue generating activity. In any manufacturing organization there are four business functions essential to its operation and growth. These are finance, production, personnel and marketing.

• Revenue generated by sales turnover has to be managed and controlled or finance for investment raised from shareholders or institutions and the function absorbs cash resources.

- Production, financed by revenues and share capital also costs the organization in terms of factors of production, raw material and warehousing for stock control.
- People need to be found, managed and administered, therefore personnel skills are essential where people are employed, for example, to manufacture the products and administer the operations, and represent an on-going cost to the organization.

Through these three additional functions, an organization can raise the finances, produce the products by employing premises, machinery and people but so far has not generated any revenue. Cash only comes into a company when it has a customer who is willing to make a transaction.

Marketing, although it requires an investment (in terms of market research, new product development and promotion), is the sole revenue generating function in any organization. The marketing function creates the customers that provide a business with the necessary sales turnover from which to release a profit. This fact is often taken for granted by production managers who use the company revenues and financial people who manage and control the money in the business.

The realization of the importance of the marketing function in creating customers and generating revenue has led many organizations to review and change their definition of what businesses they are in. Rather than thinking that they manufacture or sell, they now think in terms of what they market. For example, British Telecom Plc is no longer operating as a telephone company but is in the business of marketing telecommunication systems. W.H. Smith does not just sell books but markets and retails leisure products. In these and other organizations such as McDonald's (fast-food retailers), Amstrad (electronics) and Marks & Spencer Plc, which fully implement the marketing concept, the whole of the company becomes a marketing organization and looks to develop, manufacture and sell products and services from the marketing point of view.

Having an understanding of the purpose of an organization and the marketing concept, it is relatively easy to develop a precise meaning of the term marketing. A simple definition and illustration (Figure 1.1) of marketing is as follows.

Marketing is a human activity aimed at satisfying customer needs and wants through an exchange process, providing

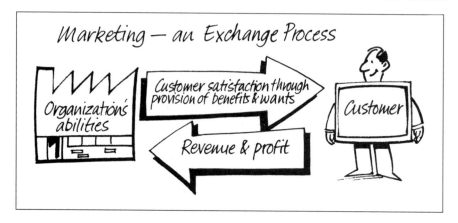

Figure 1.1   Marketing: an exchange process

customers with benefits that satisfy their wants for payment and profit.

In simple societies or when demand exceeded supply, business was a straight line transaction between a product or a supplier and consumers. Manufacturing companies made profits by concentrating on producing efficiently. Consideration of customer needs came at the end of a long chain of events. The customer was thought of as a problem solely for the sales force, whose task was to sell what had been produced.

A modern business, operating in an economy of abundant supply, is much more complex. Because consumers are under no compulsion to consume all that is available and there are numerous alternatives to choose from, organizations have to operate by focusing on meeting customer needs. A product idea or service is therefore rarely offered directly to the customers. It first has to go through research and development to meet the precise needs of a target market. Then it has to be produced in commercial quantities and qualities. It has to be carefully priced, promoted and finally distributed and sold in the marketplace. All these activities have to be co-ordinated by a policy making function. That function is marketing in its broadest sense.

Marketing, or the marketing concept, essentially focuses on all the activities of the organization on satisfying customer needs by co-ordinating and integrating with the other business functions to accomplish the organization's long-term objectives. The marketing concept as an operational philosophy does not imply that other business functions such as production and finance are secondary. Nor does it suggest that customer needs can only be met through large sales volume. The marketing concept requires integrating, co-ordinating and communicating such diverse marketing activities as product development, pricing, sales forecasting, marketing research, direct marketing, PR, advertising and selling. It is in essence the 'unifying force' within the organization and therefore closely co-ordinated with other business functions.

Figure 1.2 illustrates the co-ordinating role of marketing in an organization.

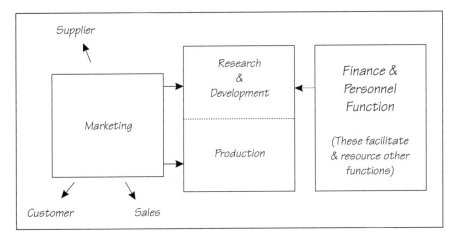

Figure 1.2   The role of marketing in an organization

Competition and the need for differential advantage

In a free market economy where competition is encouraged, there tends to be many suppliers of identical products and services. In most markets, when a new product is developed by one company, the competition will follow very quickly with 'me too' or homogeneous products. This leads to the availability of several alternatives from which the customer may choose. In some cases, such as cigarettes, chocolate and lagers, it is very difficult for customers to tell the difference between different brands in their physical form or in blind tests. A perfect example is petrol. We do not even see it when we fill the tank with this product, but we are constantly told that one brand is better than another. A service, such as a bus ride or an air journey between two locations, offered by more than one company, is identical in meeting the needs of the travelling consumer. In order to create customer preferences towards their products and services, organizations have to differentiate their offerings from those of the competition. These differences or unique selling propositions (USPs) may not be inherent in the product or service, and may be created through product planning, packaging, pricing, advertising and targeting to specific groups of customers. A good example is the way in which Heineken has been marketed as 'the only beer that reaches parts that other beers cannot reach'. There is no magic ingredient in the beer, but the difference or differential advantage has been created through creative and repetitive advertising.

The strategy of differentiation enables a company to survive amidst 'me too' products and avoid price competition. It helps a company to compete on the basis that its products are different from, and better than, competitive models. It is only through the use of marketing techniques that an organization can create and communicate differences in its products and gain a competitive advantage.

The conversion of features inherent in products and services into benefits that customers can understand is probably the most effective method of creating differences that can easily be communicated. For example, customers can readily understand that a car has new technology components that makes it much safer in wet conditions than technical details of anti-lock braking systems. In many other cases the differential advantage in selling products and services comes from the reputation or image of the organization established over a period of time. For example, consumers rarely question the quality of products marketed by Rolls-Royce, IBM or ICI. An appreciation of the need for all organizations to somehow differentiate their products or services is an essential pre-requisite to understanding the role and importance of marketing in creating and keeping customers.

Section 2 An overview of the marketing process

The marketing process, or the implementation, has three main components that are closely linked and which together with the company's stated objectives go towards the preparation of a

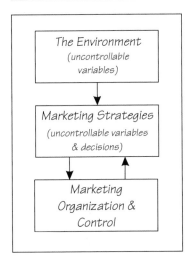

Figure 1.3 The marketing process

marketing plan. A simplified version of the marketing process is illustrated in Figure 1.3.

The marketing process consists of: environmental analysis; marketing strategies; marketing organization and control.

1. Environmental analysis

If you recognize that the only constant in business is change, the environment in which you operate becomes clearly important as your mechanism for effective change.

Environment analysis basically involves scanning, understanding and monitoring the business environment in which the company operates. This serves the purpose of analysing market opportunities and monitoring threats arising from factors beyond the company's control. All organizations operate in an environment made up of six uncontrollable variables, namely, market demand, competition, legal and political regulations, social and ethical pressures, technological change and physical environmental change.

• Demand for consumer products is heavily influenced by the condition of the national economy and interest rates.
• The dynamics of competition constantly threaten the company's share of the market.

- Legal requirements have to be taken into consideration in the design, packaging and advertising of the product.
- Social and ethical pressures increase as pressure groups have a more socially aware and interested population, highlighted by the recent calf export issue.
- New technology for component parts and/or for production influence both the way in which a company can differentiate its product or minimize its production costs.
- Physical environment changes also affect numerous industries directly and indirectly.

Demand for industrial products such as steel is derived demand and depends upon consumer demand for products such as cars, washing machines and refrigerators. A major part of the environment is the changing patterns of customers' buying behaviour and emergence of new needs and wants. Demand for new products or services may be created by competitors but which a company can profitably exploit by analysing further market opportunities or gaps in the marketplace. Marketing research can be used to provide the company with useful information on the environment in which it operates. This does not necessarily have to be expensive; the use of desk research can be cost-effective and lead to a breakthrough strategic advantage.

An organization must also gather information from the marketplace which will help it to forecast future sales of its existing products. Marketing research can provide information on the performance of the company's existing products and the effectiveness of the various marketing strategies, such as pricing, advertising and sales promotion. Marketing research also provides information on competition and the changing nature of buyer responses and behaviour. This feedback is essential for the organization constantly to modify its marketing strategies. Market and marketing research therefore contributes to the company's management information system (MIS) which aids management in its decision making process. The uncontrollable variables or factors that make up the business environment and how the Internet can be used for marketing research, how forecasting and management information systems are used in formulating marketing strategies are dealt with in greater detail in Chapter 2. In addition to scanning the environment an organization must also identify the strengths and weaknesses of the business. Strengths and weaknesses are always within an organization, whereas opportunities and threats are in the environment. Together, strength, weakness, opportunities and threats (or SWOT analysis) are the essentials of an organization's appraisal of its current situation. These are the core foundations of a marketing strategy.

2. Marketing strategies

A thorough SWOT, or situation analysis influences and often dictates an organization's corporate and marketing objectives. Marketing objectives are established from an understanding of what the organization as a whole is trying to achieve within the environmental constraints in which it operates. For example, an organization may have a long-term corporate objective of increasing the return on shareholders' capital by 2 per cent. The corresponding marketing objective set for the organization may be to increase its market share by 10 per cent. In order for the organization to realize its corporate objective, it may be necessary for management to develop various marketing strategies and programmes that would, over the stated time period, attain an increase of 10 per cent share of the market. Objectives therefore signal the level of performance the organization must achieve at some future date given the realities of its environment, opportunities, strengths and weaknesses.

As discussed earlier, because an organization cannot control the environment in which it operates, it is forced to change and adapt its methods of operation. For example, a firm has no control over the level and nature of competition or rate of technological change affecting the market. But it does have control over its own operations in terms of product design, branding, pricing, distribution, promotion and market positioning.

Increases in competition and the introduction of new technology (i.e. the environment) will influence a firm's decisions on its choice of marketing strategies, or its controllable variables. It can decide to take its product into another market, or modify the product and launch new models that may appeal to a new class of customers. It may decide to increase or reduce the price of the product, or it may decide to increase its advertising and sales promotion effort and opt for creating greater brand differentiation. All these are examples of how a firm can respond to changes in the environment by developing specific marketing strategies that help to achieve the stated objectives. The three main groups of marketing strategies are: market segmentation, marketing mix and growth strategies.

3. Marketing organization and control

An analysis of the firm's current situation, forecasting, objectives and selection of appropriate marketing strategies are the main components of a marketing plan. The other element of the plan is the consideration of how the strategies will be implemented in the organization. This includes decisions on the organization of the marketing activities, resource allocation (budgets), and control systems. It is important for decision makers to remember that the preparation of a well written marketing plan with creative strategies is only a part of the marketing process. Any marketing strategy must have potential for successful implementation by people within the organization. If the environment dictates the development of a certain marketing strategy then the firm must ensure that it has or will have the human resource available for its implementation. Marketing organization structures and budgets are the main means for co-ordinating action.

The purpose of financial control and targets is to monitor the extent to which progress towards an objective is being made and to identify the causes of any failure to achieve it so that remedial actions can be taken. This is why there is a reverse arrow in Figure 1.1, indicating that marketing organization and control also influences the formulation and revision of a firm's marketing strategies. Marketing planning must never be regarded as an annual exercise with a plan gathering dust on a bookshelf.

Marketing planning is a process which requires managers to modify objectives, strategies and organization structures in order to effectively deal with the dynamic and turbulent nature of the business environment in which they operate.

The structure of the book

This book has been structured on the marketing management process framework outlined in the above sections. The essence of the book is to demonstrate how organizations can use the Internet to aid the overall marketing function rather than merely as a promotional medium.

This book is organized into ten chapters and a number of appendices. Chapters 2 to 4 focus on information research and organization, an area in which the Internet offers major benefits. Chapters 5 to 9 look at the practical application of marketing techniques to different aspects of the Internet channel, from developing a marketing mix to creating online promotional materials and conducting sales over the net. Chapter 10 takes a look ahead to guess at some of the changes we will see in the next ten years.

Chapter 2 'Finding out about your world and your market' takes a detailed look at the six key environmental variables and demonstrates how the Internet can be used to collect valuable information from numerous sources around the world. The chapter shows, with the aid of practical examples, how information can be scanned and gathered on issues such as the economy, national and international legislation, money markets, company information, consumerism and technological innovation.

Chapter 3 outlines the scope of the Internet as a market and marketing research tool. It demonstrates the ease with which remote databases of marketing information can be accessed to collect secondary data and how the medium is developing into a communication network that will allow organizations to conduct primary marketing research from the comfort of the office. The chapter explores the potential of turning the personal computer into a virtual worldwide library.

Chapter 4 'Making your information system work' looks at the use of intranets (communication networks within organizations) to make your information system work efficiently. It then examines the best way to structure your information collection systems, with particular emphasis on the marketing information system.

Chapters 5 to 7 provide you with a detailed explanation and reference to the practical and realistic use of the Internet in the planning and implementation of the marketing strategies.

Chapter 5 'Segmentation – establishing a niche in the global market' gives you a segmentation methodology which enables you to segment your own market, breakdown the use of the Internet and find whether there is a match. It outlines market segmentation as a key marketing principle and demonstrates the potential of reaching many different individuals and groups of potential customers.

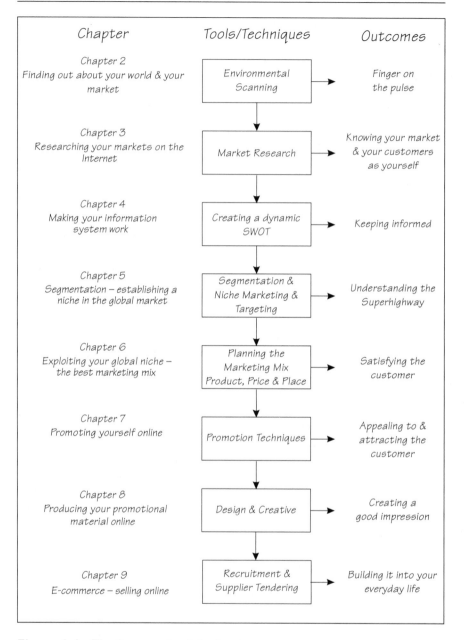

Chapter	Tools/Techniques	Outcomes
Chapter 2 Finding out about your world & your market	Environmental Scanning	Finger on the pulse
Chapter 3 Researching your markets on the Internet	Market Research	Knowing your market & your customers as yourself
Chapter 4 Making your information system work	Creating a dynamic SWOT	Keeping informed
Chapter 5 Segmentation – establishing a niche in the global market	Segmentation & Niche Marketing & Targeting	Understanding the Superhighway
Chapter 6 Exploiting your global niche – the best marketing mix	Planning the Marketing Mix Product, Price & Place	Satisfying the customer
Chapter 7 Promoting yourself online	Promotion Techniques	Appealing to & attracting the customer
Chapter 8 Producing your promotional material online	Design & Creative	Creating a good impression
Chapter 9 E-commerce – selling online	Recruitment & Supplier Tendering	Building it into your everyday life

Figure 1.4 The framework of the book

Chapter 6 'Exploiting your global niche – the best marketing mix' outlines how the Internet impacts your existing product, pricing and distribution channels. It outlines ideas of how to tailor these in tune with the use of the Internet. It deals with the application of the new technology in product planning, gaining information for pricing decisions and the Internet as a new distribution system.

Chapter 7 'Promoting yourself online' deals with the fourth element of the promotion mix – promotion. It covers all the major areas in which the Internet can act as a promotion vehicle alongside your existing promotion channels. It covers the latest ideas and developments in the art and technology of getting organizations online effectively.

Chapter 8 'Producing your promotional materials online' outlines the considerations and differences in using this new medium. It gives practical advice on the 'do's and don'ts' of producing promotional materials on the Internet.

Chapter 9 'E-commerce – selling online' provides a practical guide to creating a sales point on the web. It sets out the elements you need, and how to assemble them in the best way for your product and firm.

Chapter 10 'Where is this all taking us?' provides a look ahead, and explores the potential development of this exciting and fast-changing medium. It outlines possibilities and implications for the marketer.

The Appendices offer you background support to your use of the Internet. They enable you to get online, search and understand netiquette and newsgroups. The marketing management process, techniques, outcomes and the framework of this book are outlined in Figure 1.4.

Conclusion

This chapter has set out to explain the term marketing by developing an understanding of the purpose of any organization as a starting point. Once we can accept that the purpose of an organization is to create a customer or a customer base, then it is relatively easy to relate to the marketing concept or philosophy that gives direction to the overall business operation. Marketing – as a management orientation that places the customer as a focal point around which all operational decisions revolve – is one of the four main business functions in an organization.

The outcome of implementing the marketing concept is customer satisfaction through an exchange of benefits for payments from which an organization can release profits by being more effective and efficient than the competition. Although the marketing concept is very simple and regarded as common sense when fully understood, it is much more difficult to implement. Organizations are often burdened by weight of history and resistance to change. The inward looking management and absence of strong entrepreneurial leadership are major barriers to successful introduction of marketing philosophy in such businesses. In addition to this, most organizations are faced with many alternatives in terms of markets, customers and strategies and cannot pursue all possible courses of action due to the limitations imposed by financial and human resources.

The implementation of the marketing concept can be facilitated by adopting a planning approach based on an understanding of the marketing process. The marketing process involves a firm conducting environmental and situational analysis that lead to the reappraisal and establishment of meaningful objectives. Corporate and marketing objectives aid decision-makers in the strategies appropriate to achieve customer satisfaction. In order successfully to implement the strategies, a firm must examine its marketing organizational structures and allocate adequate human and financial resources. The whole of this process must be co-ordinated and monitored through a marketing plan.

This chapter has laid the foundations for the traditional marketing orientation which is so essential for your successful use of the Internet.

Checklist

You now know:

The purpose of an organization.	☐ Yes	☐ No
The difference between production, sales and marketing orientation.	☐ Yes	☐ No
The management orientation of your organization.	☐ Yes	☐ No
The importance of the needs, wants and values of your target audience.	☐ Yes	☐ No

Marketing is the sole revenue generating
    function in any business.   ☐ Yes   ☐ No
The formal definition of marketing and the
    marketing concept.   ☐ Yes   ☐ No
The importance of differential advantage in a
    competitive business environment.   ☐ Yes   ☐ No
The marketing process consists of environmental
    analysis, marketing strategies and marketing
    organization and control.   ☐ Yes   ☐ No
How marketing can be integrated into your
    business processes.   ☐ Yes   ☐ No
The difference between promotion and
    marketing.   ☐ Yes   ☐ No
How the book is structured.   ☐ Yes   ☐ No

What next?

The next chapter will enable you to stand back from your every-day business to assess the environment and the influences that impact your marketplace – enabling you to keep your finger on the pulse.

References

Drucker, P. (1954) *The Practice of Management*, Harper & Row, New York.

Levitt, T. (1986) *The Marketing Imagination*, The Free Press, New York.

Kotler, P. C. (1984) *Marketing Management: Analysis, Planning and Control*, 5th edition, Prentice Hall, London.

Davidson, H. (1987) *Offensive Marketing: How to Make Your Competitors Followers*, 2nd edition, Gower, London.

Chapter 2

Finding out about your world and your market

'The Internet feels like the 60's, you know there is a party going on, you just don't know where.'

Most marketing people claim that their greatest fear is that they are in abject ignorance of their place in the market. Most marketing people suspect that they may not have fully grasped their full worth in the marketplace. Very few marketers would claim with confidence that they have got their finger on the pulse at all times.

If you can relate to any of the above, this chapter is for you. It is about 'where to look' on the Internet and how to go about alleviating those fears. It will help you to design and implement the basis for an effective management information system (MIS). This can then improve strategic management decisions and lead to vastly improved marketing.

The MIS is an information system using formalized procedures to provide managers at all levels in all functions with appropriate information from all relevant sources (both internal and external to the firm) to enable them to make timely and effective decisions for planning, directing and controlling the activities for which they are responsible.

The essence of this definition is that MIS is a database of internal and external information that managers can use as an aid to their analysis, decision-making, planning and control purposes. The emphasis is on the use of information and not on how the information is processed. In this chapter, and in Chapter 3, we will focus on *information* collection and research, and we will show how the Internet can transform this activity. Chapter 4 will address the 'system' within which the data sit in order to create an effective MIS.

Know your market as yourself

Knowledge about the marketplace is key to marketing success. It is essential to effective decision-making, planning, organization and control, and knowledge has to be used to ensure that key decisions are not made without evidence or in isolation from the marketplace or other parts of an organization. The more in-tune with the market, the more successful an organization becomes. However, the environment changes the marketplace in a dynamic process over time. Forecasting, understanding and assessing the environment remains the marketer's greatest challenge and opportunity. The Internet provides a new tool to monitor and test the environment.

The environment consists of six main uncontrollable factors or variables. These are:

1 Market demand
2 Political and legal forces
3 Social and ethical influences
4 Competition

5 Technology
6 Variations in the physical environment of the marketplace.

These pose both opportunities and threats. They need to be measured, monitored and analysed by using marketing research and forecasting techniques. The information thus collected can then be incorporated with other sources of information to form a management information system, which becomes a crucial part of informed decision-making. The Internet offers a vital tool for collecting this information from worldwide sources. Indeed the Internet is such a large and diverse source of data to marketers, the challenge is efficiently to select and filter data so as to provide appropriate and up-to-date information. This is the key to using the Internet successfully to monitor the environment.

Demand

Demand for products and services varies over time. Consumer behaviour changes, but so too does the wider economy, creating cycles of demand that are critical for many businesses: a few percentage points up or down in demand will determine the difference between profit and loss on many business plans. It is surprising, therefore, how few businesses, particularly small and medium sized enterprises, invest time in predicting the way the business cycle might affect the levels of demand for particular products and services. The recession of the early 1990s, for example, was widely anticipated in the two years before it happened. Those companies that used that information and planned for its consequences were the ones that survived and even prospered in the following decade. Smaller firms in particular might think that predicting market demand by looking at the economy and government policy is a little far fetched. However, the alternative is to react only when it hits the bottom line and often this is too late to take action constructively.

Market demand is strongly affected by the policies of governments and banks. A central bank, following government or European Union targets, can control the amount of disposable income consumers have by changing the interest rate. A reduction in the interest rate releases money from consumers' mortgages and encourages them to borrow more, spend more and save less. The increase in the public's buying power fuels the economy and creates demand for all types of goods and services, creating inflationary pressures as more money chases the same number of goods. If inflation rises, central banks can increase the interest rate to slow down or control the growth of the economy. An example of this arose during 1999, when low interest rates caused inflationary pressures in the UK as consumers borrowed more to spend more. House prices in particular rose sharply. The Bank of England responded with a series of interest rate increases to try to dampen down demand.

Demand for industrial products, such as machines, chemicals and metals is also influenced by changes in interest rate policy and the levels of consumer demand for goods and services. Demand for industrial products is derived demand because industrial products and processes go into consumer products or help in the manufacture of consumer products. For example, demand for steel depends upon the demand by consumers for new cars, washing machines and new houses. Falling demand for consumer goods means falling demand for industrial components, tools and equipment too. Interest rate hikes also directly affect the profitability (and so buying power) of industrial customers for components and materials.

The importance of demand analysis for marketers

It is essential that the individual takes steps to comprehend fully the external influences on the overall marketplace. To do this, the following factors need to be continuously monitored and assessed:

- general condition of the national (international) economy – interest rates;
- regulations on hire purchase and personal loans;
- inflationary pressures;
- unemployment;
- national taxation policy;
- international trade policy.

The importance of watching how the market is changing is clear. When, for example, Bryant and May stopped producing matches in the mid-1990s, they were badly hit by production from former communist countries. This outcome could have been predicted however, by an analysis of the changes taking place in the Eastern bloc and some desk research into international competition. This would have flagged up the threat of the former Yugoslavia which had a strong and low-cost match production capability. The sooner such changes are identified, the greater the opportunity for a firm to adapt its approach to changing conditions before it is too late.

The effect of 'lifestyle' on demand

The behavioural aspects of a market such as demographic and lifestyle trends also influence the extent and nature of demand for goods and services. Changes in the demographic composition of the market and in lifestyles can give rise to new market demands and signal opportunities for new product development, thus influencing the direction of an organization's marketing strategies. Irrespective of income, many consumers will demand products and services that help them to maintain their lifestyle or the norms of behaviour and consumption defined by their personal social status. Fashion is the other behavioural determinant that influences consumers to buy products regardless of consideration of their economic situation.

Some of the important demographic and lifestyle changes affecting demand and therefore marketing strategies in the period 2000–2010 are likely to be:

- The growing importance of time. People are becoming 'money rich' and 'time poor'.
- The increase in the number of working women and their changing role in purchasing and decision-making within the family.
- Changes in the nature and size of the family unit. There are an increasing number of divorces, a greater proportion of single parents and unmarried households and more significantly the decreasing birthrate.
- Changes in the age composition of the UK population. The post-war baby boom has resulted in the largest section of the population being in their early to mid-forties. This group represents a market with most significant disposable income and is an important segment for retailers and manufacturers. The other group of people that represent many opportunities for products and services is the 65+ group. In this decade, this will become one of the largest sections of the population,

and it will have more disposable income than ever before. These people are being called the 'grey surfers'.

- The increase in the part-time and self-employed sector of society means that 35 per cent of the population are not full-time employed within organizations, according to the classic model of capitalist society. This, combined with the previous point, supports the findings of the OECD that, in the 1990s only 33 per cent of the over 55s were in full time employment. For France it was 27 per cent and for Italy this figure is 11 per cent (Handy, 1995).

- The increase in remote and home working which is becoming more and more prevalent, especially in the service sector. BT's Directory Enquiries service in Scotland is essentially a network of remote workers where an enquiry is routed out to someone working from home.

- Changes in social class and mobility. This has been facilitated by widespread home ownership, shares ownership and better education, job opportunities and lifting of European barriers – and will mean new opportunities for organizations to cater for the changing lifestyles and purchasing behaviour of many consumers with increased buying power.

- People are becoming immune to brand messages, choosing to skip TV adverts and avoid direct selling.

Political and legal factors

The political and legal processes in society greatly affect the way in which an organization operates. Changes in legal regulations and requirements give rise to many new opportunities and threats and influence the way in which products and services are marketed. Increasing pressure from government and the European Union for greater competition in the white goods, telecoms and car industries, for example, is creating huge opportunities for some players. In other sectors, such as transport and the utilities, government has shown a willingness to impose environmental, safety and service level targets which can impose controls on the way companies operate. Whole industries can be re-shaped by such decisions: history shows that even seemingly small moves can have powerful effects – like lifting the ban on advertising by such professions as dentists, opticians, architects and lawyers.

A particularly significant area in which legal requirements affect the marketing of goods and services concerns the provision of information to the consumers. At the end of the 1990s, legislation in this area was hugely contentious for the way it affected the food industry, when labelling requirements were introduced for GM foods and British beef exports. The following are just some of the legal mechanisms that regulate the marketing and advertising of products and services:

- pricing legislation;
- Trade Descriptions Act;
- Sale of Goods Act;
- government standards;
- packaging and labelling acts;
- health and safety regulations;
- consumer rights;
- data protection acts.

Social and ethical factors

The roles of the consumer in the marketing environment can never be underestimated. Active involvement by consumer and pressure groups has forced the need for social responsibility and protection of corporate reputation to the fore of marketing and operational decisions. Social responsibility has to be demonstrated by concerted action and communication to the marketplace. Organizations polluting the environment may not only face legal penalties but may lose hard-earned customer goodwill.

In order to maintain good image and reputation amongst the public, companies must avoid the following:

- misleading advertising;
- poor product performance;
- hidden financial charges;
- inadequate product information;
- unnecessary exploitation of the environment or an overseas work force;
- overcomplicated terms and conditions;
- unethical employment practices, especially relating to exploitation in the Third World.

Competition

Assessing the level and nature of demand is the starting point for the marketer. But an organization must also examine the level and nature of competition in the markets it wishes to enter. Competition is probably the most dynamic of all the environmental factors. In a free economy, any profitable market will always be subject to constant pressure from firms seeking to enter, often driving existing firms out and creating serious unpredictability in the market. Careful monitoring and evaluation of the competition enables marketing management to make informed decisions.

Competition comes from two sources. An organization normally faces competition from others in the same field as well as from organizations in other industries. For example, a butter manufacturer competes against other butter manufacturers but also against soap manufacturers who produce and market margarine from edible vegetable oils that go into the making of toilet soap. Those companies which enter your market with a by-product or subsidiary product can often be more of a threat because they may be able to cross-subsidize investment from their core products in the downturns of your market.

An organization needs to be proactive in identifying and exploiting opportunities by anticipating competitive strategies. A proactive approach requires an organization to place considerable effort and emphasis on conducting a competitive audit. Most companies have an Internet site (in the UK alone there were already almost 1 million domain names – Internet addresses ending plc.uk or co.uk – by the start of 2000). Almost all active sites present useful information about the firms running them to the public, allowing marketers to use the Internet to audit the competition without even needing to leave their offices!

An effective competitive audit would use such information to provide answers to the following questions:

- What marketing strategies are currently being pursued by the organization's main competitors?
- How are they likely to change their strategies in the future?
- What is the likely size of the market? What is the competitors' share of the market? How are they performing in terms of sales turnover, return on investment and profitability?

- What are the competitors' strengths and weaknesses in relation to the organization and the future developments in the market?

A competitive audit involves the collection of the following categories of information on the organization's main competitors:

- competitors' plans and organization;
- product strategies including new product development and product-line extension plans;
- pricing strategy;
- advertising and promotional strategy (including online activities);
- production and investment plans;
- distribution facilities and strategies for developing and using different outlets and distributors;
- other major events.

There are many legitimate methods of gathering this information, including scanning annual company reports, promotional literature, price lists, product catalogues and auditing the selling of the product, all of which can be readily obtained from the Internet (if published). Sales and market share data can be obtained from syndicated research services. Business and inside knowledge of competition is sometimes brought into the organization by head hunting and recruiting from within the industry. There are also many published sources of information on the structure, future and current trends of a particular market.

The impact of technology

The rate and nature of technological innovation is a deciding factor on the marketing and operational decisions of an organization. Technological change can be disruptive to the business models of established firms, as the rapid and chaotic development of the Internet itself demonstrates. New technologies create opportunities by providing opportunities for new product development, improvements in the methods of production, and new channels to market.

An example of how new industries emerge from investment in technological innovation is the invention of optical fibre. It was invented to meet the needs of telephone companies and has created

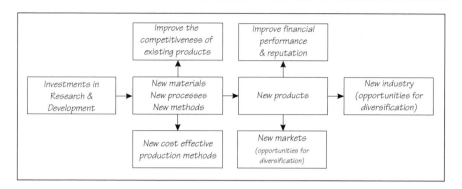

Figure 2.1   The role of technological innovation in the marketplace

new industries in the overall field of telecommunications, including cable TV, electronic banking and other consumer and business information systems.

Over-investment in technology can impose a threat to an organization. Becoming too technologically driven risks ignoring consumer needs by falling in the trap of trying to make the customers fit the product, and not the other way round. Research and development should work closely with the marketing function and develop new products around a thorough understanding of customer problems and availability of alternative products. This is particularly important in fast developing markets. In the very early phase, the market is created by product innovators, but success will often rapidly transfer to those successful at:

• fitting the innovation very closely to the needs of customers; and/or
• making the production process itself more and more efficient.

Organizations do not, therefore, have to be the first in the field of technological innovation. In fact in many industries it is high risk to be the 'first in', e.g. the video industry where Betamax was first in and technically superior but failed to establish itself as the standard. Many organizations survive by monitoring the technological developments in the market and quickly adapting their products to incorporate the latest ideas. Others improve on the research and development of their competitors and launch products with additional benefits to the consumer. It is estimated that 80 per cent of new companies are 'me too' organizations but attempt to differentiate themselves either by product or marketing differentiation.

The Internet can facilitate the marketer in three ways:

1 **To provide access to a dynamically updated reference source to technological changes**

One of the main reasons IT professionals tap into the Internet is that it lets them find out about a subject area in a fast and efficient way. You can visit a collection of IT providers and investigate their offerings, their information and their support. If your question isn't answered immediately online, you can pose the problem online and e-mail it to numerous IT support desks and forums. Their responses, and the speed of their replies, can also tell you something about the ability of different firms to react to customer needs.

Marketing and business executives do this to keep up to date with the ever-increasing pace of technological change. If you have a business concern about the impact of a certain technology, then one way is to go to the drivers of technology change and ask them about the expected growth rate, speed of adoption etc. Ensure that you post these questions to proponents of both the existing and also the new technology. Next use forums to ask how the end users feel about the prospect of this new technology. In this way you are likely to be able to build up a picture of how this technology might affect your business.

Is the innovation demand-led or technologically driven? Often IT companies develop technical innovations, and then look for business needs to attach to them (creating solutions in search of a problem). Often these business needs are contrived and not a genuine concern of end business users and ultimately the technology fails to make an impact. Neural networks and expert systems were two examples of technological push rather than user demand and have not entered the general business application market because of this. Yet much of the press cited these as 'changing the world as we know it'; marketing people spent time trying to assess the impact on their business but many forums revealed how disappointed business people were with the time taken to utilize and leverage the technology.

Take another example. If you are an office furniture producer, remote working and portable technology would pose a threat to your organization. But will this happen? How quickly? The secret is to assess where the drivers are coming from – is the widespread discussion of home-working an example of demand pull, or technology push? Toshiba, Compaq and IBM have been investing heavily to promote remote working as a solution to the needs of business, i.e. they are claiming their technology will satisfy demand. In fact, remote working was a term created by the IT world and the idea was not on the business agenda before the PC revolution. There is little evidence existing to prove the business benefits of remote working or the supposedly huge demand from organizations. Here, you, as a marketing or business executive, must assess the conflicting messages in the environment, examine their sources, and decide for yourself what outcomes are possible. In this case, the driving force is the IT and telecoms companies with access to substantial investment and therefore it is easy to predict the successful development of the technology, with broadband links and remote computer access. The extent to which this translates into a widespread take-up of executive home-working is a completely different, and more important debate. The technology may develop quickly, the take-up is likely to be much slower. This kind of analysis is central to business planning.

2 **To provide access to your competitors' use of advanced technology**

Companies often promote themselves with reference to their advanced R&D and often give indications of which technology they are experimenting with. This, of course, can be a bluff. The effectiveness of different companies' adaptation to the Internet is itself an indicator of how easily and quickly your competitors absorb and utilize new technology.

3 **To provide a medium to investigate and gauge customers' reaction and need for new technology**

Many companies use the Internet to test market products and services. This is cost-effective but is not always low risk. As obvious as it may seem, a good product development idea posted on an open forum can travel the world as fast as it has taken to type and this is the best way to reveal confidential information to your competitor. Please be warned!

Assessing the physical environment

The environmental factors mentioned above have a human origin. They result from human activity. But markets are also at the mercy of the physical environment, made up of geography, location, climate, seasonality and accessibility of the market. Retailers find an Indian summer can damage their annual profit figures, and water companies need to be ready for the random appearance of dry years. The timing of such environmental events is difficult or impossible to predict, but a careful use of past records does make it possible to assess levels of risk and contingency for the surprisingly large number of businesses affected directly by the environment. The Internet is also widely used by environmentalists, and it is possible to use the medium to gather high-quality data on the environmental politics and issues that affect business.

The Internet can provide you with:

• meteorology references;
• climate forecasts;
• geographical references;
• data sources that underpin the environmental debate.

How the Internet makes monitoring the business environment easier

The MarketingNet website (www.marketingnet.com/cybermarketing) provides you with a tour of reference sites to aid you in the task of environmental analysis. Most Internet browsers enable you to book-mark sites of interest to make returning to these areas of interest easier. By book-marking, you can regularly look up relevant indicators and this can become a vital part of your management information system. Maintaining a dynamic on-going monitoring system of your market and the environment is one of the most important aspects of the marketing.

If you really want to make the process even slicker, you can set up an automatic search for updates on sites of interest. Simply use the browser to bookmark sites of interest and set the browser to check for updates at regular intervals.

Conclusion

World-class marketers know their market and the environment. This chapter has outlined how the Internet can help you in this task. It has provided you with references of where to find vital information to assess your environment. It has not been intended to be exhaustive but a starting point for your own exploration. The important point is to keep re-thinking the market you operate in as it changes – and to act on your findings.

This chapter has helped you strengthen your knowledge of your environment, appreciate whether your organization is in touch with external factors and enable you to feel confident that you have got your finger on the pulse. We have taken you back to the necessary theory but provided you with a fast and easy solution to move forward and answer the questions posed for your organization. So are you in touch with your environment? Is your finger on the pulse? How in touch is your organization?

Checklist

You now know:

The six variables you need to monitor in the environment.	☐ Yes	☐ No
Where to look on the Internet to have access to these six environmental indicators.	☐ Yes	☐ No
Factors which impact market demand.	☐ Yes	☐ No
How to assess the political and legal influences on your organization.	☐ Yes	☐ No
The importance of assessing social and ethical influences.	☐ Yes	☐ No
How to size up the competition.	☐ Yes	☐ No
How to assess the physical environment.	☐ Yes	☐ No
How to keep your fingers on the pulse with book-marking.	☐ Yes	☐ No

References

Charles Handy (1995) *The Empty Raincoat – Making Sense of the Future*, Arrow Books published by Cox and Wyman Ltd, Reading.

What next?

Chapter 3 takes you from the general to the specific – helping you explore and research your marketplace and your place within it.

Chapter 3

Researching your markets on the Internet

During the 1990s the Internet has become a principal medium for market research. As marketing research involves gathering information from many different sources, the Internet has become a very powerful medium for companies to scan published data from around the world quickly. It also enables them to gain feedback directly and instantaneously from target groups of customers. This enables people like you to understand individual customer needs more cheaply and effectively than ever before.

All major suppliers of marketing data are online, selling their services directly through the Internet using online credit taking facilities. The advantage for the marketer is that this data can then be fed straight into the marketing information system and kept dynamically updated through the Internet.

This chapter however is aimed mainly at **non-specialists** looking for an insight into the sort of market research information that can be gained from the Internet, as well as marketers looking at the potential online market for their products and services.

There is a heavy emphasis in the chapter on what can be done at **low cost**, or even for **free**. There are a large number of market research agencies selling information over the web – often at a hefty price. However, not many companies can afford to pay for these – and with so much free information available, it's possible for you to glean a large amount of pertinent, up-to-date information that will meet much of your needs.

The importance of market research

Now, it is all too easy to see the Internet as an extension of your own marketplace. Your existing customers may be online and it is tempting to use this purely as a new medium to communicate with them. This is the first trap companies fall into. They jump straight in to 'promotion' rather than taking a disciplined marketing approach. This is counter-productive in two respects: firstly existing customers act differently using this medium; and secondly, it fails to take advantage of potential new markets.

Market research will give you the ability to understand how your target segment uses this new medium, what they are looking to achieve and how you can add value to their activity. It will also enable you to identify new target sectors and understand their needs. Again, remembering the 10/90 rule (90 per cent of what you do on the Internet must add value, 10 per cent can sell – any other combination fails), unless you fail to add value to your target audiences you will fail to achieve results. You can only add value if you know what is of value to them.

This chapter has two broad aims. First, it has been designed to provide **an overview of the market research processes** and methods as used in conventional marketing. These can be used to understand your customers and their use of the Internet. Second, it details **the sources of marketing information that can be accessed on the Internet**, i.e. using it to actually conduct the research. Marketing research is a significant discipline in its own right within the very broad marketing function. The scope of the book only allows for an introductory coverage of this important aspect of marketing.

What is marketing research?

Prior to examining the Internet as a research medium, it is useful to have an understanding of what marketing research entails in conventional marketing. There are many definitions of marketing research, and clarification is not helped by the introduction of the term 'market research'. To simplify matters, the term **market research** should be used to mean the collection of information on a potential market that the organization may be interested in entering. Because the organization is not already marketing to that market, the research is concerned with finding out the state, nature, size and buying behaviour of the market. It may include investigations concentrating on researching the needs, wants and values of the potential customers in that market to guide the organization's efforts to develop a new product. It also includes the development and testing of the prototype of the concept to the test marketing stages of an eventual product launch.

Marketing research refers to the research undertaken when an organization is already marketing its products and services. Marketing research is used to provide the constant feedback from the market so that management can formulate the most effective marketing strategies and change their short-term tactics, if needed, to counter the effects of competitive actions.

Similar techniques and sources are used to collect both market and marketing research data, but which may be modified depending on the objectives of the investigation. Marketing research is much wider in its range of functions than merely to investigate and analyse data on markets. The scope of marketing research can be seen from following two definitions:

(i) 'Marketing research is the systematic problem analysis, model building, and fact finding for the purpose of improved decision making and control in the marketing of goods and services.' (Philip Kotler)
(ii) 'Marketing research is the systematic and objective search for and analysis of information relevant to the identification and solution of any problem in the field of Marketing.' (Green and Tull)

In summary then, marketing research is concerned with the scientific investigation of all factors affecting the marketing of goods and services. Its scope is virtually limitless, answering such questions as: Who? What? When? How? and Why?

Marketing research is employed in the provision of information to aid the decision-making process in the following main fields of marketing.

Research on markets

- Analysis of market size and level of competition including value, volume and share distribution for products and services.
- Competitive audit of strengths and weaknesses.

- Market demand including buying behaviour, frequency, repeat buying, motivations and demand factors such as seasonal and other fluctuations.
- Market structure, who buys, by age, sex and social class groupings, and industrial buying patterns.
- Market trends and business forecasting, including industry changes and impact of technology.
- Studies of export markets and other opportunities.

Research on products and services

- Determining present uses of existing products' characteristics that are most important, and research alternative uses of the products.
- Comparing consumer or customer acceptance of existing products with similar competitor products' strengths and weaknesses.
- Studies aimed at product line simplification.
- Packaging research, design or physical characteristics.
- Test marketing of new or improved products.
- Determination of advantages and limitations of proposed new products.

Research on marketing policy and strategy

- Studies of prices – their influence on sales, and in relation to competitors' pricing.
- Evaluation of price policies – discount structures/distribution.
- Appraisal of current sales methods and practices.
- Studies of distribution methods – costs, alternative channels, effectiveness.
- Territorial and individual salesperson effectiveness/variations.
- Evaluation of sales incentive schemes – prizes, bonuses.
- Effectiveness and importance of sales/after sales service.
- Analysis of the effectiveness of sales promotion activity – exhibitions, PR, merchandising and point-of-sale material, special offers.

Research on advertising

- Analysis of competitor practices in relation to current policy.
- Research prior to and during the development of advertising campaigns.

- Pre-testing and post-testing of advertisements.
- Evaluation and selection of media.
- Studies in advertising effectiveness.

Other possible areas

- Economic forecasting – both financial/budgets, and model building.
- Transport and logistical studies – distribution planning optimal allocations.
- Plant location studies.
- Marketing intelligence, analysis and evaluation with a view to acquisitions and licensing agreements/joint ventures.
- Legal aspects of patents, legislation affecting products, labelling, restriction and sale – importance in export evaluation.

Where do I start my online marketing research?

Before deciding on what methods should be used to collect information, it is necessary to be clear about the marketing problem, the aims of the research, the budget available and sources and methods of collecting data. An overview of the marketing research process, sources and methods of collecting data is given in Figure 3.1.

There are two main sources of marketing research data:

1 Secondary sources (or desk research).
2 Primary sources (own research).

Secondary sources

Secondary data is information that has been collected by research carried out by the company, other organizations or official bodies and that is readily available in a published form. Although secondary data is collected for purposes other than meeting the organization's objectives, it is nevertheless a very useful first source

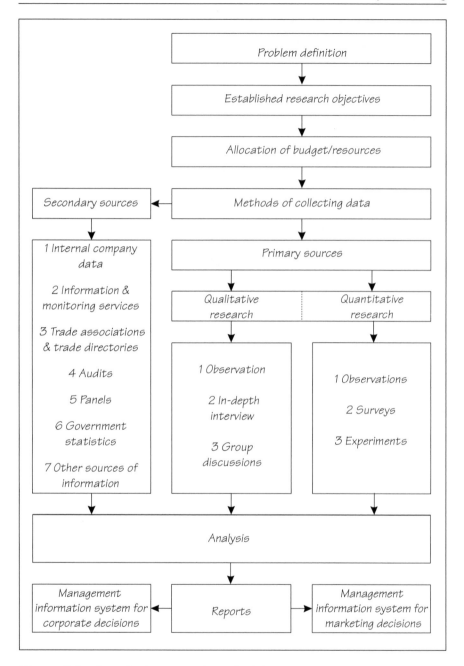

Figure 3.1 A marketing research methodology

that should be consulted to gain an overall impression of the marketplace. Secondary sources of information cost little or nothing, but require effort and knowledge of the various publications and reports available.

Finding good research on your marketplace is often the most frustrating but most fruitful place to start. The availability of this information will vary considerably according to the specific market concerned. Consumer and retail market information are still a lot more readily available than that for business-to-business markets.

1. Internal company data

Before wasting hours of your valuable time on the web, a good starting point is to look internally to your organization and find out what has worked and what hasn't. What product ranges sell best off the page and which ones demand a different approach? If you are looking to promote your organization online this sort of information can be essential.

It is very hard to decide how company data should be used and what data is needed as it will depend on the job in hand and the information available. Sales records are usually a good place to start when analysing the market. The sources of internal company data that can be used to gain a useful impression of potential company performance in the marketplace are highlighted here.

Marketing data
- Price lists
- Customer lists categorized by business sector; by amount spent with the organization; by location; by product type
- PR releases, articles and editorials
- Adverts placed
- Direct mail produced.

Sales data obtained through analysis of invoices
- By product
- By product line
- By customer class
- By cost centre
- By region
- By salesperson
- By competitors.

Annual reports
- Financial report for the organization: P&L, balance sheet, etc.
- Financial report for customers
- Financial report for competitors
- Financial report for suppliers
- Trade association data
- Payroll
- Departmental budgets
- Manufacturing cost reports
- Accounts receivable
- Inventory reports
- Trade journals
- Sales call reports
- Manning tables
- Personnel department reports
- Census data
- Marketing cost reports.

Market research data that already exists in the company
- Audit and panel data
- Special projects
- Customer demand schedules
- Questionnaire replies.

Marketing personnel
- Turnover ratio
- Hiring ratio
- Transfers
- Promotion
- Absenteeism.

Financial information
- Credit
- Discount analysis
- Promotional allowances
- Budgets
- Customer list
- New accounts.

This data is an essential ingredient for the marketing information system described in Chapter 4 for which the use of the Internet as the publishing medium can be very powerful. A good overview of information is essential also when it comes to promoting the organization on the Internet (Chapter 8) because it enables the implementer to have easy access to factual information which can be used to build the credibility of the organization online.

2. Online information and monitoring services

As you will have gathered, there is a vast amount of business data on the web. Much of it is out-of-date and worthless; some of it is invaluable.

If you can afford it, our advice to you is, don't waste valuable company time and money searching aimlessly for marketing reports online, buy them direct from existing data suppliers or contact some of the suppliers listed in this section. All of the principal market research agencies are online. These include:

Nielsen: www.acnielsen.com
Mintel: www.mintel.co.uk
Keynote: www.keynote.co.uk
Gartner: www.gartner.com
Forrester: www.forrester.com

> **Quick Tip 1:** A comprehensive list of online UK market research agencies is available at **www.bmra.org.uk** which has been compiled by the British Market Research Association. The same site provides links to international equivalents. **http://www.green-book.org/** provides an online search facility for market research agencies worldwide, whilst the BMRA provides a free online Select-line service which enables you to select a service online to match your needs.

However, for the majority of us who cannot afford to spend several thousand pounds on online market research, there is a wealth of free/low-cost information on the web that will help you do your job. We start therefore looking at general business information sources, before turning to country, market and company specific information.

General business sources
For marketers looking for up-to-date information upon their competitive environment, the Internet is probably the best external source of targeted daily marketing information. With so many free sites of information, we've been very selective. A more comprehensive list is included on www.marketingnet.com/cyber-marketing, but this selective list – geared towards the non-US marketing manager – is indicative of the wealth of information available.

Marketing information about the Internet
A clear health warning should be attached to Internet market forecasts. It is difficult to project market growth rates in mature industries; in a highly dynamic, hyper-competitive e-commerce environment even more so.

To give some indication of the difficulties, it is sufficient for instance simply to compare the projected worldwide consumer shopping revenues from some of the leading Internet research agencies. These vary from $10 billion to $32 billion for the year 2000 alone.

With such a disparity, it is scarcely surprising that market projections for later years will be hugely wrong.

The situation is exacerbated by:

- different collection methods
- different survey sizes
- different definitions of e-commerce
- different industry coverage

to name but a few variables. The projections need also to be put in the context of one of the longest bull runs in US history, uncertain churn rates for ISPs, the dot.com 'bubble' valuations and an unprecedented increase in venture capital going into high tech industries.

Our point is to treat individual Internet market growth projections with a high degree of scepticism. If most major market research agencies are going to be wrong, you would be wise to present colleagues with a likely forecast range – anything more specific and you are highly likely to be wrong!

> **Quick Tip 2:** Good online sources of Internet statistics include **www.Nua.ie**. This Irish agency was one of the first organizations to send out a **free weekly online newsletter for e-commerce professionals**, detailing market growth and usage statistics. Unlike many of the US sources of Internet statistics, it is genuinely international. It was recently quoted in the foreword to a major US government report on the emerging digital economy.

General business sites: where to go first

There are a number of business websites that are potentially invaluable to marketers. These include:

www.thebiz.co.uk	A useful starting point for the novice business information researcher.
www.brint.com	One of the first – and still one of the best – catalogues of online business information sources. At first, it can be difficult to use and it's American, but if it's online and any good, it should be listed here.
www.ft.com	The new *Financial Times* site is a distinct improvement on earlier versions. Its parent company has invested a lot of money in this service, and it shows. Particularly useful for marketers are the **free e-mail newsletters**. Unlike other newspaper e-mail services, these are market-specific, and save you having to read the newspaper every morning!

> **Quick Tip 3:** Still confused about where to go first? Download a complete free list of the best market research web links from www.marketingnet.com/cybermarketing – and get surfing.

Market survey and monitoring reports

Published surveys and reports are a low-cost/no-cost starting point as these are the established way of collecting information on markets, products, media, customers and competitors. **Quick Tip 1** provides two lists of the main online market research agencies. Specialist research agencies in this relatively new area include Forrester.com and Gartner.com in the USA, and Continental in the UK.

3. Trade associations and trade directories

Most industries have trade associations with the aim of providing members with information and assistance that is useful for their operation and expansion. Trade associations therefore publish data on new products, markets and technologies that has been gained from surveys of the industry.

Studies can, however, be very limited in scope and statistics may be difficult to interpret if important companies or groups of companies are omitted. Because of the restricted number of secondary data for industrial marketing research, trade associations studies can sometimes be very useful in providing a starting point of researching industrial markets.

Quick Tip 4: Industry bodies and business schools in the UK provide useful starting points for marketing managers looking for online management information – here are a few:

- **www.inst-mgt.org.uk/external/man-sorc.html** The UK Institute of Management provides a carefully selected list of European business websites; a good starting point.
- **http://www.dma.org.uk** The UK Direct Marketing Association.
- **www.cim.co.uk** The Chartered Institute of Marketing.
- **www.cranfield.ac.uk/cils/library/subjects/coinfo.htm** An excellent select list of the best free company information sites on the web.

Online trade directories can also provide useful information on companies within industry. For a list of specific industry bodies online, see the Trade Association Forum, which is sponsored by the UK Department of Trade and Industry at **http://www.taforum.org.uk/**. Information on suppliers of products is often a useful starting point of studying the level and nature of competition in the marketplace. The main online international and UK trade directories for marketing research purposes are as follows:

- Dun and Bradstreet: **www.dunandbrad.co.uk**
- Kompass: **www.kompass.com**
- Kelly's Directory: **www.kellys.co.uk**
- Key Note Reports: **www.keynote.co.uk**

4. Audits

Again, if you are in the consumer or retail industry, desk research on competitive products is likely to be fruitful, especially audits.

Audits for individual companies can be very expensive, and host companies wishing to use retail or wholesale audits tend to use a syndicated service such as A.C. Nielsen. This information is now available online at **http://www.acnielsen.com/**.

The method of data collection is retail sampling. Every two months actual stock levels on display are recorded in a series of sample shops. These are classified into different retail organizations, multiples, co-operatives and ordinary retailers and the total sales per month are recorded. Clients may specify particular brands or package sizes to investigate and whether in special areas or the whole of the UK market. In addition clients may commission special analyses or tables on particular products, for example, the effect of special offers. Nielsen also covers advertising expenditure on newspapers, magazines and TV on each brand that is investigated and collates this information with stock movements. It also supplies data for every brand in the market during the period of the report. This is itself secondary data supplied by the Media Expenditure Analysis Ltd. The main use of the Nielsen Index is to provide information on the distribution of the product in the various retail organizations and the level of stocks and rate of turnover, particularly for new products.

Additional information such as where the stocks are placed, source of supply, are also included in the auditor's record. The data is scrutinized and then itemized and finally grossed up to universal levels. The standard type of information that is computed from these audits is:

- consumer sales – actual sales in volume and sterling;
- retail deliveries;
- retail stock;
- stock cover;
- average stocks and average sales per shop handling;

- average price paid;
- distribution;
- showings, i.e. point of sales materials.

All this information is broken down by region and shop type. Additional information is available from the data, the most important of which is probably breakdowns of forward and reserve stocks.

The major disadvantage of audit reports to the market researcher is that the Nielsen Index is confidential and may only be used by those who have permission from the client.

The main advantage of audit information is the trend patterns which emerge from national data. Audits are becoming increasingly dependent on the large multiples and if a company such as Boots refuses to participate, the results of the audit can be somewhat suspect. However, the audit does have another disadvantage in that it has a long reporting period of two months, which is not always quick enough.

5. Panels

A panel consists of a representative sample of individuals, households, shops, stores, wholesalers or organizations from which data is obtained at regular intervals. It is similar to a focus group in which a group of people are brought together to focus on a key issue or discussion. The main difference between a panel and a focus group is the latter is usually a one-off activity whereas the former is used to describe a set of people who may be used again and again by your organization. They provide a continuous process and set of data which can be compared over time to provide trend information. The use of panels to obtain information about particular groups, organizations and their behaviour has the following advantages.

Trends can be studied – including sales, brand share, source of purchase, consumer attitudes, behaviour and usage. Although trends can be studied by using a series of separate samples, the use of the panel has some important additional benefits. Use of the same sample provides more accurate information and greater precision in results as sample variations are avoided.

As the sample remains the same the behavioural patterns can be followed through time for individual members – useful for brand switching/loyalty, repeat purchase behaviour.

Costs of sample selection and recruitment are spread over many surveys, and reduce the need for subsequent planning and supervising of fieldwork. Panel members learn instructional procedures, and are usually co-operative in supplying complete data. If interviewing is involved, time is saved, but mainly the benefit is in the quality of the data obtained.

Panels are valuable for conducting experiments under controlled conditions where the reactions of different groups or reactions to different marketing activity can be measured and compared. This is useful for new product development and for assessing the effect of changes to advertising or the effects of sales promotion campaigns. Most importantly, it is one of the best ways to investigate customers' response to the Internet as a marketing medium. One example of this is the collection of TV audience viewing figures run by BARB (Broadcaster's Audience Research Board) where a panel of households around the country have a monitor which records which channel is viewed. The household is also required to complete a diary to record the number of people who were actually watching a given programme.

There are several panel services available in the UK. Examples include Taylor Nelson AGB for household products as well as for spending habits, savings and insurance **www.tnagb.com**.

6. Government statistics

The Government Statistical Service is made up of statistics divisions of all the major departments plus the Business Statistics Office and the Office of Population Censuses and Surveys and the Central Statistical Office which co-ordinates the system. It is considered to be the largest single provider of statistics in the country.

Quick Tip 5: There are dozens of high-quality downloadable market research reports available from governmental sources. These are listed separately at **www.marketingnet.com/cybermarketing**. The only problem with these is that they rapidly date. The best in our view published in the last two years has been produced by the US Government which is downloadable free from **www.ecommerce.gov**.

The Government Statistical Service exists primarily to serve the needs of government but it is readily used by business managers. It is not expensive, but does not claim to give tailor-made answers to individual organizations' problems.

7. Creating your own marketing information
The most commonly adopted approaches are:

(a) Benchmarking of key players
This is where you would identify and monitor the five to ten key players in your given market. This assumes that they are limited companies and therefore publish accounts. CompuServe makes this particularly easy by enabling you to set up a regular search which is run overnight on their servers, which then reports back results to you. This means that the costs are kept to a minimum. Likewise you can set up bookmarks on the Internet (see Appendix 2) to reference the activity of key players.

Company Sleuth also scours the web for information upon target companies (**www.companysleuth.com**) – very useful if you are undertaking an initial competitive benchmarking exercise, but overkill otherwise. Another free individual company service is available from **http://edgarscan.pwcglobal.com**. Unfortunately this lists only US companies, but is indicative of the sort of benchmarking details that are available. Business consumer sites like **www.uk-invest.co.uk** provide helpful insights into publicly-quoted companies (in addition to free real-time share prices across a number of stock exchanges).

(b) Independent sales pooling
This is where an independent organization (most commonly banks, but sometimes trade associations) will act as a sales pooling agent working alongside a market research consultant. Here the key players in a given market agree to pool their sales figures through this intermediary. Confidentiality is critical and each member's sales figures are only seen by the sales pooling agent who then publishes the total accumulated figure to identify the size of the market. Each member is also given their share of the market and this is usually monitored on a quarterly basis or monthly basis. Each member agrees to pay the sales pooling agent a fee for providing this service but this is usually a relatively small investment. The most common approach to setting up a sales pooling syndicate is

to contact a market research company who will then liaise with an intermediary (e.g. bank) on your behalf.

The most innovative sales pooling organizations use the Internet to collect information from the syndicate online which help them to:

- collect information from each member quickly and cost effectively;
- assimilate and cumulate the data automatically;
- disseminate the results at the touch of a button.

Many Internet marketing companies offer to do this service for a fraction of the cost of using conventional methods. Some organizations may perceive using a marketing company through the Internet as less secure than going through a bank and the postal system, but in reality there is no security threat and the contractual arrangements on both sides are identical.

A successful sales data pooling company has been Whitaker's BookTrack, which monitors the sales of books through UK retail outlets. Whitaker tracks the sales of the top 5000 titles each week going through over 2000 retail outlets. It also has specialist services tracking sales through specific book outlets such as college bookstores. Virtually all main UK book publishers subscribe to the invaluable service – a service that did not exist six years ago and would be impossible to administer without Internet technology.

(c) Networking

With so many new market entrants into such a chaotic market, it is scarcely surprising that there has been a huge increase in informal networks of like-minded business people. One of the best known is the First Tuesday club, a mixture of venture capitalists, e-commerce pioneers and marketers that meets online and offline to swap ideas, problems and solutions.

Quick Tip 6: Visiting **www.imab.co.uk** and **www.firsttuesday.com** are very good places to start finding out about where e-commerce is going, along with opportunities to network with people who know a lot about the problems you are facing.

Secondary sources of information for industrial products

There are fewer sources of online information on industrial products and markets than on consumer goods, though this is changing as business-to-business e-commerce rapidly grows in Europe.

The main sources of information are:

1 **Business monitors:** These give data on output by industry and cover almost all the industrial activity in the economy. These are listed above and on the marketingnet.com website.
2 **Government publications:** Many of the government publications cover industrial production, employment, competition, regulation, etc.

Quick Tip 7: The best places to go for government statistics on markets and e-commerce in general include:

- **www.oecd.org** probably the best independent source of non-US statistics available on the web.
- **http://europa.eu.int/en/comm/eurostat/serven/home.htm** the EU's statistical service – hardly gripping stuff, but it provides you with a useful general overview of e-commerce in Europe.

---

3 **Trade journals:** There are many trade journals for each of the industrial sectors and these provide useful information on the state and future trends in that industry. A list of online journals is provided in the BRAD Media Directory.

Primary sources

Primary sources of information are those which have originated directly as a result of the particular problem under investigation. Online primary research is normally carried out by an organization's marketing research department or commissioned through a marketing research agency or company. Since this subject is worthy of a book in its own right, we focus here upon the pros and cons of online market research, and where to make a start.

Methods of collecting primary data

Methods of collecting primary data can be categorized into two groups:

* qualitative research;
* quantitative research.

Qualitative research

The main characteristics of qualitative research are:

* It is usually exploratory or diagnostic and is normally used to 'get a feel' of the situation. As such it is the starting point on which other research methods can be developed.
* It involves small numbers of people who are not sampled on any statistical basis, that is the sample selected may not be representative of the population.
* Participants may be selected to represent different categories of people or organizations. No hard and fast rules can be made from the data collected by these methods. It is, however, possible to subject it to statistical analysis.
* The findings are impressionistic rather than definitive.
* The researchers are interested in quality of information rather than in quantifiable data.

Qualitative research gives the marketer the best insight into the use of the Internet by their desired target audience. We cannot stress enough how vital this is in order to appreciate the relevance of the Internet, the target audience's current use of the net and what potential there is for using it as a promotion and merchandising tool.

There are three main methods of collecting qualitative data, namely by:

1 observation;
2 group discussions;
3 in-depth interviews.

1. Observation

Observation research is used in many areas of investigation where people would not answer interview questions correctly because:

- They do not know the correct reply.
- They are unwilling to tell because of embarrassment or from reasons of pride or prestige.

In this research method the information is collected by observing some action of the respondent rather than by asking questions. It is a cost-effective method of collecting primary marketing information and can be used as a scientific technique when it:

(a) serves a formulated research purpose;
(b) is planned systematically;
(c) is recorded systematically and related to the general proposition;
(d) is subject to checks and controls on validity and reliability.

Information can be gathered by personal or mechanical observation.

Personal method involves a researcher to observe respondents taking some action, such as buying behaviour in a store, and recording the observations. The personal observations can be followed by interviews with a sample of respondents to obtain additional information. Mechanical observation normally involves the use of electronic or mechanical devices to record or count the action by people or vehicles. In online terms, much research has gone into the effect of 'click-throughs' and banner ads.

The methods of collecting data by observation have been successfully employed in the following types of fields of study:

- new product development (for example, cars, kitchen fittings and other appliances);
- merchandising (store layout and stocking of products);
- behavioural research;
- advertising copy.

The problems associated with this method of collecting data include: high costs involved in training people, writing up the results, not being able to give underlying reasons for behaviour and the method being unrepresentative of the target market concerned.

The secret to success on the Internet
The best way successfully to promote your organization on the Internet is to:

- Get into the hearts and minds of your potential customers who are using the Internet. The best way of doing this is to watch how people use the Internet. Finding out the first place people go when they start using the Internet, what they choose to bookmark and why, and what they like to see on a web page or newsgroup. A good starting point in developing primary research methodology is to look at previous primary research findings. **http://www.nopres.co.uk** contains several full reports on opinion surveys of UK Internet usage, including numbers using the net, gender, and age profile of users.

• Find out what your competitors are doing both nationally and internationally by observing their presence on the Internet or in some cases their distinct lack of activity. Newsletters such as those provided by Nua (**www.Nua.ie**) give helpful indications of what is being spent offline in promoting dot.com businesses.

2. In-depth interviews

In-depth interviews are carried out amongst small samples of people to explore a particular issue and to gain a better understanding of a given problem or situation. It requires the researchers to identify respondents who would represent the target market and conduct an in-depth interview using a schedule of topics or an unstructured questionnaire. Depth interviews are normally recorded on a small tape recorder or notes are taken verbatim. Interviewers use visual aids or other material to help illustrate the topics of research. Tape recordings are then transcribed and quotations are used for analysis and reporting of the interviews. Quotations and overall analysis of depth interviews are then used in planning group discussions and/or questionnaire design for quantitative research.

One innovative and popular way to elicit general online feedback (a little quick and dirty but practically free) is to raise a general subject area and post it into a newsgroup or forum in CompuServe. You would write a message saying 'We are looking for your reaction to . . . Please reply giving your response, your background, your interest etc.' Typically you need to offer an incentive which could be a summary of the total responses received.

In order to investigate the potential popularity of this book, Butterworth-Heinemann posted a brief summary and positioning statement into an Internet marketing newsgroup on the Internet. They received over 30 responses, fortunately virtually all positive, and primarily based on this, they decided to go ahead with commissioning the book.

3. Group discussions

Group discussions provide valuable information by encouraging the interaction amongst a group of people to discuss a topic under investigation. The group consists of eight to twelve participants who take a part in open-ended discussions moderated by a trained researcher. The group discussion provides the researcher with an opportunity to observe the group process directly and helps to chart their reactions to specific questions or to the physical product under investigation. The group also provides the researcher with information on the dynamics of attitudes and opinions that can be provoked with great spontaneity. As with in-depth interviews, the discussions can be recorded and transcriptions are then used in analysis and reporting.

Online, this can be done through chat rooms. Any organization can set up a chat room for free. See for example, the Yahoo Chatroom service, which allows you to screen members before joining (see **www.yahoo.com**). Many innovative marketers use this form of interview as a starting point for designing offline interview questions.

The other methods of collecting qualitative data are case studies and longitudinal studies. Case studies examine people or organizations in great detail over a short period in time and provide useful information on customer or organizational buying behaviour. A longitudinal study is a detailed examination by observation of a person, setting or an organization over a long period of time. The best free examples of longitudinal attitude research into online behaviour is available at **http://www.gvu.gatech.edu/gvu/user_survey**. You need to be careful however about direct comparisons between US and European consumer online behaviour.

Quantitative research

There are three widely used methods of collecting primary quantitative data: observation, surveys and experimentation. Very rarely do researchers use all three methods on any one project. The choice of method depends upon the nature of the research problem, the amount of money, time and personnel available.

1. Observation

This is very similar to the observation technique described under qualitative research but here a much larger sample is involved.

2. Surveys

A survey consists of collecting a large volume of information from a significant number of people selected from a large group. A survey provides an original source of information and is regarded as the only way of finding out the motives, opinions and buying intentions of a large number of people. Survey research is carried out by gathering information by telephone interviews, postal or e-mail surveys and personal interviews. The method selected for a given project depends on flexibility, amount and accuracy of information required, time and money available.

Telephone interviews
This method has the advantages of speed, low cost and face-to-face communication. Against the advantages there are a number of disadvantages:

1 Telephones are not universal – industrial versus consumer surveys.
2 Location of respondent, non-contact.
3 Difficulty of establishing credentials.
4 Interviews need to be kept short.
5 One can't use visual cues, illustrations, motivational techniques.

Postal surveys
This method involves mailing a questionnaire to potential respondents and having them return the completed form by mail/e-mail.

As no interviewers are required, this type of survey is not diluted by interviewer bias and problems associated with the management of interviewers.

The following are some of the advantages and disadvantages of using postal/e-mail surveys.

Advantages
1 Cheaper than any other method despite postal increases – interviewer wages/travelling costs, and telephone charges have all increased dramatically.
2 Immunity from interviewer variations.
3 Respondent can work at own pace.
4 Information may be required from household or group which would be time consuming using personal interview.
5 People more willing to make responses to personal questions, e.g. reporting behaviour which is not socially acceptable.

6 Avoids problem of non-contact.
7 Responsiveness to different parts of the questionnaire may indicate different levels of interest.
8 It is reliable in the sense that it can be used repeatedly.
9 Useful in locating rare populations for which sampling frames don't exist.

Disadvantages
1 Questions must be simple and straightforward; lowest common denominator.
2 Explanation of survey purposes and covering letter very important.
3 Reduces flexibility in questionnaire design – avoidance of routings/codings/dependent questions.
4 Answers have to be accepted whether vague or misunderstood.
5 All questions can be seen beforehand: can't therefore be used to test knowledge, brand awareness, etc.
6 Can't ensure validity of respondent.
7 Can't supplement the questionnaire with observational data.
8 You may get a low response. This can mean that it is expensive. One way around this is to use an independent organization to carry out the questionnaire for you. Another is to use incentives (although you may get a biased sample if you do this). If the information is critical it is best to consult a market research company who can give you advice on which approach is best suited to your objectives.

E-mail questionnaires
This is the most cost-effective way to collect data. You can create a questionnaire form on the Internet and request members of a specific newsgroup, e-mail customer list or forum to fill it in. Typically like any questionnaire you need to offer an incentive but this can be the results of the survey. This is normally enough.

If you are looking for a large number of respondents and you are not asking a large number of questions, we would recommend offering an attractive competition. In the entry form you can ask demographic questions which you can use to analyse the results and abstract more targeted data and embed the market research questions within the entry form. So long as you inform the respondent that you are using the data for market research, this is not illegal.

Personal interviews
Personal interviews are more flexible than the other two methods because the interviewer can change the questions and clarify the

issues as and when they arise. The main advantages and disadvantages of this method are listed below. The main disadvantages are cost, organization and fieldworker variations, control and supervision. Costs of using personal interviews are often prohibitive, may be £40 or more per completed questionnaire for industrial or commercial surveys where highly trained interviewers need to be used. Non-response is a major problem and requires costly recalls to be made when using probability samples.

Advantages
1 Advantages are to be had in questionnaire design. This can be more complicated, hence shorter, and can be used directly as data processing input.
2 Interviewer can explain purposes of survey and can indicate the benefits – use of persuasion.
3 Interviewer can explain meaning of questions.
4 Where responses are irrelevant, partial, or inaccurate, the interviewer can probe further.
5 Use of visual matter, checklists, diagrams, rating scales, etc.
6 Can be used to test a respondent's knowledge as the possibility of interaction is removed.
7 Can be used where spontaneous replies are required, for example in measuring attitudes.
8 Can ensure validity of the respondent.
9 Interviewer can supplement questionnaire with observational data.

3. Experiments
Experimentation is used where the researcher is trying to establish a cause-and-effect relationship. The most important cause-and-effect relationship is between marketing variables such as advertising, sales effort, pricing and sales results. In order to establish cause-and-effect the researcher must attempt to collect data from an experiment that involves the control of all extraneous factors so that any variation in the effect (for example, sales turnover) can be attributed to the change in the marketing variable that is being tested (for example, price or amount and type of advertising).

On the Internet, you can actually change the way that a page is displayed according to the audience you are appealing to. This allows you to experiment with which is the best message to use across different cultures, countries and audiences. Most e-commerce providers now allow customers to customize the way their website is presented to them; many provide detailed order histories and personalized stock information. A good example of this is **www.rswww.com** – one of the largest suppliers of electronic components in the world, and a leading profitable e-commerce player.

Conclusion

We have covered some of the principal sources of marketing information on the Internet. We have also looked briefly at the pros and cons of doing primary market research online. The advantages of online marketing research is that it can be fed easily into a company's management information system as outlined in Chapter 4.

In this chapter we have tried:

- to strengthen your knowledge of your place in the online market;
- to help you appreciate whether your organization has fully grasped its online potential;
- to enable you to feel confident that you know the issues behind online market research.

Together, this knowledge should enable you to gain a deeper, more profound understanding of the opportunities of the Internet, and to avoid making some expensive mistakes.

Checklist

You now know:

The difference between marketing research and market research.	☐ Yes	☐ No
The importance of research in understanding your customers and their buying behaviour.	☐ Yes	☐ No
The importance of online research in scanning your marketing environment.	☐ Yes	☐ No

The difference between secondary and primary research.	☐ Yes	☐ No
The range of low-cost/no-cost publications available on the Internet.	☐ Yes	☐ No
The difference between online qualitative and quantitative research.	☐ Yes	☐ No
The use of the Internet to cost-effectively conduct initial qualitative research, involving small samples.	☐ Yes	☐ No

What next?

Chapter 4 outlines how you can integrate this information to create an effective decision-making tool – the MIS system. This is the key ingredient for intelligence gathering and leverage.

References

Kotler, P. (1994) *Marketing Management: Analysis, Planning, Implementation and Control.* 8th edition, Prentice Hall International, London.

Green, P. and Tull, D. (1977) *Research for Marketing Decisions.* 4th edition, Prentice Hall International, London.

Where to go if you want to find out more

Crouch, S. and Housden, M. (1995) *Marketing Research for Managers.* Butterworth-Heinemann. (Useful practical introduction to offline market research.)

Hagel, J. and Armstrong, A. (1997) *Netgain: Expanding Markets Through Virtual Communications.* Harvard Business School Press. (Hard-headed view of e-commerce potential by McKinsey consultants.)

Moore, G.A. (1998) *Inside the Tornado.* HarperCollins. (Discusses the impact of Internet technologies in the context of wider technological change.)

Tapscott, D. (1998) *Growing Up Digital: The rise of the net generation.*
McGraw-Hill. (Visionary book on the impact of the Internet on
the buying habits of the under-20s.)

> **Quick Tip 8:** For a complete list of web-links mentioned in this chapter,
> **download free** from **www.marketingnet.com/cybermarketing**. If
> you can recommend good websites for market researchers not
> mentioned here, please let us know.

Chapter 4

Making your information system work

We have seen how the Internet can transform your ability to research the dynamic environmental factors affecting your business, and the changing markets in which you operate. Internet technology makes this sort of research much easier. But carrying out research does not help unless the data gathered is kept up to date, and even then it's no use unless the people who will **use** the research can get hold of it when they need it. Fortunately, the net can help.

This chapter will explain how an 'intranet' (a company-only, private communications network) can make it easier to keep vital research information up to date, and to communicate the findings across a company to ensure people at all levels are properly informed about the changing world in which they operate. It will also examine the issues you will face in developing the right management information system for your company.

What is an intranet?

The Internet is a public space. Information on the Internet can generally be accessed by anybody able to go online, and anyone can post information for others to read. An intranet uses similar technology to create a pool of information only accessible to people within one organization. The system can be provided using a private cable network (a local area network or a wide area network) or it can be delivered across the same communications lines that carry Internet traffic. But the effect is the same. Technology allows organizations to have a private, interactive communications system which allows messages, information and documents to be shared across users.

An organization will purchase a web-server, or hire web space to host its own Internet site to the outside world. To create an intranet, it uses an internal web-server or it partitions a part of the site to host its internal website, which customers and competitors cannot access because they are protected by a security 'firewall' (security is discussed in Chapter 9). This is used as an internal communications area.

The result is a powerful communication facility within the organization, in which there is considerable control over who can communicate with whom. Private sub-areas can be created for communication within particular departments or job functions within an organization, and it is possible to control the rights to publish material on the system. The technology makes it easier for firms to share vital internal research data with those who need it. Similarly, it becomes much easier for people collecting information to share it with colleagues who analyse it.

The effect on an organization can be dramatic. Historically, most organizations have accepted the need for formal systems of disseminating information produced by the various departments or functions. These have included reports, operating statements, special analysis, variance returns, balance sheets, and other financial and performance related data. Such methods had the advantage of being comprehensive, accurate and consistent. But these traditional approaches suffered from inflexibility and produced information that quickly goes out of date. It was also often the case that some functions were better at producing internal communications than others. Accountants, for example, regularly produce figures for cash flow, costs, and turnover. There is often a poorer supply of essential information about the way the market, competition and demand is changing – even though without following these changes closely there might soon be no turnover to report on!

The intranet, in effect an electronic internal publisher, makes it easier for outward-facing disciplines like marketing to share vital information across an organization and to influence planning. Accounting figures are useful, but they tend to look inside the organization, and to look backwards. There is now an opportunity to use technology to focus minds on the external environment and the future as well.

What sort of organizations should develop intranets?

An intranet is particularly important in complex and decentralized organizations, in which it is not possible for managers to observe and experience all the operations and activities in an organization. They therefore need formal channels of information for their routine, short- and long-term planning and control purposes.

The feasibility of this option also depends heavily on the size of the organization and its budget. This may well not be the best option for an SME (small or medium enterprise of less than 100 people) because it requires a significant investment in having an internal web-server. Small organizations, however, can still use e-mail to share files and research data with appropriate users. Similarly, e-mail is an excellent vehicle for data collection. If a rep, for example, hears of a competitor's move, or gets important feedback on an idea or product, it's important this information is shared. E-mail will allow that to happen easily, but don't forget whatever technology you have in place, people won't use it unless they're encouraged to do so. Make sure you have a culture of sharing information and ideas first – then choose your technical solution.

Among medium sized organizations, there has been a rapid growth in the use of intranets for information collection and sharing in the past decade. In the mid-1990s, most marketing directors from medium sized organizations (100–500 employees) did have a marketing information system (our survey showed 32 out of 35 did so). But in those days, nearly all were paper-based format (just over 5 per cent had decided to go to an electronic format). Today, most firms of this size have switched to an electronic solution. This is enabling directors who were concerned at the costs of a dynamic information collection system to reconsider their approach, and abandon the paper-based tradition of an annual 'big push'. The survey of marketing directors also reveals that most conducted an annual SWOT review, and analysed how external factors should affect internal decisions on pricing, product development and promotion. But the development of good internal information systems was less advanced. It is now highly likely that this problem has been solved by intranet technology, which can make information sharing within an organization so much easier.

The intranet as an internal communication tool

Not only can it be expensive and time-consuming to communicate even the most simple of initiatives across the whole of a large organization, but it can also be ineffective. Pockets of the organization can become saturated whereas others can be left in ignorant bliss. Often it is the sales people who get left out, staff who are not within the organization's physical location every day. Ironically it is exactly these people who need to understand and relate to major changes within the organization.

The research findings discussed in Chapter 3 are examples of information which, once shared with the whole organization, can help build commitment to your Internet marketing campaign. What better communication tool to build support for the use of the Internet than Internet technology itself?

In this way:

- The corporate business plan can be posted throughout an organization and kept dynamically updated.
- The marketing plan can be integrated with the marketing activities so that internal team members can see how the overall plan is being implemented.
- The corporate policy documents (appraisals, expenses, holiday entitlement, etc.) can be stored in one place and updated regularly without having the paperwork mountain that so many organizations wrestle with.
- The company's newsletter can be read online.
- Price lists and product descriptions can be referenced throughout the organization, even by salespeople who work remotely.
- Interactive forms could be used to configure, price and print quotes for fast delivery to customers.
- Stock levels can be queried remotely.
- Discussion forums can be hosted to improve intra- and inter-departmental communication.
- A quality control feedback system can be implemented and all the documentation and proformas can be stored and updated without incurring the huge paperwork changeover process.

- A suggestion scheme can be initiated with anonymity built in.
- New versions of software can be collected by employees and so enable them to receive the latest version of software.

Centrally publishing internal communication is only one benefit. Further benefits come from the support an intranet gives to employee interaction. Senior managers can create response forms which enable employees to give feedback, ask questions, comment or extend corporate 'thinking'. Just as the Internet can provide a closer link between the manufacturer and the customer, so too can it create a closer link between staff at different levels within an organization. It is a brave step to implement, and has been shown to have powerful effects on the structure of organizations, removing some middle management positions which formerly were dominated by information handling. IT can flatten the structure and accelerate a change process which would otherwise take years to implement. Many of the large American organizations use intranets primarily for this purpose and have found the benefits greatly outweigh the initial investment needed to build the IT infrastructure.

There is now a wide variety of products and specialists aiming to support the introduction and management of intranets. All the main software houses produce 'internal web-publishing' tools, making it easy for senior managers to design their own internal web pages, and there are now hundreds of consultancy firms providing advice. The key to planning in this area, however, is to focus on the outputs, not the technology. The outputs are simple – they are about what people do, how they communicate, how they share information. The watchword is to 'think people', not technology, when planning an intranet. The project should not be lead by IT people, but by the people who are going to use the system. When considering each aspect of the system, ask yourself the following questions:

- Will this system make it easier for people to work together, or more difficult?
- Does the system make it easy for the people who need information to get hold of it?
- Does the system make it easy for people who gather information to share it?
- What value-adding activities will become easier as a result of this system?

If you're building an intranet that creates lots of work and delivers no tangible rewards, then think again. The structure you have put on the information you are collecting probably isn't clear or appropriate to your needs. Collecting and sharing data is pointless unless the system within which it sits, the 'architecture' of the information, is right for your organization.

Two security tips

It is essential that your intranet is secure. You will have to satisfy yourself that the product you are buying or installing is robust enough to meet your needs. However, even a good system can become vulnerable if security is not taken seriously. To avoid this, make sure that:

• You appoint a named individual (preferably someone senior) to take charge of security. He or she will need to keep abreast of changes in the field, and to monitor usage of the system to ensure that security remains a top priority. Giving this responsibility to an individual is better than placing it generally with a department, which runs the risk of no-one feeling security is really their job.
• Ensure that you have a system that copes easily when people leave the organization. Name-based entry codes are harder to manage than position-based ones. For example, a university will give students a codename that includes initials, course and year. As each year graduates, it is very easy to terminate access to the system. Make sure that leavers will really leave, and not be able to access your files from your competitors' offices.

The structure of a management information system

Information must not be collected and made readily available to managers working in all parts of an organization. Intranet technology enables this data sharing. But it is also important that the data shared is well organized and structured. It has become a cliché of the information age to observe that too much information can be as bad as too little, but this is true. The key is to make data useful and accessible through a well thought through, integrated Management Information System or MIS.

We have already seen that the Internet can support the collection of the environmental and market data necessary that sit within a firm's MIS. We have seen that the marketing information system is an integral part of the whole. Structuring information, and designing an MIS that works depends, however, on the character and focus of the organization in question.

Influences on the type of MIS

The main factors determining or influencing the type and overall structure of the MIS that is appropriate for a given organization are listed below.

1 The primary function of the organization. The type of business – manufacturing, wholesaling, retailing, services or public authority – is the main influence on the type of MIS that will be required.
2 The scale structure and levels of the organization:
   • number of departments, sections and levels;
   • degree of autonomy of departments and sections;
   • number of people employed/sales turnover/capital employed;
   • degree of centralization or decentralization.
3 Interaction with the marketing environment:
   • Importance of external information?
   • In what ways does the organization need to communicate with customers, suppliers, trade unions, government departments etc.?
4 The types of decisions that need to be taken:
   • systematic decision-making;
   • corporate, long-term and strategic timing or urgency of decisions.
5 The management style: autocratic or participative.
6 Investment available for using latest technology for storing and dissemination of information.

Irrespective of the size of an organization and whether the information is in a manual or electronic form, the fundamental structure and the typical sources are common to all designs of MIS. A typical MIS is illustrated in Figure 4.1.

The outputs of an MIS reach managers in a variety of forms, from analyses to statistics and statements. These are generally referred to as reports and fall into three broad categories.

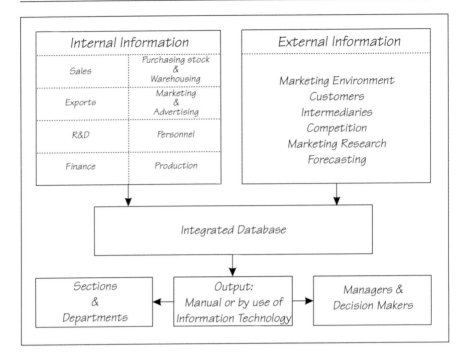

Figure 4.1   Typical inputs and outputs of an MIS

1 Reports providing passive background information. These are normally produced at lengthy intervals and give details of assets, records, depreciation, summaries of annual production statistics and balance sheets.
2 Reports providing control information. These reports are produced more regularly and provide useful information and influence current and short-term tactical and operational decisions. Examples of reports include cost variance reports, credit control information, working capital statements and sales, market trends.
3 Reports providing statistical data for planning. These reports include information necessary for forecasting, corporate short-term planning or for longer-term strategic planning. Examples of statistical reports include investment appraisals, budget models, market research reports and analysis and selective economic trends and data.

As with all types of information, an MIS has no intrinsic value of its own. The value which may be attributed to any MIS can only come from actions of managers that can be measured and evaluated. For example, the use of information must lead to decisions that increase profits, or reduce costs, or utilize resources more effectively or increase the current and future efficiency of the organization.

The marketing information system (MkIS)

A marketing information system is a sub-section of an organization's overall MIS. The MkIS provides data for marketing management decisions and has been defined by Kotler (1994) in the following terms:

> *A marketing information system consists of people, equipment and procedures to gather, sort, analyse, evaluate and distribute needed, timely and accurate information to marketing decision makers.*

A total and integrated MkIS is one which is fully integrated with other functional information systems into the organization's overall MIS. As outlined in Figure 4.2, an MkIS relies heavily on marketing research information from the organization's environment and forecasting of the future state of the economy and market demand for goods and services (these sources are summarized in Chapter 3). The value of an MkIS can be illustrated by examining the inputs and outputs that make an effective information system.

The main benefits of using an MkIS are:

- It can contribute to the improvement of managerial performance.
- It integrates and disseminates complex marketing information for decentralized firms that may be dealing in several markets with a large number of products.
- It allows management to exploit and implement the marketing concept more fully.
- It encourages management to use information that the organization has invested in.
- It contributes to better control of operations, in particular in such decision areas as product withdrawal, modifications, response to competitors' advertising and marketing effort.

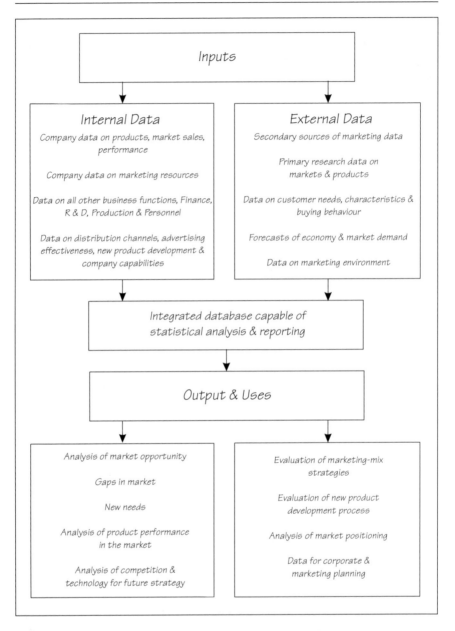

Figure 4.2 Inputs, outputs and uses of a marketing information system

The design of an MkIS

1. External and environmental intelligence

The marketing environment consists of all the factors that affect an organization's ability to create and satisfy customers profitably. The external environment consists of many factors. The six factors that have a major impact on decision-making are market demand, political and legal forces, social and ethical influences, competition, technology and variations in the physical environment of the marketplace as outlined in Chapter 2.

This information is the basis and foundation of an effective marketing information system. Successful marketers store this information, disseminate it and make it as widely accessible as possible within their organization – security issues permitting. They then monitor it by enabling dynamic input from as many sources as possible: shareholders, salespeople, market research organizations, PR agencies etc.

This information becomes the front windscreen for the organization to widen their vision of the world and focus and prioritize on what is important. It can dramatically change an internally focused organization into a rapidly evolving and adaptive one.

Just as the web page which accompanies Chapter 2 references sources, where you as a marketer can find information about the external environment, you would provide a window to relevant information for your employees about your organization's environment. Here you would publish market reports, key note reports, internally conducted research about your market and the environment. Again the same core concepts highlighted in Chapter 8 apply to attracting your target audience, inviting their response etc. which is still very valid. You would design your internal website with the same care and attention as one you would produce for your customers.

2. Internal control

Some of the organization's internal information will be published purely as an internal communication tool in order to disseminate information uniformly across the company.

However, within the remit of a marketing information system, you would focus on internal information which enabled you to ascertain how effective the match is between the external variables and your internal competencies. This information is likely to include many if not all the factors listed in Chapter 3 within the section titled 'Internal company data' (page 43).

In this way you can build an overview of what your organization can offer, achieve and deliver – uniformly communicated across the organization.

3. Policy decisions

The MkIS monitors and evaluates an organization's opportunities and threats (external and environmental intelligence) against its strengths and weaknesses (internal control). This provides you with a dynamic, self-maintaining SWOT analysis. This provides marketing management with the information necessary to manipulate the variables that can be controlled and changed in response to the changes in the environment. The Internet ensures that this data is kept maintained and you are not left with a decaying MkIS.

Policy decisions result from this dynamic SWOT analysis which includes changes to products, pricing, promotion, channels of distribution, type(s) of target markets served and line of business. These types of policy decisions can determine the success or failure of an organization. Therefore, it is imperative that the system provides accurate and timely information which people trust, respect and regularly reference. A key role in this process is to set up a filter mechanism which enables information to be checked before it is published into the Internet. In most cases this filter is the marketing department who validate the external information coming in and ensure that the internal control information is correct at any point in time.

A good MkIS will also document why a policy decision was taken, highlighting the underlying thinking and assumptions which were paramount at the time enabling a historical review of good and bad decisions. This enables the organization to learn and improve its decision-making capabilities. It is a brave act on behalf of senior management to reveal this to the whole organization and most commonly this is kept with restricted access only to those involved in the decision-making process. However, this still enables those involved to review previous decisions and understand why and how they worked (or didn't if the case may be!). Documenting this information is also an excellent way to help smooth the process of succession management and alleviate the turning wheel effect where new management unknowingly repeat the same mistakes as those that preceded them.

It is important for an organization to trap the background reasons why a policy decision was taken. This is typically forgotten in the echelons of time and needed when this policy is revisited and needing to be renewed. Understanding why policy decisions were taken, the environmental and internal variables that impacted the decision is critical for organization learning. Often companies carefully trap external data but fail to trap the impact this then had on the internal change process. A successful marketer monitors the environment, monitors the impact on the organization and captures the resulting actions and bottom-line impact on performance. This not only builds a powerful professional record of success but creates a knowledge bank which is a powerful and valuable corporate asset. It is true that 'the future isn't what it used to be' but the business process does follow patterns and the lessons from yesterday are valid for tomorrow if the variables that impacted the decisions are captured. Examples of this are where price wars repeat and damage all major players in the market. The reason why they repeat is that the knowledge of how badly they affected each player is not harnessed and evaluated at the time the decision was taken.

Using an intranet to create a dynamic marketing information system

Using an intranet, the information taken from internal sources can be collected, stored and displayed in an easy to use manner as soon as the data becomes available. In this way a dynamic SWOT analysis can be created and maintained for the organization. The strengths and weaknesses of the organization are stored in an internal section; the opportunities and threats are maintained in the other. These databases can then be used for analysis, decision-making, planning and control purposes throughout the organization. The emphasis is on the use of this information as a dynamic source of knowledge and should not focus on how the information is then processed.

The MkIS system can be used to collect dynamic information from salespeople about the environment and competitors: if orders have been lost, to whom and why? How does the organization's pricing policy compare to moves by rivals? What feedback has there been to product innovations? Up-to-the-minute information on, for example, pricing decisions or new product developments, can be a vital tool for firms in dynamic markets. An intranet can massively decrease the effort of sharing this sort of information, and the technology offers an exciting tool used effectively by many innovative organizations.

Conclusion

Just as the Internet makes research and data gathering easier, so intranet technology offers a radical tool to improve the analysis and dissemination of information within an organization. But the benefits this can deliver will not be realized unless technology is made to serve the interests of the people who use it. The sort of information collected must suit the needs of the organization in question, and it is essential that it is organized and presented in a coherent, easy-to-use structure that makes it easier for people to work together. But properly thought through, a good management information system will be clear, easy to update and will make the networks of people within your organization more effective, and more responsive to change.

Checklist

You now know:

The difference between an MIS and an MkIS.	☐ Yes	☐ No
The key ingredients, inputs and outputs of an MIS and an MkIS.	☐ Yes	☐ No
The issues relevant for the design of an MIS to your organization.	☐ Yes	☐ No
The value of an MIS system to your organization.	☐ Yes	☐ No
The use of a webserver as an MIS and MkIS publishing and monitoring facility.	☐ Yes	☐ No
The use of a webserver as an internal communication tool with remote workers and for cascading information quickly throughout the organization.	☐ Yes	☐ No
The use of the MIS to monitor, record and trace policy decisions to changes in internal or external factors.	☐ Yes	☐ No
The security issues surrounding the use of an internet as an MIS tool.	☐ Yes	☐ No

What next?

You have now seen how to consolidate your internal and your external marketing information to provide a marketing intelligence system for your organization. Next we will look outwards and examine one of the golden rules of marketing – segmenting your markets. Chapter 5 provides you with the theory behind segmentation and then shows how the principles of segmentation still apply on the Internet.

References

Kotler, P.C. (1994) *Marketing Management: Analysis, Planning, Implementation and Control*, 8th edition, Prentice Hall, London.

Chapter 5

Segmentation – establishing a niche in the global market

Successful marketers break down markets into sub-groupings by reference to the different needs and characteristics of customers. This process is essential to producing targeted effective promotion rather than a machine-gun approach which is not only costly but ineffective.

In the previous chapters we have shown how you investigate the environment and your marketplace. You now need to use this information to define customer groupings. These are collections of people who are your target markets. If you are at the conception stage, where you have no previous sales history information to analyse, you may need to conduct further research to identify your target audiences. In this case, we recommend that you return to Chapter 3 to investigate this further.

The main objective of this chapter is to give the marketer an understanding of the process of segmentation and assess the business opportunity the Internet provides as a method of reaching and communicating with identified segments. The chapter is broken into four sections – What is segmentation? Channel choice – will the Internet reach your target market segment? How the Internet can help identify market segments. How to decide whether to invest in online marketing.

What is segmentation?

Segmentation, or target marketing approach to business operations, centres around the recognition that different customers require different things from what may seem like the same products. For example, some people may buy bread on price and convenience (long-lasting, cheap, sliced bread). Others may only want bread that is 'healthy', and others want bread that is 'fresh and tasty'. Each group chooses according to different criteria, and are all willing to pay different amounts for the product. Consequently, a baker only making cheap sliced white bread will be missing sales that could be made to customers prepared to pay more for freshly baked brown, or for special breads containing nuts. Not only will income be lost, but so too might the marketing budget. A campaign that sells sliced white needs to target the people likely to buy it, and to understand what motivates their purchasing decisions. A campaign that also hopes to draw in fresh brown bread lovers will not only fail to do so, but will also dilute the messages that the real potential purchaser wants to hear.

Segmentation, therefore, is about understanding the values and desires of subgroups, and making sure the products and the messages are right to sell to them. This is a central principle of marketing. If you sell jewellery, for example, there is no point in producing a good average product for the average woman. She doesn't exist. You need to know what specific groups like best, and make sure you can offer something they like more than your competitors. It has been a failing of production-orientated businesses that they have tried to sell the same product or service to everybody, through mass distribution and mass marketing. This no longer works. Some businesses adopt the 'half-way' approach and produce two or more products that have different features, styles, quality, size, etc. and offer variety to a large number of buyers rather than appeal to different groups of customers.

A simple definition of the term segmentation is given below.

Segmentation is the breaking down of supposedly uniform markets into sub-groupings by reference to the different needs and character-istics of the customers.

We can further simplify this definition by examining its main components.

Supposedly uniform markets

Many organizations that adopt the 'shotgun' or mass marketing approach make the mistake of believing that the market in which they sell is uniform, that is, that all the customers are the same and that they will buy whatever is available. This is also the classic approach adopted by many companies on the Internet, seeing it as one homogeneous entity. Markets are only uniform when the product or service is very new and there is little or no competition. For example, when computers were first invented, the market was uniform – anybody who had a need for a computer was a potential customer for the products on offer. All markets slowly attract competition and many 'me too' similar or homogeneous products become available on the market. In order for many businesses to survive in such competitive markets, different organizations start to differentiate their products by addressing the different groups of customers that make up the market. Gradually the market becomes fragmented and offers opportunities for organizations to target their products to distinct groups or segments of the market.

Different needs and characteristics of the customers

The essence of a market orientation is that the customer is the focal point in running the business. The starting point or the foundation therefore of any business is its market or customer base built upon an understanding of customers' needs and characteristics. Customers for consumer products such as clothes, cosmetics, jewellery, cars, electrical appliances, holidays, trains and buses can be grouped as segments by reference to their age, sex, social class and life style. Customers for industrial products can be grouped by analysing their geographical location, types of industry, end use of products and customer size. Analysis of all types of markets can also give rise to the identification of gaps in needs that are not currently met.

Criteria for successful segmentation

Segmentation takes place within the context of overall market analysis. To successfully target a market, an organization must ensure that it meets the following basic requirements before manufacturing products for that segment.

1 **Identification of a target market.** This requires imagination and an ability to interpret market research information (both statistical and

qualitative) and to identify the characteristics that can be employed to segment a market. Segmentation can take place along a number of different axes: geographic, demographic, psychographic and behavioural. These concepts are explained later in this chapter, which describes how the adoption of the Internet can be analysed using this segmentation approach.

2 **Measurability of the size of the identified sub-market**. Once a target market has been identified, it must be measured to ensure that it is large enough to make it viable for the organization to enter. The organization must be able to gain information on the make-up, nature, size and any variations in demand of the sub-market.

3 **Accessibility**. If it has been decided that the sub-market is substantial enough to justify investment in manufacture and marketing, the organization must research whether it can reach that group of people. The organization must be able to communicate with the sub-market and therefore ensure the availability of media that will reach them. Also the product has to have channels or outlets for distribution to reach the target customers.

4 **Appropriateness**. The company must be able to match the needs of the target with the ability to produce the right product at the right price in the right quantities. These considerations may prevent the organization from entering a recognized market segment. For example, it would be inappropriate for a plastic toys manufacturing company to attempt to enter a market segment that requires wooden toys. Essentially the organization has to decide whether the needs of the target market are within its agreed definition of 'what business are we in?'

Channel choice – will the Internet reach your target market segment?

The challenge for the marketing-oriented firm is to identify an attractive segment in the market, understand its needs, create a product or service that meets those needs better than any rival, and then to establish the most effective channels to communicate the offer to the market. It sounds obvious. But when we are dealing with a communications technology that is **not** used universally, it can be harder to do than you think. The Internet itself is a service which is well established in some segments of the population, and less so in others. Before you can take advantage of the possibilities the net offers, you first have to know that the market segments you want to reach are accessible via the net.

For example, in the early days of the Internet, a cosmetic company set out to target 30–40-year-old women who had an AB demographic profile and worked in London. Unfortunately, less than 5 per cent of them then used the Internet and therefore it was not an appropriate or cost effective mechanism to reach these people. Another cosmetic company researched and identified a market for a luxury gift ordering and delivery service for packaged cosmetics. They wished to target 30–40-year-old males with high disposable income. The Internet offered this company a huge target audience.

Your target market segment (TMS) defines the maximum number of customers you hope to reach. The choice of channel should be guided by the need to reach as many of these people as you can, as efficiently as possible. It is crucial, therefore, to understand the fit between the segment you want to reach, and their attitudes to the net: knowing what percentage of your TMS you can reach online will be an important figure as you build a business case to support your online channel.

It should be noted, however, that even when you know how many of your TMS are accessible online, predicting what happens when an online offer goes live can be difficult. For example, Iceland (the frozen food company) set up an e-commerce outlet, and found that online customers bought in much larger quantities than customers in retail outlets (£50 per transaction, instead of around £10). Given Iceland's brand positioning this was a wholly unpredictable outcome.

The pattern of Internet use is changing

To understand the usage of the Internet, it is necessary to understand the concept of diffusion. Diffusion describes the process whereby new ideas or technologies spread through communities. Sometimes diffusion is slow (the take-up of vaccination in nineteenth century England took many years, and many waves of illness before it reached the whole population). Many recent technology innovations have diffused very rapidly, with the VCR climbing from less than 20 per cent penetration into UK households in 1984 to over 70 per cent ten years later. The CD player, and the mobile phone have also grown at astonishing rates. As technologies spread, it is inevitable that the sorts of people who own them also change. The first buyers of CD players were very wealthy technophiles who had a 'serious' love of music. Most of them were male, and they tended to be urban. Today the CD player is relatively cheap, and it's the main home music device for the great mass of the population.

The point to notice is that as technology spreads through a population, so it moves through different segments. Consequently, with a technology that is still spreading (like the Internet) even the 'latest study' of the segments of the population who have adopted it is likely to be out of date. This makes the marketer's job difficult, as a serious Internet investment has to pay off over a period of many years, during which time the audience for the net is likely to change. Fortunately, the trend is only that it gets bigger.

Before looking at what we know about Internet usage among different segments today, a pointer that will help you keep track of the way the uptake of the technology develops.

The pattern of Internet diffusion varies little between countries

This is an important and useful point to notice. There are now thousands of studies of the way the Internet is developing in Finland, the US, Sweden, Germany, Singapore, Australia . . . the list is endless. At first sight, if you're targeting the UK market, this might seem frustrating. But the evidence is that the pattern of what's happening in different countries varies relatively little – even if some countries are 'ahead' of others. So if you see a good report on the growth in, say, Germany, look for the patterns, and consider whether the same thing might not be going on here. This way you will vastly increase the range of intelligence you can draw on as you look at the markets you are targeting.

What we know now about Internet usage

To develop your business case, you need to know how many of your target market segment use the Internet. To make this easier, we have approached Internet take-up in the same way you might segment your market. If you are not familiar with the principles of market segmentation, this section will also provide you with an overview of the main techniques.

There are many ways of segmenting a market. An organization has to apply different variables such as age, sex and social class, either singly or in combination. The various consumer characteristics and patterns of behaviour can be clarified into the following four main groups.

1. Geographic segmentation

Markets can be segmented into sub-groups by reference to the different geographical locations of the customers. The sub-groups can then be defined as towns, cities, counties, regions or countries.

There is an increasing amount of information available on the breakdown of users by country, and even by town – remember, though, that this information only gives a snapshot of a dynamic process.

Netwatch published figures in late 1999 that suggested the following breakdown of Internet users by country:

Country	Percentage of population using the Internet
Canada	38
Australia	25
Singapore	25
USA	25
New Zealand	24
UK	15
Germany	14
Hong Kong	14
Taiwan	12
France	11

The UK (with the Nordic countries) has seen some of the fastest adoption of the Internet in Europe. Digital television and WAP is advancing more quickly in the UK than in other European markets which will further accelerate the pace of Internet take-up. This is a continuation of a pattern identified by GVU (Georgia Tech's Graphic, Visualisation and Usability Centre) in their Third Internet Survey. GVU discovered back in 1995 that the UK had the fourth largest population of Internet users in the world (after California, New York and Texas). The survey showed the UK to be the most interested European country, followed by Germany. Other interest came (in descending order) from the Netherlands, Sweden, Finland, Switzerland, France, Norway, Italy, Belgium, Denmark, Austria, Ireland, Iceland, and finally Spain. Given the Internet's strong American base, the UK has a clear language advantage in adopting the net, and it is likely that this has helped the relatively strong UK uptake of the technology.

Within countries, the evidence is that penetration has been highest in the big urban centres, and lowest in rural areas. The OECD, for example, published studies in their Information Technology Outlook showing that Australian PC ownership was more than one third higher in urban areas than rural ones. Similar studies in the UK have shown that Internet usage is highest in big cities, with London and the south east leading the way. Internet penetration in London was estimated to be nearly double that in Yorkshire. These sorts of patterns are typical for the take-up of new technologies which tend (not always!) to find a foothold first in metropolitan areas. It is likely that the pattern will become less pronounced as the Internet becomes more mature.

2. Demographic segmentation

Demographic segmentation involves analysing the observable and measurable features of the population. Such features or variables include age, sex, family size, stage of the family life cycle, income, occupation, education, religion, race and nationality. Segmentation by reference to demographic variables is used most extensively because consumers' needs, preferences and usage rates are directly related to these variables. As many of the variables are observable, they can be measured and used more readily than other methods of segmentation. The main demographic variables are expanded below.

Income

Income is used as the basis for segmenting markets for cars, holidays, clothing, houses, furniture and many services. Incomes can be grouped to give rise to target markets for given products. The level of income does not always directly link with people's occupation (or social class) and occasionally there is high demand for the product from people belonging to the lower social class. For example, plumbers and carpenters are skilled manual workers but may earn more money than a teacher or a doctor.

Income is the most important factor determining the likelihood of owning a computer, or having access to the net. The OECD found that for every increase in average household income of $10,000, the likelihood of owning a computer rose by 7 per cent. The study also showed that PC ownership and web access was higher in wealthier areas. The UK bears this pattern out. In Canada too, the three provinces with PC ownership above the national average turn out to be the three with average incomes above the national average.

This is a very important statistic. It means, particularly in the early years of PC-based Internet access, that the typical user will come from the wealthier sections of society. Ernst and Young, in a study for the National Retail Federation in the US, found that 46 per cent of online shoppers had an income above $50,000, compared with a national average of 17 per cent for all households. If your target market segment is in a low income bracket, it may be that the Internet will not be the best channel until penetration spreads more evenly across society (digital television might allow this to happen).

Age and family life-cycle stage
Most consumer markets can be segmented by reference to age groups. For example, the market for toys starts at birth, for such products as rattles, teddy bears and pram toys, and then expands to 1–3 years, 4–9 years, 10–13 years and so on. An organization has to identify or construct such groups and analyse the customer needs prior to develop products for each target group.

Family life-cycle refers to the progress of life through its various stages, which can be classified and used as a useful method of segmenting markets for such products and services as insurance, cars, domestic appliances and furniture. Life-cycle stages can be grouped as follows:

- young and single;
- young and married;
- young, married with child under 6;
- young, married with youngest child 6 or over;
- older, married with children;
- older, married with no children under 18;
- older, married with grandchildren.

There is now a significant amount of data describing the diffusion of Internet technology and online purchasing among these groups.

The pattern is simple. The age breakdown of online buyers does not reflect the age breakdown of the population, but is biased towards under 40s, with the under 30s age group being most likely to buy. This is not to suggest that the market amongst older buyers is small, simply that a greater proportion of younger buyers are using the net.

There is also a significant link between PC ownership and family status. PC ownership is highest in households in which children and teenagers are most likely to be present. Teenagers are the most avid domestic computer users, and a number of studies suggest that wealthy families with teenagers are the most likely of all households with children to be wired.

The 'typical' online household has a head of household in his or her mid-thirties. This figure has increased slowly as the Internet has developed, although European users tend to be slightly younger than the Americans. (The figures may reveal something about the slightly later take-up of the technology in Europe, suggesting that it is first adopted among younger users, but shifts rapidly to slightly older users, often with children.) However, the concentration of first-time buyers on the net is among the 40–49 year old age group, reflecting the continuing spread of the technology across the age groups.

Sex

Segmentation by sex of consumers is most common in marketing fashion goods, jewellery, hairdressing, magazines, cosmetics and certain food products. Recently there has been a trend to market products such as cosmetics and diet products to men and cars, beer and cigarettes (such as Kim) exclusively to appeal to women.

In 1999, there were 5 male Internet purchasers for every 4 females. But again, the gender bias in the Internet is changing. The April 1995 GVU survey reported 15.5 per cent of users were female and 82 per cent were male (2.5 per cent would rather not say!). But by 1998, the Georgia Institute of Technology reported that 55 per cent of Internet users were male (compared to 48 per cent of the US population). Once again, this highlights the rapidity of the maturing process that the Internet has undergone.

In Europe, by the same date, the process was not so well advanced. Eighty-four per cent of Internet users were male, down from 90 per cent in 1995. Given the historic parallels in the patterns of acceptance of new technologies, it is likely that the European figure will quickly follow the US trend.

Education
Another important factor determining PC ownership and Internet access is education. There is a strong correlation between levels of education and the likelihood of being online. This is a well-established fact of Internet life supported by dozens of studies. Perhaps it should not be surprising. The Internet has strong roots in academia, and people with a good educational background are more likely to fall into the higher income brackets that also indicate a tendency to own PCs and have Internet access. But for marketers interested in the educational markets, and information industries, this is a significant fact. It also helps explain why one of the biggest e-commerce providers (Amazon) sells books! There is a perfect fit between the booksellers' TMS and the pattern of early Internet diffusion.

3. Psychographic segmentation
Segmentation by reference to customers' psychographics involves sub-dividing the market on the basis of how they live rather than on how much they earn. The maintenance of quality or standards of living are determined by social class, lifestyle and personality.

Social class
Social class of a person is based on his/her or the head of the household's occupation. The head of the household is that member of the household who assumes the financial responsibility for the welfare of the family and for the maintenance of the household. The numerous occupations are grouped into four categories commonly known as AB, C1, C2 and DE. Social class can be used in conjunction with age and income to provide a strong base for targeting such products as cars, clothes, home furnishing, leisure activity, entertainment, etc.

There is, of course, a strong correlation between social class and income. Not surprising, therefore, that GVU discovered that Europe's surfers were largely made up of ABCs, civil servants, college lecturers, college students, engineers, those in the entertainment business, homemakers, those working with Info systems, micro-computer specialists or people who are networking.

Lifestyle
Lifestyle aspirations influence individual choices about consumption and buying. Lifestyle refers to the patterns and modes of living

that have been adopted by people as their approach to life. Target segments are formed on the basis of differences in which products and brands are used to facilitate and improve the life style. In order to identify lifestyle segments, organizations have to measure consumers' interests, activities and opinions. For example, there can be five lifestyle segments for men's clothes:

1 The conservative consumer
2 The fashionable consumer
3 The brand-conscious consumer
4 The outgoing consumer
5 The price-orientated consumer.

This will vary according to the product type and is an ideal area of discussion within a forum with your customers. This can be particularly advantageous to investigate prior to moving to promoting on the Internet. Understanding this can help you assess the appropriateness of the Internet channel, and enable you to customize the website according to the brand image your customer will find most attractive. For example, conservative consumers may find the online experience in itself a deterrent, while price-oriented customers, or fashionable customers may feel it adds to their shopping experience. They may feel they have 'discovered' a bargain, or have shopped using fashionable new technology. Think how many people tell their friends and family when they first make an Internet purchase. The Internet medium will not always have such allure, but while it does it can be exploited.

Personality
Segmentation by personality types is used in marketing products and services such as sports cars, luxury items, expensive holidays, credit cards, leisure and sports activities. The analysis of personalities of end users is employed to design features into the products and the ways in which they are advertised. Personality characteristics such as extrovert, introvert, risk taking, sense of adventure and self-confidence help to build the product's personality and helps with the messages that go into the advertising. For example, from a demographic study it can be seen that the heavier users of shotgun ammunition tend to be men aged 25–44 in a skilled trade, with lower income range and often from a rural area. The psychographic

data show that the shotgun user is an outdoor type, more attracted to violence, less worried about risk and with lower levels of internal control (conscious). This type of information helps with decisions on where the product should be sold and what should go in an advertisement.

As the Internet becomes increasingly pervasive, it is becoming harder to suggest that any one personality type dominates. Instead, different products and sites can attract communities of like-minded people, amongst whom personality traits can be identified. Marketers have the opportunity to listen in to the conversations on the more interactive sites to assess the personalities involved. Newsgroups and chatrooms on the Internet, and forums on CompuServe or CIX (for example) are open areas in which marketers can detect a great deal of helpful information about the draw of particular products for different personality groupings.

4. Behaviour segmentation

Behaviour segmentation involves dividing people into sub-groups on the basis of their knowledge, attitudes and use of a product or service. These behavioural characteristics can be used to analyse customers and group them according to their:

- user status;
- usage rate;
- buying habits; and
- motivation factors.

User status

The user status of customers makes a big difference to the way you approach them. They can be non-users, ex-users, potential users, first-time users and regular users of a product or service. During the phase of rapid expansion in Internet access, firms competed to attract as many non-users as possible. This meant running huge offline advertising campaigns to draw non-users in, and encourage them to try online services. In the US, in 1999, dotcom companies spent $755m advertising in traditional media, a three-fold increase on the previous year. The aim here was to attract non-users, because the business plans of hundreds of firms depended on winning a significant share of the business of people who still had not gone online.

A service aimed at new users would need to be very simple, with lots of help features and reassurance. By contrast, a service targeted at regular users might be very cut-down, offering extra speed and responsiveness and choice because it didn't have to worry about losing new customers. Understanding the user status of your customers, therefore, is important. It is most likely that in the first decade of the Internet, your priority will be attracting non-users, and helping new users.

Having established the level of use of the Internet amongst your customers, you must next ask 'how' they use the net. Again, people behave in very different ways online. The following three characterizations will help you think through the type of use your customers want to make of the net. Do they want to be a *global villager* a *global beachcomber* or a *global worker*?

The global villagers

Some people see the net primarily as a means of communication. They use it for e-mail to communicate, or exchange ideas in global Usenet 'newsgroups' or forums dedicated to particular subjects. Typically people like this subscribe to CIX or CompuServe, or they might use MS Hotmail to allow them to keep in touch with dispersed friends while on the move. They may use the Internet for searching for specific information but their primary focus is networking, communication and information sharing. The extreme version is the self-employed consultant who is looking to sell his/her services online. They come home after a hard day and tap into their virtual office and find out who has been talking to whom, about what. They are anxious about how they appear online and often state their judgements in black and white to retain the ethos of an expert. Many genuine experts go online to talk to the populace and declare that the responses they get take a huge amount of time to answer and are often of low value. Another common type here is the travelling student who uses the Internet as their main resource for keeping tabs on friends, family and news from home. Jupiter Communications estimated that 70 per cent of teenagers went online to read and write e-mail, and that 50 per cent would use chatrooms during an Internet session. Girls were more likely to adopt this use of the technology than boys. If you are setting up a website with no chat area, and you want to reach these people, you may well fail.

The global beachcombers

Others use the net to search, abstract, source and order. They are looking for something for nothing. When they find something of value, they have proved that they can be a loyal advocate of the provider. At the extreme, these people scour magazines for interesting places to visit, desperate not to miss out on hidden treasure. This is a significant group on the net, and explains why one recent study found that the word 'free' was the second most widely searched word on the Internet. These are the people who routinely download free software, free newspapers, free pictures, free music, and see this as the main benefit the net has to offer. These surfers regularly use the search databases and would boast that they know the Internet as a Londoner knows the Underground. If they buy online, they will want to be sure they are getting a good price.

The global workers
These people use the net as part of their everyday process of working. Contacting customers and suppliers. Referencing suppliers as bookmarks on the world wide web and using it as a communication tool with that supplier. Asking and answering business questions online. Researching issues and technological changes. At the extreme, these people very rarely use the telephone but prefer e-mail. They see the Internet as a critical information base to draw knowledge from and will remain loyal to sites which enhance their knowledge, ability to perform better or give them some leading edge information. For this group, the net offers real commercial value, and they are often willing to pay for services like access to the FT archive or online databases. Many of these workers are 'cash rich' but 'time poor', and see the Internet as a useful way to make convenience purchases – hotels for holidays, presents, books, CDs, etc. Time can matter more than price to these people.

Usage rate
Markets can be segmented into light, medium and heavy usage groups. Heavy use of a product tends to go with greater price sensitivity, or demands for a higher level of service. Losing a heavy user matters much more than losing a light user, a fact which explains the explosion of loyalty card schemes on the high street. The shopper who spends £100 with you every week will spend over £50,000 in ten years, and it's worth spending not to lose the business. Keeping a heavy user also saves on customer acquisition costs – marketing – and should be a priority. Lots of light users are going to cost more per head to attract, and consequently will deliver poorer margins.

Similar principles apply online. The heavy Internet user is more likely to come back to your site than the light user. Similarly a heavy Internet purchaser pays for the acquisition cost over and over again.

There is now some evidence on the intensity of Internet use, showing that it is rising. In 1999, Nielsen//Net Ratings Inc reported that the 'average web user' had 16 web sessions per month, and spent just over 7 hours online. Remember that these figures will be hugely influenced by American usage patterns, as most users are still American. European telephone charges create a significant hurdle to achieving such high levels over here. But it is clear that a large proportion of Internet users commit a considerable amount of time to the medium. This fact explains too the emerging pattern whereby – particularly amongst younger users – the Internet is displacing television as a recreational medium in the home.

Buying habits

Buying habits vary by product, and within products. Some products require regular repeat purchasing, while others are bought infrequently. Some customers will buy (for example, books) regularly, while others only occasionally. Understanding the customer's attitude to purchasing your product will help you tailor the process to suit his or her needs. Evidence is emerging about some categories of customers' willingness to buy online. Ernst and Young found the patterns shown in Table 5.1. Notice the way some categories exploded in only one year.

Table 5.1 Percentage of households that have purchased products online

	1997	1998	Change
Computer-related products	40%	39%	−1%
Books	20%	39%	+19%
Clothing	10%	21%	+11%
Recorded music	6%	21%	+15%
Gifts	5%	20%	+15%
Consumer electronics	NA	19%	
Travel	16%	14%	−2%
Movies, videos	NA	14%	
Subscriptions to online publications	6%	11%	+5%

Source: Ernst & Young Internet Shopping Report 1999 for the National Retail Federation

More and people use the Internet as a part of their buying process. Chapter 6 will highlight ways in which products and Internet offers can be moulded to make this easier for customers. But by examining the processes used and information offered by successful sites in the fast-growing categories listed in Table 5.1, you will be able to work out what ideas can be copied in your own field.

Motivation factors
What people do on the Internet reveals something about what motivates them. If you can appreciate what motivates your potential customers, you can attract attention and so have a good chance of eliciting action. Many companies promote themselves online without the first understanding of who it is they are trying to attract and what motivates them.

This method of segmentation is much less rigorous and heavily subjective. However, it is a useful and practical way of conceptualizing the rapid evolution of the Internet. We have already seen that demographic analysis helps us get a handle on the way the net is changing. Understanding the changing motivation of users helps too.

The first Internet users were technical enthusiasts. They were simply excited by the technology, and used the technology to share information. Their drivers were the motivation to understand and create an emerging system, to develop programming. Outsiders would probably have found their conversations impossible to understand. A tiny handful of this group had the vision to see that transforming the technicians' playground into a mass market product would change the world – and make them hugely rich in the process. These were some of the first people to use the Internet and as such remain an established community with some common behaviour traits.

Starting around the same time is the academic community who instigated the growth of the Internet. They remain another established and cohesive subgroup, who use the Internet primarily for the sharing of ideas, publishing academic knowledge and networking. The Internet experience of many in this group is completely different to the experience of a non-technical new user today. They are likely to use different search engines, and spend a great deal of time in specialist subscription databases where modern academic journals reside.

The next community online were the growing army of IT professionals. For them, the networking power of the technology was key,

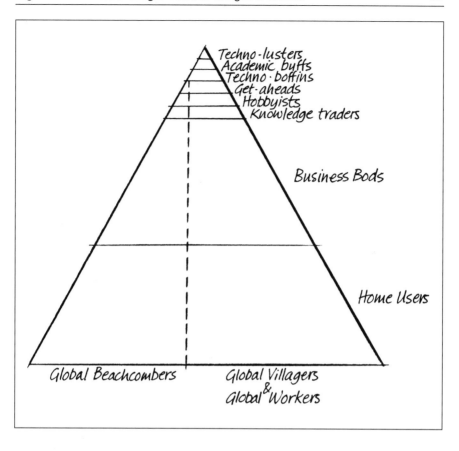

as it offered a support mechanism for dealing with technical problems. There was a great deal of sharing experience, as a virtual community saved itself from re-inventing the wheel again and again. The vast majority of the early forums on CompuServe and

many early newsgroups on the Internet had a strong IT focus specifically for this target audience.

Next, a range of other professionals went online. They valued the Internet for the vast amounts of knowledge that was appearing on it, and for its power as a research tool. Journalists, business researchers, and campaigners mined the net as a vehicle to share or gather information and opinion. They have a clear perception of their goals and are using the Internet as one mechanism to achieve them. E-mail is the main driving force behind their use of the Internet and speed of communication is of paramount importance to these people.

Alongside these people are a band of 'hobbyists' who use the Internet as a means of achieving desired outcomes. This time the desired outcome has less of a professional focus, but can be more personal. Almost every hobby and leisure pursuit is covered and these people will use the Internet to meet people of common mind, share ideas, source information and purchase products from referrals. A significant sub-sector within the hobbyist community are the music enthusiasts who want to interact with their favourite group, or with other group fans.

But the real volume growth of the Internet is coming from two other much bigger segments. Business users account for an increasing

proportion of online accounts, as virtually every medium-sized enterprise (or bigger) goes online. As remote working and portable computing grow, the Internet offers the glue to hold virtual teams together, and a mechanism to carry company knowledge and information. The second mass market, and the area of biggest growth as the Internet matures, is the non-technical domestic user. These users are the target audiences of all the major Internet providers, and most of the new consumer e-commerce ventures. The light at the end of the tunnel and the gold at the end of the rainbow!

So what motivates this emerging mass market? Fortunately (and unsurprisingly) there has been considerable effort to find out. Most of the surveys point in one direction. Customers want to save money, shop when they want to, and get real choice. Life has to get easier and less expensive – in other words the mass market wants what it's always wanted, better value for the money and time invested in shopping. It sounds like an obvious point, but notice what's happened. Technically motivated users have given way to non-technical people. Once users would be drawn by clever software, and innovative sites (even if they were slow to use). Now the mass market is here, the technology must give way completely to delivering the customer what he or she wants. And that is? Something easy to use (so it doesn't feel technical), time saving (so it's fast), reliable, and that delivers **value**. If your firm is still in love with the technology, watch out. The new mass-market consumer is not.

How can the Internet help me identify segments in my market?

The Internet can be used to help the marketer identify more sharply the segments in the market.

An approach which works for products and services that focus 'communities' (music, technical products, professions like teaching or medicine) is to tap into the Internet as a meeting place for people with common interests, needs and worries.

Forums, newsgroups and discussion areas offer a virtual meeting room for people to discuss relevant issues. These may be run by Internet service providers, portals and even by your own rivals. You can take advantage of any of them. If you can identify the people who are most likely to be interested in your product, you can then eavesdrop on their meeting and see what they are interested in, what concerns they have. You will have an ear to the ground, constantly listening to your customers. For example, the

Times Educational Supplement website includes discussion areas for teachers. If you are in the education business, you can easily read into these areas to see what motivates your potential customers, and what their real concerns are.

The best way to keep in touch with your customer base is to talk to them every day. Offline this is, for the most part, impractical for marketing and senior business executives. Online it becomes a possibility. For the large IT companies, the Internet has offered a dream come true. They set up a forum and invite their customers to talk to them and to each other. They have created an instant dialogue with their target audience and by listening to what they say to other customers they can see where they are failing and where they are succeeding. This dynamic interchange has enabled IT companies to be closer to their customers. This has enabled them to react faster to customer service offerings, product development and new product planning.

The first question you need to ask yourself is 'Are my customers online using forums or newsgroups?' If they are, then the Internet has got something to offer you as a mechanism for effective segmentation. If not then you have two options: either return to traditional marketing research techniques such as questionnaires, as highlighted in Chapter 3, or get your users talking by creating a forum for yourself, or using the net to run surveys and opinion polls. Many companies create user clubs and host forums just for the purpose of market research and segmentation whilst providing their customers with added value services such as a direct link with the organization, support and other customer contact.

Assuming your customers are online using forums, there are different approaches according to whether you are in consumer marketing or business-to-business marketing.

Consumer marketing

If you are a consumer marketer and need a clearer segmentation of your market, the Internet may offer a great observational starting point.

If you sell photographic equipment, you can discuss in a photographers' forum what people look for when they are about to buy a new piece of equipment. You may be able to elicit a response about how they liked your product. But what you are really interested in here is what your customers really value about the kind of products you sell. You may get a few surprises. When British Airways set out to study its customers' preferences, it assumed that safety, and on-time arrivals would be at the top of the list. But what customers most often cited as key differentiators were the attitudes of staff, their ability to cope when things went wrong, and their willingness to be flexible when dealing with customers. The same might be true of the health service. Good medical care is expected, but staff attitudes, food, waiting times and the aesthetics of hospital buildings are more likely to be talked about by patients. Observing the discussions between customers online can be a key ingredient to understanding how they really make their choices.

A word of warning: the culture of the Internet is open, honest and caring to the most part. There are of course exceptions. Generally speaking though, people offer advice, opinions and reactions freely. Often the motivation is egotistical (people like being asked for their advice) but more often than not it is to be friendly as one would help somebody who is lost in the street. This friendliness and openness is one of the main cultural attractions of the medium. While the rapidly increasing commercialism of the net will change the cultural rules, there might still be heavy penalties for firms which break them. If you are looking in forums and newsgroups to identify target sectors, you may be tempted to ask personal questions and in doing so offend. Please take note here to observe all the rules of netiquette outlined in Appendix 4, before contributing to any forum or newsgroup.

Business-to-business marketing

The character and content of a firm's Internet sites reveals a great deal about the way they see themselves, their skills and their strategy. But it is harder to use the net to 'eavesdrop' on conversations within your market if you are in the business-to-business sector: the forums that exist online tend to be grouped by interest area or by company, but what you often need is typically information about job functions. It is worth looking to see whether appropriate conferences or forums exist, but it is also possible to set up your own dialogue with potential customers. The key rule here is to avoid 'spam' – sending lots of unsolicited e-mails which will only annoy. But if you have a serious interest in something that others care about you will find that you can make contacts this way.

Our best advice is to use observational research to investigate where your customers go when they use the Internet, which forums they subscribe to and what magazines they subscribe to online. All you need to do is follow their route around and listen to them, elicit feedback in every way possible and use that feedback to increase your understanding of your target market. This book is all about finding your customers on the Internet and attracting them to your products and services. This sounds obvious but the simple trick of investigating your customers' use of the Internet is often forgotten. It can teach you a lot.

By getting really close to your customers by way of a forum, you have the opportunity of identifying what products and services they are failing to be supplied with – in other words niche marketing.

Gap analysis or niche marketing

The methods of segmenting described above can be employed to market existing products and services to distinct target groups. The other approach to differentiating the company's products, increasing sales turnover and market share is finding and filling a gap(s) in the market. This involves the thorough analysis of all existing products offered in the marketplace and ascertaining what needs are not currently being met. The identification of a possible gap or niche in the Internet is easy and potentially very lucrative, but is then subject to the criteria for successful segmentation and by deliberate design, manufacture and marketing of a product that would meet the needs of the customers.

How do I decide whether to use the Internet to reach my target segment?

We have looked in some detail at the process of segmentation, and we have seen that the Internet itself is better suited to targeting some segments than others. By this stage you should be very clear about whom you are targeting, and what will make your customers choose your product over a rival's. You must also be clear about their attitudes to different communications channels, and know how they use the net and why.

Having done this analysis, you should have a sense of the match between the Internet channel and your target audience. You will also realize that the coverage of the Internet is changing daily, as more users come online. But *exactly* how it is developing will seem very uncertain. So how do you decide whether to invest in the channel?

The key here is to develop a business plan that incorporates the uncertainties you are faced with. Trying to turn the problem into numbers will help you make the right decision. Start by working out how big your target market segment is. Then work out what percentage of these people are likely to be online now. Next, use your knowledge of your customers, and industry benchmarking (assessing the performance of rivals) to work out what sorts of conversion rates can be achieved online. This will give you a target revenue stream for an Internet investment at current levels of take-up. You should compare this revenue to the costs involved and work out whether you are better off spending the money on traditional channels. £10,000 spent on traditional media that reach 1 million customers and achieves a 2 per cent conversion rate is worth more than £10,000 spent online that reaches 0.5 million customers, even if they offer a 3 per cent conversion rate.

So far, so simple. But then you have to look to the future. Try to project the way Internet coverage of your segment will change over the coming five years. The answer will be uncertain, but you should be able to suggest two possible figures, one for a fast roll-out of the net, another for a slower rate of growth. Once you have these figures, you can project revenue streams for each rate of growth, and work out how your business plan looks in the medium term. The different revenue figures (high and low) you get will reflect the uncertainty and risk of operating in an emerging market, and will help you assess the best strategy. (Projections are also useful in that they give you a benchmark against which to compare actual trends, which will help you monitor the level of your investment as the Internet develops.)

If you think your segment is offline now, but will soon go online, it may make sense to invest now, learn about Internet marketing and develop your site ready for when your customers start to come online. It is relatively inexpensive and the learning curve that you will develop as a result may put you years ahead of your competitors. This is the strategy of a great many dotcom businesses which are building sites and brands ready for when e-commerce really starts to take off.

You may find that you have reviewed the demographics and conducted some research with your target audience, and not seen a correlation or a desire in your target audience in the medium term. If so, it is wise decision to do nothing. You have to follow your own analysis, and not be swayed by the hype and press excitement about the Internet. There are no prizes for spending valuable marketing resources in a medium which will not produce maximum returns. Remember, it is quite possible that, for your business, the Internet may act as a great diversion for your competitors while you can gain competitive edge through the use of another medium.

Conclusion

The key to making the best use of the Internet is segmentation. It is the only way to be successful in the long term as well as the short term. Segmentation, very simply, is the breaking down of supposedly uniform markets into sub-groupings by reference to customer needs and characteristics.

In this chapter we have explained the concept of segmentation, and shown that the Internet itself can be analysed in terms of the segments it covers. We have also seen how the Internet can be used to help you refine your own market segmentation. Finally, we have seen how to tackle the all-important decision on investment in online marketing. The techniques and concepts explained here complement the structured, targeted research skills outlined in Chapter 3. Together, they allow you to encapsulate who your target/s should be, how they use the Internet and how you can approach and attract these people to your company's products and services. This sets the foundations for developing your marketing strategy, which is outlined in Chapters 6 and 7.

Checklist

You now know:

What segmentation means and why it is critical
    to your organization.   □ Yes   □ No

What factors you need to consider when you attempt to segment your marketplace.	☐ Yes	☐ No
How the Internet can be geographically segmented.	☐ Yes	☐ No
How the Internet can be demographically segmented.	☐ Yes	☐ No
How the Internet can be psychographically segmented.	☐ Yes	☐ No
How behaviour patterns can be used to segment Internet users.	☐ Yes	☐ No
How you can use the Internet to refine your own market segments.	☐ Yes	☐ No
How to assess the fit between the Internet and your target market.	☐ Yes	☐ No
The techniques for deciding whether to invest in the Internet channel.	☐ Yes	☐ No

What next?

You should now be clear about the market segments you are targeting, and the extent to which the Internet is capable of reaching them. It is now time to develop your 'marketing mix' – to take the series of detailed steps needed to ensure you provide exactly the right product, in the right way, at the right price, to the right people. These sorts of choices arise when selling any product or service, and you may know how to use the concepts offline, in the 'real' world. Online, however, some of the rules have changed. In Chapter 6 you will discover how to work out the right marketing mix for your product or service as you plan to launch on the net.

Exploiting your global niche – the best marketing mix

The 'marketing mix' is one of the essential concepts in modern marketing. Every business, whatever it sells, has got one – even if some of them don't even know it. The marketing mix simply refers to the set of choices a firm makes to influence the buyers' responses towards the company's products or services. Planning the marketing mix properly is an essential part of business success, and it's a common failing of production-orientated organizations that they fail to realize just how important this is. It's only through getting the detail right that your brilliant products and services actually sell, and gain the maximum possible return for the business.

The marketing mix is very simple to understand. In a free market economy, we cannot force people to buy our products. All we can do is to understand their needs and wants, and plan our offerings in such a way that they will attract buyers towards our products or services rather than choosing what competitors have to offer.

The marketing mix consists of all the things the management can do to influence a potential purchaser's choice. This involves a whole series of decisions which can be grouped into four sets of variables, namely:

- **Product:** the goods or services that the firm offers its target markets.
- **Price:** the amount of money that is charged by the firm to its customers, including decisions on discounts and allowances.
- **Place:** the location of sale, and the distribution of the product/service to the customer.

- **Promotion:** the communications that are needed to make customers aware and persuade them to buy goods and services.

The marketing mix is known as the 'four Ps', and the Internet affects each of them in a unique and distinct way. This chapter will focus on how decisions about product, price and place have been changed, and in some cases been revolutionized, by the Internet. Chapter 7 will deal with promotion, one of the areas in which the Internet has had its most powerful effect.

At the end of this section, you should be able to review your own marketing mix, and work out how to change it for the Internet. Each of the 'four Ps' requires a detailed, properly costed plan, and this section is designed to help you draw up a comprehensive approach that covers all of the important decisions you will face.

The real challenge, as we go into the detail, is to retain the wider picture we developed in the last chapter. By this stage you should have decided which segment of the market you are targeting, and know a great deal about the way your targets use all of the different media at your disposal. The overriding message now is that your organization's efforts online must integrate and reinforce all aspects of your existing marketing strategy. The Internet should not be seen as a separate variable but as an additional dimension, which supports and is supported by all the traditional marketing activities.

Product

By this stage, you will have identified whether there is a marketing opportunity using the Internet. You will know whether your target audience is approachable online.

Your next step should be to establish if your target audience is currently buying your type of product on the Internet. It is increasingly likely that they will be, and this gives you a basis to research what they look for and how they make their buying decisions. You can identify opportunities to position and sell your product online in a way that differentiates it from other online retailers. Here we recommend conducting primary and secondary research into the buying behaviour of online shoppers to answer the following key questions about their choice of product or service. What is it that allows them to differentiate between one product and another? How do they evaluate alternatives?

- By the physical look of the product?
- By product features and options?
- By the brand name?
- By the packaging?
- By the quality of the product?
- By the fit inside an established product line?
- By the service level provided?
- By the guarantee or warrantee?

Going through this checklist helps you clarify exactly what it is that makes the customer choose one company's offer over another. Next you have to do two things. You must work out how best to highlight on the net the qualities that matter most – this means using all of the promotional skills outlined in Chapter 7. But you also have to discover how to use the Internet to enhance your product or service, so that you can deliver *more of the qualities that matter than your rivals.*

The rapid pace of development of the Internet means that this process of research and product development is unlikely to have been comprehensively conducted by your competitors. Clear, customer-focused research is the key mechanism by which you can leapfrog the existing online retailers. The opportunities are vast here, and, handled well, can produce a strong, original value proposition which can create revenue with relatively low set-up costs. The key is to adapt your product or service to take full advantage of the new online medium.

How do I adapt my product to succeed online?

1. Research your opposition

The huge explosion in e-commerce means that firms going online now can benefit from a wealth of other people's experience. In 1999, US e-commerce was worth $20.2bn, and Europe is forecast to reach the same figure by 2003. What this means is that thousands of companies have spent millions of dollars working out what works on the net, and by careful research you can benefit from their experience. The very fact they're online means they have made their investments in a very public place. It is very important that you find out exactly what your rivals are doing and it is worth drawing up a list of exactly how they have tried to adapt their products and services online. Compare this list to your own list of product differentiators and this will help you focus very tightly on exactly what makes your own offer unique.

The information you can gather this way can be extraordinarily helpful, as some academics from Surrey University found recently when they looked at the way hotels are using the Internet. In the hotel industry, one of the best ways to increase profits is to make sure your guests come back – it is calculated that a 2 per cent increase in the numbers returning is equivalent to a 10 per cent reduction in costs. So, building relationships with your customers is crucial in this business, as it is in so many others. In the hotel industry, relationships might develop if you offer special features and options to returning customers, or a special level of service. You might also be able to use the web to offer them a personal service – contact them by name, and offer them the things you know they like when they come back. To find out how the hotels were using the net to create stronger relationships, the academics did what you should do – they logged on and trawled through site after site. (They looked at 143. You can get away with less than that!)

Their findings show how much detailed valuable information you can get online. A few of them are shown in Table 6.1.

Table 6.1

Feature	Percentage of hotel websites
Online directory	93
Online reservation form	61
Real time reservation processing	21
Online cancellation	16
Loyalty programme information	20
Language localization	18
Virtual hotel tour	5
E-mail newsletter	4

It looks like providing an 'online directory' is now expected in the hotel industry. But if you can offer real-time reservation processing online you are giving your customers something better than 79 per cent of your competitors. Even fewer of them are able to provide information in different languages, show people round their hotels, or send their customers newsletters which might encourage them to come back. As you think through ways to use the Internet to enhance your service or product, you can see that this sort of information is a goldmine. It is also available free on the Internet, if you are methodical and take time to look. The key is to focus on the needs of the consumer, and ask how the special characteristics of the Internet are being harnessed by your rivals to meet them: by adopting this approach you can discover ways to get ahead of the competition.

2. Rethink your product

Having looked at your rivals, you must now look at your own product or service. Your analysis of the competition will already have given you some useful ideas. You should now go through each different characteristic of your own product or service, and ask yourself how these can be improved or adapted for online. Each one of the product's characteristics – its perceived quality, its branding, its appearance, styling and packaging, its fit inside your product line, and the associated service and warranties – will have been considered in great depth when the product was planned in respect to conventional marketing. Now you must look at these issues again, step by step, to ensure you can maximize the online opportunity.

Quality

The quality of the product has to be communicated to the customer. If the consumer has any doubts about quality, they will have a reason not to buy. Offline, in a retail outlet, the marketer has a whole array of techniques to communicate quality. All five senses are affected as you walk off the street into a warm, well-designed delicatessen – you can taste the food at the counter, smell the freshly ground coffee, and pick up the vegetables before purchase. Online, you can only hear and see, and this creates challenges in promoting products that rely on other senses: you can't pick up the new jumper, or feel the balance of a new tennis racquet through your computer.

For some products this is not a problem. If customers can easily assess your product before buying from pictures and text, then communicating quality online is easy. The customer will want information – about the product type, the price, delivery conditions and so on. Once they know these details, their questions about quality will have been answered. Pharmacy products, office equipment, branded tinned and bottled foods, computers, and travel tickets are all examples of this sort of product. If this is your business, then rethinking your product will involve using the Internet to provide all the information customers need to make buying decisions.

This has been the approach of the Internet bookseller, Amazon. Amazon recognized that it doesn't matter who sells a book – books are the same, no matter which firm sells them. What influences a reader's choice is information, whether it comes from newspaper book reviews or the recommendations of friends. In a bookstore space is limited, and it is possible only to show a few reviews of particularly strong titles. Online, Amazon has been able to make thousands of reviews easily available, which makes the purchasing decision easier. Recently, for example, Amazon decided to promote a list of the best books of the twentieth century. One of them was *Ship Fever*, by Andrea Barratt. Amazon published two full reviews, the highlights of three others, a synopsis, and eleven reviews by customers who'd read the book. The effect is to remove barriers to purchase in a way that offline stores find hard to rival, by making the quality of the product on sale clear to potential customers.

Another group of businesses offers services or products that can be tried out online. If you sell advice, information, or entertainment, you might well be in this category. You should consider a second proven approach to demonstrating quality on the Internet, which has been to let customers sample your products online. There are thousands of examples of firms doing this. One of the most innovative in recent years was Sony Pictures which promoted its film *Muppets from Space* by creating a website that allowed viewers to experience short sequences of Muppet characters and hear music from the film. It was even possible to access a game, download a screensaver and see previews by clicking on a banner advertisement posted on the web. The point here is that the user has a chance to sample the quality of the film, which Sony hopes will whet the appetites of potential viewers. The same approach is used to promote music, radio stations and magazines which offer free access to recent editions to encourage people to buy or use the product offline. Dorling Kindersley, the book publisher, has taken the tactic to its limit, promising to make available the content of all of its books on the Internet. Consumers will be able to see the quality of the products in amazing detail, which DK hope will encourage them to buy books online or in shops. You should consider whether your target customers could sample your products or services online, and whether you can take advantage of the capacity of the Internet to communicate quality in new ways.

Books, of course, rely on text, and so are very amenable to Internet selling, and information and entertainment businesses are easier to sample online than many others. What if your product – like perfume, or a pair of shoes – can't be sampled over the net, and usually sells by affecting senses that cannot be reached online? How do you communicate its quality?

Later in this chapter we will look at branding, labelling and packaging which can help build consumers' confidence in products they cannot try out online. Quality can also be communicated by warranties, guarantees and returns policies. But if you are selling this type of product, it is important that you are clear about the role the net will take in the product's wider marketing strategy. While you can support a product's reputation for quality online, you can also trade off a reputation gained offline, and simply use the Internet for selling. This is the approach of, for example, the online perfume retailer www.ibeauty.com. Their website provides only a small photograph and a sparse description of the products (Chanel's *Allure* is 'citrus, spicy, oriental, romantic/sensual'). The ibeauty site relies on customers already being familiar with the products, and hopes they will buy online for convenience and price. Ibeauty's service takes advantage of the limitations of the Internet to create an offer which is markedly different from that of high street perfume retailers. The quality of the product is established entirely offline, while the online service (convenient, competitive prices, simple to use) offers an approach which is qualitatively different to the scented, glamorous high street shops.

Consumers judge the quality of different types of products, therefore, in different ways. The key to getting quality right for your product is to make sure you can answer the following questions.

- Do my target customers judge quality on the basis of *factual information*? What sort matters most? How can I excel in providing this information online?
- Do they judge quality by *experiencing* the product? How can I let them experience what I can do online?
- Will my target consumers make most of their quality judgements offline? How can I use the online selling channel to capitalize on their perceptions of quality?

By being clear on these points you will be in a position to approach quality in a way appropriate to your own unique product or service:

Features and options

Every product should incorporate distinctive features and options that will attract customers away from competitors' products. Often these special features will be the key differentiator that makes a customer choose one product or service over another. The Internet allows you to create a whole range of new variations in your products or services. Those that work will be the ones that translate into real benefits for the end customer.

The Internet is a communication medium. It allows you to:

- share *more* information with your customers than you can offline;
- talk to your customers as *individuals*, and not as groups;
- *listen* to your customers' views and preferences.

Each one of these Internet characteristics can be developed to create special features for your products and services.

Sharing information with your customers

Sharing information on the Internet is easy and need not be expensive. But the benefits can be powerful. Sharing information can prove to your customers that you're doing a good job. This has been the approach of Federal Express and UPS who allow their customers to access their package tracking system and monitor the progress of their parcels. Or, it can simply make life easier for the companies and individuals you are doing business with. This has been the approach of firms running Public Refrigerated Warehouses in the US. They are introducing systems to allow customers to track the levels of inventory in the store at any time, helping them with their order management systems.

Schlumberger, an oil field services provider, used online technology to allow customers to access extremely time-sensitive data about work in the oil fields. This has allowed much closer working relations between Schlumberger and its customers.

Examine the information you hold within your business, and ask yourself whether you can help your customers by making it available to them. Have you set up a 'Frequently Asked Questions' area? Is it easy to search, easy to use? Does it answer the right questions?

Sharing information gives you a real opportunity to enhance your products and services online.

Talking to your customers as individuals
The Internet offers great opportunities to learn about individual customers. How long do they spend at a site? What other sites do they visit? What kinds of goods do they buy? Internet technology allows you to learn about the individuals who make up your market.

Once again, Amazon provide a good example of this approach succeeding. The Amazon site will remember the preferences and interests of individual customers, and target them with individualized book recommendations when they next visit the site.

Learning about your customers and targeting them as individuals may offer great benefits. But be careful. Personalizing the way you communicate will not work for every business. Here is a checklist to help you decide whether you should consider it:

- Does your site offer a content or product range so wide that users will be helped by a targeting system?
- Will you get a high level of repeat users, allowing your software to learn about individuals' preferences?
- Is the historical information you pick up on your customers a useful predictor of their future behaviour?

The online bookstore passes all three tests. It also offers benefits to users, who are likely to see more material that they are interested in. But the technology has failed on many occasions where these criteria have not been met. They key is to use it only when it is appropriate to your business.

A second approach to personal communication comes straight from the text-book of old-fashioned direct marketing. Use incentives to persuade people who contact your website to reveal their profiles. This allows you to target the right messages at the right individuals. A typical recent example of this sort of data collection occurred on the Go Network, the Internet search engine. Users of the service received a pop up screen which began 'Win a Panasonic Portable CD-Player!' The Go Network was 'interested in learning more about your interests and opinions', and in exchange for completing a five minute survey, you had the chance to win a prize. Once the survey was complete, the company would have your personal details and, most important, your e-mail address.

Mailing lists can cost money to compile offline, and the Internet is no different in this respect. You should consider how much the chance to talk to potential customers as individuals is worth, and decide whether this approach will help you.

Listening to your customers' views
The Internet allows your customers to talk back. It is important that you let them do so, listen to what they say, and use their feedback:

- Feedback can improve your products. SAM Learning, a UK software company, began supplying the Freeserve Internet site with educational materials when the site launched. As soon as the site launched SAM Learning began to receive real-time feedback from customers which gave it valuable insights into its markets of a sort that were simply unavailable before. But you will only receive this sort of response if your site encourages people to get in touch, and makes it easy for them to do so.
- Feedback can improve your communications. When you know what your clients most value about your site, you can ensure that their priorities are properly reflected in your marketing.

So, the Internet will revolutionize the way you can communicate with customers. For one particular class of products and services, this creates a further opportunity. If your business can *deliver its goods via the net* (e.g. online software, news, magazines, databases, online trading, online search engines, online advice services), you can produce different versions of your product to target different groups of users. This allows you to discriminate between those who will pay more for what you do, and those for whom it is less valuable.

Creating online versions can be valuable in two ways. Sometimes you can target a range of different groups online, and sometimes the online channel allows you to reach the segments your offline channels miss. Creating online versions also allows customers to differentiate between your products online and offline. Online versions can be created by offering different levels of service.

- **Speed:** business information, for example, is worth a great deal to traders if it is provided instantly. But to non-professionals, it can be provided at a lower price with a slight delay.

- **Control:** text provided in a read-only format is worth less than text you can download and change. Lexis-Nexis, for example, has charged customers for the right to download text.
- **Range:** casual users of a magazine site may be drawn in by the right to read the current edition. But business users, journalists and academics may require searchable access to the archives. *The Economist* (in common with many newspapers) divides its site in this way to target different groups with different interests.
- **Support:** some users will be happy with a phone-based, chargeable support service, while others may require more written support materials and greater back-up. This distinction may allow you to segment your online offer (e.g. take out a subscription for a fully supported service, but access to basic content is free), or you can use the online channel to reach the market segments missed by offline business. This is the approach of Desktop Lawyer, a service offering interactive software that allows clients to draw up agreements online. Up to 70 services are supported including partnership agreements and wills. The price is much lower than the average high street firm, and users pay to contact the helpline to sort out queries. Here the Internet is being used to reach new segments with an offer that is radically different to that on the high street. Online banking too can be differentiated from the offline service: customers can be denied access to high street advice and counter services, but charged less than high street customers.

Style

If your products or services can be delivered over the net, then you have a chance to replan their styling to suit the Internet. The core principles are the same as for physical products. Styling must reflect the aesthetic tastes of your target market, and help communicate to them the reasons why your product is preferable. The multi-coloured housings of the 1998 Apple Mac computer range were a classic example of good styling. The assertive, radical design conveys very deliberate messages. Apple is making a virtue of being different, being outside the Windows/Intel-dominated mainstream. It is using styling to claim that being different is more exciting, more leading edge. In a market in which hardware manufacturers find it hard to differentiate themselves, and computers are becoming commodities, this is a sensible approach.

Online it is essential to follow the same market-focused approach. A good example is Versaware, a supplier of online publishing software. Versaware serves book publishers who often lack the software skills to put their materials online. Versaware has designed its website to require anyone entering to watch a short, sophisticated sequence of moving graphics. This creates an impression of technical and design sophistication, which colours potential customers' views of the firm's services. The style of the packaging underlines the firm's marketing message. Style can be used as a powerful means of achieving differentiation from your competitors. The opportunity of re-styling the product online are huge and the costs of doing so are negligible compared to the costs of re-styling in conventional terms. The greatest advantage the Internet offers in this respect is that of experimentation. You can assess how attractive a product is to the target audience by the number of hit rates (number of visitors clicking on pages that reference that product). You can then re-style it to find the most suitable fit with your target audience.

Branding

Every product and service has the potential for branding. A brand name helps to establish and differentiate a product from the competition. Brand names are very important on the Internet where the ability of customers to compare prices creates a downward pressure on pricing. Brand names are one way of protecting yourself against this pressure.

Leveraging offline brands

A brand name helps reduce the uncertainty that can stop a potential customer buying. Brands imply a reputation for quality, reliability, value, service. In a new environment like the Internet, these qualities will be in short supply, and so using the credit you have built up in years of offline trading makes sense.

This is why Kellogg's for example, include a time-line at the top of their website. This emphasizes the very long relationship the company has had with consumers, which is the source of their very strong brand reputation. Similarly, the *New York Times* banner online is the same as the offline newspaper – old fashioned typography that underlines the history and reputation of the paper. The research shows that this approach works. Hotel companies with an existing brand name have found significant advantages on the Internet compared to lesser known hotel suppliers. This has been due to the fact that people like to reduce the risks of purchase by going with a name they know and trust. If you have an established brand name with international respect, you have a significant competitive advantage over your competitors when it comes to Internet marketing.

Using other people's offline reputations
If you don't have a strong offline brand, then you can link your product or service to people and organizations that do have a reputation. A shaving oil company called King of Shaves® used Will Carling (captain of the English rugby team) to endorse their new product. This conveyed the quality because it was used and endorsed by a 'quality' person. This worked well on the Internet because they positioned their product alongside a picture of Will Carling. Another example of drawing on another's reputation is that of J. Sainsbury Plc who used the British wine critic Jancis Robinson to review wine on their website.

Building a new brand online
If you haven't already got an established brand name, one of the opportunities open to early adopters on the Internet is to build up a reputation by being among the first online. This is getting harder and harder as a flood of companies enter the market, and increasingly you will need to use offline marketing tactics as well as build

an online presence. Direct mail, press and bill-board advertising, and telephone sales should be considered. This has been the approach of the British e-commerce providers Jungle.Com. Jungle used bill-board, press and bus advertisements to try to establish a name for their online site. Online, they tried to 'buy customers' by offering free goods to people prepared to register.

Managing a brand online
Brands not only have to be established online, but they have to be managed. Once you have taken your brand online you will have new tools to manage it. The leading Internet research group Forrester says that the effect is to change the nature of the consumer's relationship with your brand. Offline, you can use logos, copy and colours to communicate the benefits, values and personality of your product. Online you can allow customers to experience your brand, as they interact with you and your site. This is where the capacity of the net to offer personalized communication, tools to solve problems, and detailed information marks a great change from the offline world. When you design your site, therefore, you must ask yourselves these questions:

- How would customers like to interact with my brand online?
- What constitutes an effective, quality relationship with my customers online?
- How can dialogue be created and maintained online?
- What sort of online experience would enhance my customers' perception of my brand?

Answering these questions will help you identify the link between the experience of using your site, and your brand reputation. Understanding this link will enable you to maintain and build your brand over time.

Packaging
The customers' sense of the perceived value of your products can be enhanced by the way that they are packaged and presented. Packaging is an integral part of the product and is sometimes the first point of contact with the customer. If the product is to be sold online, the Internet offers the marketer a great opportunity to get this right, because they can test the effectiveness of different packaging at the touch of a button. The presentation of the product

online can be finely tuned to suit the target audience interactively by careful monitoring of viewing figures (hit rates). There are negligible costs in re-packaging your products online.

If the customer actually receives the product online, the packaging on receipt also needs careful planning. Buying books online is less aesthetically pleasing than seeing the cover and presentation of a physical book. Downloading music does not give the customer the all important box and sleeve cover. It is important to look for creative ways around this. One approach to packaging is to tie the online product or service to an offline product. This is the tactic used by American college textbook publishers, who 'give' access to online teacher support materials to colleges that adopt their books. The price of the online product is bundled with the physical textbook, which then has an added value to the consumer who is buying 'books plus'. This approach can be adopted for a wide range of products, and is a useful way round the packaging problem.

If you are providing an online service, it is particularly hard to find a way to package your offer to emphasize its value. But there are other techniques you can use to emphasize the value of the product or service you are offering:

- Periodic e-mails or phone calls can emphasize the quality and value of your service.
- Send out 'newsletters' that underscore the expertise your firm provides.
- Inform your customers of ways your service is improving.
- Create industry forums that provide a useful networking service for you and your customers.

People are prepared to pay a substantial amount for good packaging and the ability to convey and deliver this remains a major challenge to most online marketers.

Product line

A product line is a group of products that are closely related in terms of their similar function and are aimed at the same group of customers through the same type of outlets and that fall within a similar price range. For example, Kellogg's Branflakes have a product line with Branflakes with sultanas, Branflakes with fruit and All-Bran. In this example, the product line has been extended and this helps the company to use its manufacturing and marketing capacity to its fullest and ensure that they provide the customers with a choice. The basic product is the same but variety has been introduced at a similar price range. Product line extension is a useful strategy with which to fight off competition.

On the Internet, we have seen that 'versions' can be created to broaden your product line without incurring great expense (see 'Features and options'). The capacity of the Internet to record the time and numbers of users of different aspects of your site means that 'versioning' your product creates a fantastic mechanism to find out about customers' preferences in detail, and to work out what it is they really value about your products.

As well as considering your own product line, you should also consider the full range of products and services that would interest your type of customer. Inevitably, this will include things you cannot make or do yourself. But if you can make these things available at your site as well as your own offerings you will increase the number of reasons customers have to visit your site. This will make it more effective. A good example of this approach can be seen on the Levi's Jeans website. Levi's does not produce music, but recognizes that its customers will be attracted to a site that makes online music available. Levi's has therefore set up a large music area where users can play tracks and find out about concerts supported by Levi's. There are no special prizes for going it alone, and you should list the firms producing goods that are complementary to your own, and consider whether you can pool content so you both can benefit from greater traffic. This is known as affiliate marketing.

Guarantees and warranties
Customers can be influenced to buy a particular brand by giving them peace of mind. Guarantees and warranties are very much a part of the product because, like the benefits and features, customers look for how the inconvenience of paying for a product failure or breakdown can be avoided or minimized. Every product should carry a guarantee or a warranty which has been designed with customer satisfaction in mind. The customer's post-purchase doubt about the product can be reduced by the completion and postage of a guarantee registration card.

The Internet allows any individual or organization to set up shop. With good creative design this can make it very difficult for the end customer to differentiate between established reputable organizations and cowboys. Because of this consumers are correctly dubious of company names or product names that they are not familiar with. Guarantees offered in a published format online are legally enforceable and therefore this can be very important for the peace of mind of the customer.

Guarantees and warranties can either be provided by the company running the online site, or by third parties. Travel providers can offer guarantee schemes run by the industry, and retailers sell products with warranties provided by manufacturers. Consumers in shops know that the warranties are there, and expect the shop to be around when they start using the product. Online, they are more worried, so it is important to emphasize the security and value of any warranties and guarantees that you offer more forcibly than you do offline. This is why Amazon.com's online shopping cart has 'Shopping is 100% safe with us. Guaranteed' emblazoned on the button. By recognizing the doubts in the back of consumers' minds and confronting them, you can increase the levels of usage of your site.

You can achieve a real competitive advantage here. In mid-1999, the US Federal Trade Commission found that only 26 per cent of companies surveyed posted their refund policy on their site. Only 9 per cent revealed their order cancellation terms. Making these details clear builds trust with your customers. Another route is to use companies like 'www.bizrate.com', which offer consumers star ratings of online retailers by ease of ordering, product selection, product information, price, website quality, on-time delivery, product representation, customer support, privacy policies, and shipping and handling. The online retailer includes a 'bizrate' button at their site, and potential purchasers can see the firm's record as assessed by an independent body. This reduces uncertainty and takes perceived risk out of buying, making it easier.

N.B. One word of warning, the costs involved in suing an international company outside of your own legal domain are expensive, and consumers are usually aware of this, so guarantees and warranties usually only offer benefits to those within your own country.

Service level

Customer service either before, during or after the sale of a product is another important factor in planning and making the product (or service) complete. A customer buying a washing machine or a car must be assured that the company can provide an adequate service backup in case of repairs or spare parts. In respect to service products such as consultancy and training, the level of service should be demonstrated in terms of customer care and attention.

The lowest viable benchmark for an Internet service is that it matches the standards on offer in the 'real world'. Breaking down offline services by quality, speed, dependability, flexibility and cost will help you establish the standards that you need to match online. But the goal of service provision on the Internet should be to exceed what can be offered offline. This can be done by personalizing responses, or providing new services. Dell's provision of 450,000 searchable pages of information online is an example of a new service made available online. The particular beauty of it is that it, in effect, employs customers to answer their own queries: Dell's site includes the 'Dell Knowledge Base' which encourages customers 'before calling for assistance' to look up the answers to their queries themselves. This is both cheaper than an offline information service, and of higher quality.

There are four key points to remember when designing your online services.

First impressions matter

The customer judges the future level of service that a company is likely to provide right at the first point of contact. On the Internet this will mean that they will assess the quality of online information for the hints it gives concerning future service provision. Ensuring that you obey the 10:90 ratio of salespitch to value, your customers will perceive you as giving good service. You need to do more than simply promote your products. The more added value you provide (helpful information, links, contacts) the better perceived level of service you are providing.

Your responsiveness matters

An important indication of service is the organization's responsiveness to online requests. We asked for further information from 26 organizations online, five came back the same day, five came back the following day, ten came back within one week. two came back within a month and four never responded. The Internet is an immediate, reactive medium, so your organization's responsiveness online should be faster than you can achieve through conventional communication mediums. Customers want to know if they message you that you're really there. If you respond quickly, they'll know that you'll respond if something goes wrong.

The technical quality of your site matters
If your site is full of screens that don't work, or links that have gone out of date, then you're sending a bad message to your customer. You're telling them that you don't care about quality. They will be put off buying from you because they know you don't fix things that go wrong.

Your understanding of the customer matters
Every organization tries to make the buying process as easy and friendly as possible for their customers. On the Internet, this means your site must be simple to use, and it must let the customer do whatever he or she wants. This will mean recognizing that some customers will want to contact you or buy by phone, others by fax or by post, and still others online. Many companies make it difficult for their customers to use the ordering mechanism that suits them best, which sends another bad signal. It implies that the customer has to fit in with the company, when good service is the other way round.

You have now examined the key techniques for developing your product for the Internet. You have seen how researching your competitors and breaking down the dimensions of your own products will help you re-focus what you do for the Internet. But many Internet companies are start-ups with no product to adapt, and in any dynamic market companies have to develop wholly new products to respond to changes in demand and competition. The next section lists key principles for developing Internet products and services, and it describes how the Internet can be used to support the new product development process.

Principles for new products on the net

The Internet has seen an explosion of new product development. Not all of these new products will succeed. But there are some central principles you can follow to ensure that your Internet product can be successful.

- Does it deliver value to the consumer? People will buy products and services that give them perceived value, and the price they pay must be less than the value they feel they receive. Value can be created online by targeting the value chains of offline businesses. High street banks or retail outlets, paper-based publishing and distribution systems all represent costs that you can avoid online. When developing your product, be sure that you are offering real value.

- Is it simple to understand and easy to use? Complex products that require explanation will take off more slowly than the simple solution. This is particularly true online where technology can be confusing, it is expensive being online and there is an increasingly loud noise of the competition.
- Is it easy to distinguish from its nearest rivals? If you plan to be the fifth or sixth Internet music store or bookshop, you must be able to convince your customer very quickly that you have something special to offer that they can't get elsewhere.
- Do you have the skills to do everything yourself? Designing a website, running it, providing customer service, and running a top quality back office operation requires a diverse range of skills. If you can't deliver on all of these, find a partner who can, or your customers will quickly pick up negative messages about your products.
- Can you get the product noticed? Chapter 7 will deal with online promotion in more detail and suggest strategies to get maximum value from your online promotion budget. The importance of visibility should be considered right at the conception stage of a new product. Ask yourself whether you really are developing something that is strong enough to get noticed in the noisy Internet marketplace.

Using the net to support new product development

The Internet can be a powerful tool to support a new product development programme, which is an essential aspect of all businesses. If the segment you are targeting can be contacted online, you have a powerful medium for dynamic interaction with your customers, which can let you test concepts and new product ideas. The Internet is, of course, a very public place, so it must be used in the knowledge that your competitors are watching what you are doing. But we believe that the Internet can be integrated with the traditional approach to product development (as outlined below), and that it can bring significant benefits to the process.

The product development process

The traditional approach to new product development can be understood as a series of seven steps. Internet technology can be used to enhance many of these.

1. Product development objectives

It is imperative that the objectives of product development are clear. Which target audience the product is designed for; what revenue stream is it expected to produce; over what period; to what cost, etc.

2. Idea generation and product screening

Both these tasks are components of formal product planning and their efficient organization and control can reduce the high risk of waste and product failure. The Internet is particularly helpful in allowing distributed product development teams to work together. No longer do you need only to use the people you can gather together in one office. One British publishing firm has used this approach to develop a reading scheme for use in three different international markets. The design team was distributed across three continents, and communicated by e-mail.

It is estimated that the overall success rate for new products (both consumer and industrial) is only 65 per cent. The main reasons why new products fail include:

- Investment in managerial ego – that is, management or a high-ranking executive pursue a favourite idea and the product is developed without much market research.
- Over-estimation of the size of the market.
- Bad or inappropriate product design to meet customer needs.
- Lack of resources allocation for advertising and marketing.

The new product ideas have to be screened in order to eliminate the greatest number from further considerations. Successful screening requires the use of a systematic method of appraising and shifting the alternatives. One such system is the use of a score-card that requires the company to score points (say out of 10) to a series of considerations for each idea. The ideas with low total scores are rejected. The key areas for scoring including such questions as:

- Is it a unique product or with a number of unique features?
- Is it patentable?

- Is it within the 'business we are in' category?
- Can it be manufactured with existing plant and skills?
- Will it sell to existing customers or is there a ready-made market for it?

The Internet can act as a good link with academic research institutions for their knowledge and understanding of this field especially if the product lies within a high technology or engineering field. It can also be used as a supplier search directory to find interested parties who may wish to manufacture your product and be able to give you an indication of manufacturing process issues and costs. The Internet, then, can offer a one-stop shop to feasibility and can save you a huge amount of time and effort searching for information by conventional means. (Please read Appendix 5 on searching.)

3. Concept testing

Once a large number of ideas have been screened and rejected, those remaining can be taken to the next stage. Concept testing involves explaining and demonstrating the product idea to a sample of the potential market to gather their views on them. This requires the production of prototypes (and/or graphic illustrations) and use of qualitative and some quantitative research. It is also useful, at this stage, to research the views of retailers, wholesalers and experts in the field.

The Internet enables you to talk to customers about the concept. This is now widespread. A typical example is the small US manufacturer of noise cancellation technology, Andrea Electronics. The firm produces equipment that will reduce background noise in busy environments. The firm's website asks customers where they perceive the next best uses of Andrea's products – videoconferencing, speech dictation, Internet telephony or to support voice command and control technologies. The danger here is that the Internet is also open to your competitors. This will limit the detail you can go into in online surveys. A way round this problem is to put a general request out on a forum, collect interested parties' e-mail addresses and talk to them privately away from the forum or even using traditional forms of communication.

If you are dealing with other businesses, however, you can use a secure server which permits only carefully vetted people to access the information through a password front screen. This technology is very powerful. Increasingly, good designers are trying to involve their customers in their product development. Boeing, for example, asked its eight largest customers (including British Airways and Qantas) to participate in the design of the 777. Using online communications, smaller firms can now tie their customers into the design process early on, saving costs, improving product quality and strengthening customer relations.

4. Technical feasibility analysis
Concept testing usually results in the rejection of more ideas and the remaining ideas are then subjected to technical feasibility studies to:

- Determine if the firm can design a product which implements the new product idea.
- Estimate the investment required for development and manufacture.
- Estimate unit cost of production.

The Internet can be used for tendering, where you invite manufacturers to request a fully documented specification for them to reply to giving implementation plans, prices and service agreements. The invitation to tender can be posted on a forum or a website and the full documentation sent by post after various vetting processes have taken place. This is widely used by large organizations and the government.

5. Product testing
Product testing provides information on the following and is used on only one or two of the ideas remaining from the elimination process.

- product shelf life;
- product wear-out rates;
- problems that may result from its improper usage or consumption;
- potential defects that will require replacement;
- appropriate maintenance schedules.

The Internet is unlikely to offer much assistance here because this stage relies on the prototype being tested in physical reality.

6. Profitability analysis
Many new products fail to survive in the market because the company fails to achieve acceptable levels of profit contribution. Profitability analysis is therefore an important stage of the new product development process that provides information on break-

even points, operational costs, cash flow projections, profit contributions and return on investment.

However, testing the market's elasticity of demand can be done in a painless and cost-effective manner by asking customers online how much they are prepared to spend on a given product. This is very rough but a result of a price which is close to the cost margins will give an early indication of the potential unprofitability of the product before further costs are invested. The reverse is also true where consumers may be prepared to pay premium prices for a product. Many companies constrain their product development based on perceived low margins without first testing the propensity of their customers to buy. There are many ways to do this online. Mailing lists can be purchased, opinion can be canvassed in chat-rooms, and informants can be offered rewards for taking part in surveys.

7. Test marketing and market introduction

All new products should be subjected to test marketing amongst a sample of the potential market. Although test marketing can be an expensive and time-consuming exercise (that can give competition time to launch a similar product first), it is justified because it can provide a valuable trial run prior to national launch. Test marketing provides information on product acceptability, reactions to pricing policy, effectiveness of advertising and other sales and distribution policies.

The Internet can be used as an effective way to invite customers to test market the product. While the demographic bias of the Internet towards younger, urban customers may mean that you get a skewed sample this way, you can balance online testing with work with offline customers. The online sample should be highly cost-effective, enabling you to canvass a larger sample than would be possible without the net.

If it is software that you wish to test, the Internet can be used to distribute the product for testing. Server security systems can ensure you restrict assess to the prototype to exclude all but your target group. Many IT companies use the Internet to test early releases of their software, e.g. Netscape.

Product re-planning in summary

The Internet offers both a challenge to your existing line of products and services, and a tool to make them better. Every aspect of the goods your firm offers the market should be reviewed in this light – their quality, features and options, styling, branding, packaging, the range of products in the line and the service you offer. Using the Internet to your advantage, you can replan your products and services to make them more competitive. The net also offers a powerful tool for new product development. You can now be closer to your customers early on in the process, and you can use virtual teams that span different markets and parts of the organization.

Pricing

Pricing is a central issue for marketers, and the Internet poses a major challenge for pricing policy. This section will explain why pricing online can be so difficult, and provide you with the tools to think through the right pricing policy for your products and services. The key is to be clear about what it is you are selling, why it is that customers will buy, and what are your goals in setting prices. Having understood these points you can adapt traditional pricing mechanisms to the Internet channel.

Why pricing on the Internet is difficult

The Internet has the potential to change the rules on price for your product or service. In many cases, the effect is to drive the price down. It is important to understand why this can happen before you start to draw up your own pricing policy.

The Internet can force prices down for three main reasons: it can make it *easier for customers to choose* between products; it can *reduce overheads* making price cuts possible; and as the *scale of competition increases*, customers' choice increases, forcing prices to fall.

It is easier for customers to compare prices

If you're buying a computer on the high street, the process of making comparisons between different shops can be long and tiring. Economists call this the 'cost of search', and even for something like computers, most customers tend not to spend too much on it. They might visit three or four stores before deciding that it's not worth trying any more. They know, however, that more effort might be rewarded with better value. That customers are not prepared to try all the shops in their area means, in effect, that if they end up buying a machine that costs £20 more than one down the road, they don't mind. The impact of this is to support higher prices. Online, however, the cost of search is reduced. To compare prices of computers online, you only have to click the mouse. Indeed one click can let you compare the same goods from all over the world, and it is as easy to access the small firm as it is to search the major players. This means more consumers will find the better value offers, and average prices will be brought down.

Product overheads are reduced

The price of the high street computer has to include the rent and rates for the shop, and the costs of holding stock in shop windows, paying for the staff, and delivering the goods to the store. Online, these costs can disappear. There is no shop and, instead of the firm paying for the goods to go to the store, the customer pays for them to be delivered from the warehouse. This reduces the cost base, creating the potential for cheaper prices.

The scale of competition increases

The Internet has no boundaries. Whereas books in the UK were once sold on the high street – or by mail order – now they can come from American and German online booksellers. A Taiwanese direct sales computer firm can now compete directly with European companies, and music can be distributed globally via PC. This means that the process of globalization is speeded up, which increases the scale of competition. More competition brings greater choice and, with it, greater pressure on prices. In this way the Internet drives down prices. The Internet can, therefore, be a hostile environment for marketers. The customer, it seems, has everything to gain. The way forward for marketers to combat this potential global price war is to plan their marketing mix in such a way as it clearly differentiates their products in areas other than price. The first step is to be very clear about what it is that you are selling.

Prices for 'bits' versus 'atoms'

Pricing issues will vary according to what it is that you are selling. Right at the start of the Internet, Nicholas Negroponte identified this as a key issue. He argued that firms selling 'atoms' – goods that exist in the real world – face different pressures to those firms selling 'bits' – goods and services that can themselves be distributed as bytes of information over the Internet. Books are 'atoms', but online music is 'bits'. A supermarket online shopping service is selling 'atoms', but an online phone directory is selling (or giving away) bits. The economics of the two different uses of the Internet are very different, and you should be clear what the balance of your own business is before trying to fix a price.

Selling 'atoms' online

If you are using the Internet to promote or sell 'real goods', like food, white goods or cars, then the key pricing issues will concern marketing and distribution costs. By-passing the retail outlet creates a potential cost saving, which you or your competitors might exploit to reduce prices to the consumer. If you have no offline business, you will want to do this in order to create a competitive offer. But firms with existing offline businesses face special challenges as they start to sell real goods online.

- Firms that own their own retail outlets can only cut prices online by undercutting their own stores. This is known as 'channel conflict', and can alienate consumers.
- Firms which offer discounts to retailers offline could pass savings onto the consumer online. But here there is a danger that they alienate their offline outlets which contribute a large percentage of their sales.

These challenges cannot be avoided. Remember that the Internet is always open to new firms which do not have a conflict of loyalties between the offline and online channel.

To solve these dilemmas, we recommend that you focus very clearly on your company's profitability, both now and in the future. You should set prices to maximize profits, and to secure the future of the business. By now you have much of the information needed to do this. You will know:

- What percentage of your existing customers are on the Internet?
- How quickly this percentage is likely to grow?
- What are the key factors that customers use to discriminate between different firms' products (price, service, features, guarantees, warranties, etc)?

- How can these key factors be enhanced online?
- What are your competitors doing (are they developing the online channel aggressively, what is their price and product mix)?
- Is there any advantage to being first to establish an online brand? (Do not assume it's always best to be first. Often it will be, but not always. One British educational software company invested heavily in being first online, but the market was moving only slowly in that direction. The result was that they created a great deal of online material that quickly looked dated, without establishing a position that could stop other firms entering the market.)
- How will online selling change your cost structure? (The effect could be dramatic. Andersen Consulting estimated that conducting a banking transaction online could cost less than 1 per cent of the price of doing it in a high street branch.)

Using this information you will be able to estimate the extent to which your market will migrate to the Internet, and how fast this is likely to happen. These factors should influence your pricing policy.

If the online market is likely to develop only slowly, and is unlikely to replace the offline market, then prices should not be set aggressively online. Pushing sales online might damage your profitable offline business. Indeed, some firms like Schuh, the shoe retailer, believe that need to touch and feel shoes means that the Internet will never be a good medium for transactions, and so they use the web for brand building but not online selling. They have no special online pricing policy.

If the online market is likely to take off very quickly, and replace the offline market, you will have to re-engineer you business so that you can deliver competitive prices and establish a strong online position very quickly. This will be particularly important if you have competitors who are using price to establish and dominate the online channel. If you are in this position, your firm will need to take tough decisions to cut back your cost base to ensure that you can compete.

Second, your analysis should tell you how much price matters to your customers. Remember, just because the Internet generally promotes price competition, it does not mean price competition is the key driver now in your industry. A good example comes from the book industry, which is now increasingly price sensitive. In the early days of the net, many were surprised by a study by the OECD which showed (in 1997) that the prices for books were *not* lower online than in offline stores. But the explanation was simple. Most of the people buying then were affluent, well educated, busy males aged 25–39. These people valued the time saved by shopping online, and were prepared to pay for convenience. As the range of Internet users has expanded, more people are online who are concerned about price, and today most online book sellers have to undercut the high street to attract business. It is important, therefore, to know who is buying and what they value before you set your prices. Do not set prices that are too low if your customers are really buying from you because of choice, convenience, service, or another aspect of your overall product or service.

The underlying pricing issue for online retailers of goods available offline is *channel conflict*. It is very important to avoid this. Selling your goods more cheaply online than in the shops may make offline goods seem overpriced. The section on 'Price' (below) explains how to use pricing packages to ameliorate this problem. Another solution is to create a product variant, or new online brand that will allow you not to damage your offline market. This was the tactic used by British Airways when they launched their budget brand, 'Go' airlines. BA was aware that there was a growing market for budget airlines, which substantially undercut established firms. But there were risks. Launching a 'British Airways' budget airline would encourage passengers paying for full BA tickets to ask why they were so expensive. Creating a new brand for the budget airline allowed BA to differentiate the cheaper service from the rest, reducing the possibility that BA would simply tempt its own customers to buy cheaper seats. The same approach can be used on the Internet, where a firm with a well established offline brand can create a new online brand in order to compete in an emerging price competitive online market without damaging continuing offline sales.

Some issues facing companies selling 'real' goods online, however, are not changed by the Internet. This is because the cost of producing the goods themselves is not affected by the choice of the Internet as a marketing channel. A washing machine still has to be designed, the materials have to be bought, the labour hired, and manufacture paid for. The issues facing firms which sell 'bits' – goods and services that can be delivered wholly online – are more challenging.

Selling 'bits' online

If your firms' products can be distributed directly through the Internet, you will face special issues when you come to pricing. The explanation for this lies in economics. Economists have long argued that, in a *competitive market*, prices will tend towards the *'marginal cost'* of the good being sold. This means that the price will get closer and closer to the cost of producing the next copy of the item for sale, as firms try to maximize their volumes. We have already seen how the Internet promotes competition, so we can be sure that the Internet is a 'competitive market'. When we look at marginal costs of reproduction on the Internet, the problem becomes stark. For most products sold and consumed online, the marginal cost is virtually zero. It doesn't cost anything to produce the next copy of, say a musical track, or an online newspaper. There are no printing costs and virtually no distribution costs. The effect of this economic theory is visible everywhere on the Internet where so much information is free. If your products are delivered electronically, you will need to understand what is happening.

An illustration of the process comes from the US. Today, anyone visiting a site like www.switchboard.com can type in a name, and find a phone number from a directory of 90 million entries. The service is free. Content which today commands no price was worth, only a few years ago, $10,000 per copy printed on an early CD. But the CD contents were rapidly copied and prices fell, first to a few hundred dollars, and then down to less than 10. The price of the CD was plummeting towards the marginal cost of printing the next copy. When the Internet came along, the listings became worthless, and the information is now given away. This is a dramatic example of economics in action, and the implications are very important if you are selling a product that is transmitted via the net.

The process does not just apply to phone directories. The growth in MP3 technology, which allows Internet users to download digital copies of music tracks, provides another example of the same trend. By August 1999, the MP3.com site had 154,000 free songs ready for users to download onto their machines. All of these tracks would have been 'for sale' before the Internet.

To set prices in this challenging field, we recommend that you start by looking again at your product, and ask yourself what differentiates it from your competitors. If you have a copy of the phone directory, and your competitors also have one, it will be hard to sustain a price. But if you have something that is distinctive you will be able to avoid the huge erosion of value outlined above. Check that you have explored all of the following techniques to ensure that you have a something which cannot easily be copied, despite the technology of the Internet.

- **Personalization:** do you produce different versions of your product or service in response to individual interests and needs?
- **Versioning:** do you offer different versions of your goods to capture the different values of different segments of the market?
- **Service:** have you worked out ways to offer more than a one-off sale of data, and to offer instead a long-term service relationship with your customers? As the Internet guru Esther Dyson puts, it 'the likely best defence for content providers . . . is to distribute intellectual property free in order to sell services and relationships'. A great example of this process in action is the software industry where prices have reduced vastly but companies have recouped their margins by charging for support and training. In this way, they move from being software vendors to service providers. Many industries are following along the same lines, where they sell the product at near cost but make their profits by selling services.
- **'Must-have' content:** is your product unique? Do you own something your customers simply must have? Must-have content is often another way of describing branding. *The Financial Times*, for example, know that businesses will want to search *their* archives before any other because of their enduring reputation for business news – and so the FT can charge for the right to search back issues. Similarly the Reed group attempt to publish professional information that their users have to read, thus securing a good market price despite the negligible marginal cost of production.

The key, therefore, is to plan the marketing mix in such a way as it clearly differentiates your products in areas other than price. This brings into play all eight factors mentioned in the product section of this chapter (quality, features and options, style, branding, packaging, product line, guarantees and warranties and service). These can be carefully planned and presented so that the consumer clearly sees the reason for premium prices. Branding still remains the most effective way to differentiate your product online – people will always be attracted to a name that they know online.

Having established that you can provide an ongoing service of high-quality, hard-to-copy, branded information, you should use the Internet to support market research to assess willingness to pay. You will need to look at competitors' pricing, and speak to your own target customers directly.

The Internet has, therefore, the potential to change the pricing structure of an industry. You should now understand why the medium poses such a threat to prices, and understand the ways in which your products and services can be developed to secure value even in this competitive environment.

The next step is to examine the strategic issues you will face as you prepare to set prices. The two key issues relate to your firm's *pricing objectives*, and its *business model*.

Pricing objectives

As with other components of the marketing mix, a vital step in setting prices should be to establish objectives. Pricing objectives should flow from the company's corporate goals, and pricing plays an important part in realizing corporate strategy. Some firms will have a corporate goal of achieving 12 per cent return on shareholders' investment every year, which creates a framework for marketing managers to guide pricing. Likewise, a firm that establishes a corporate aim to establish a dominant position in a market requires marketing managers to engineer prices in a flexible way so as to ensure high market share. Many firms have this long-term strategy on the Internet.

Any pricing strategy adopted by a company, therefore, must flow from the overall objectives that the corporation is trying to achieve. There are five possible overall goals that can guide pricing. The first four are most common online:

1 To achieve a given target of profitability.
2 To win a particular position in the market.
3 To pre-empt, meet or follow competition.
4 To support product differentiation or company image.
5 To achieve an overall stabilization of prices in the market.

Business models

A second factor is the business model your firm is using. For most 'atom' based firms, this will be simple. The Internet is used as a new channel to market to drive sales of the offline product. In this approach, the new channel can be used to cut costs, creating a more competitive offer to consumers, and traditional price-setting tools can be used. Some firms selling products and services that can be delivered over the net will be able to use the same 'direct income' model. Other firms, however will use a model which has no direct income. Depending on the group you are in, the issues will be quite different.

Business models with direct income

Firms selling 'atom' products, and some selling products and services that can be delivered over the net will be able to use a traditional model. They will produce a product or service, set a price for it, and sell it. They might sell it directly online, or use the online environment to drive sales offline. Those firms selling products directly like this, which also can be delivered over the net, will have a particular advantage of low marginal costs. They might hope to be highly profitable.

Business models without direct income

For some firms selling 'bits' things are not so simple. They may have to use a business model which involves giving their intellectual property away for free. These firms cannot set prices at all.

In this approach, income is expected to come from other sources:

- **Advertising revenue:** the site is intended to create a high level of use, which will attract advertisers who will pay for space.
- **Telephony income:** in Europe where Internet access incurs phone charges, the site will generate revenue for phone companies who can pay the site for traffic generated. This source of income is often limited to Internet service providers.
- **E-commerce income:** the site might have links to (or partnerships with) other firms which provide e-commerce services. These will create revenue which should provide commission to the site owner and hence a source of income for the content producer.

Companies using this model include Freeserve, the British ISP which does not charge for the information on its site, or for its e-mail and Internet access service. It hopes that its 1.3 million users will generate large amounts of advertising, telephony and e-commerce income. Many information businesses have found themselves having to adopt this 'free to user' model in order to attract and retain site users. Another good example is *Slate*, the Microsoft online magazine which was set up for sale online for $19.95. But by February 1999 only 28,000 out of 400,000 site visitors had bothered to subscribe, advertising revenue was very low, and the magazine didn't pay its way. Then the entire magazine was made available free, and by June, there were 1 million visitors per month. Revenue then increased as advertisers spent more.

Charging nothing for your core product can seem counter-intuitive. The Microsoft example works because the site can draw heavy advertising income, and the magazine promotes the MS brand (creating value in other ways). If you are in a sector in which online products and services might be made available for nothing, the key is to work out the wider business model that will make the give-away policy pay in the long run.

Methods of setting prices

For the majority of firms which do sell their products and services offline as well as online, there are several formalized methods of determining price levels. Some allow the firm to set its own prices, while others ask the firm to be a price taker. The main methods are outlined here. (Notice that firms become price takers because of the particular Internet channel they have to use – they sell into markets organized by purchasers or by independent market makers. There is further discussion on this important aspect of the net in the final part of this chapter, 'Place'.)

Price setters

1. Cost-plus pricing

Cost-plus pricing is the simplest and most commonly used technique of building a price by allocating costs to the product and adding on a percentage profit margin. This may sound like a common-sense approach, but in fact deciding what costs to attach to any one product involves a great many arbitrary decisions (what proportion of rates, if any? Or heating? What about recovering R&D for new products?). Also, this method does not consider the market, and does not respond to volume. Applied to the Internet, the cost-plus method might simply impose a downward pressure on prices (reflecting lower costs) which the whole product development and branding strategy is designed to prevent.

2. Breakeven analysis and target profit pricing

Target profit pricing applies the concept of a breakeven chart. An analysis of the breakeven chart shows the total cost and total revenue that can be expected at different sales volume levels and different prices. This method is an improvement on cost-plus pricing because the firm can examine the interrelationship between fixed and variable costs and also the effect price has on sales volume. Once the firm decides on the price to charge, fixed costs cease to be a relevant factor – the simple objective of pricing then becomes to maximize contribution to fixed costs. Maximizing contribution is the logic behind the cheap, late-ticket offers made available by www.lastminute.com. The firms selling through this site know that the marginal cost of filling one more seat is very low, and so any extra revenue they can generate represents a contribution to fixed costs.

Given a sales forecast, this technique will also tell you when you will break even with different prices. But it does not help you work out what level of penetration a particular price will deliver – a serious weakness given that establishing market share online may be your key pricing objective.

3. Competition-based pricing

In this method, the firm bases its price largely on competitors' prices, without paying too much attention to its own costs or demand. The firm decides to price above competition, below competition or the same as competition, and then re-engineers its business to make different prices work. This approach is necessary in markets in which it is hard to differentiate one firm's offer from another. Much unbranded computer hardware falls into this category. In other differentiated markets examining competitors' pricing structures is a helpful way of seeing how much your target consumers are willing to pay for different products. This approach will give you a scale of perceived values into which you can slot your own products.

4. Market-orientated pricing

In market-orientated pricing methods, costs and profitability are considered but the primary basis for setting price is the 'elasticity of demand'. How reactive are customers to changes in prices? What price will achieve the firm's pricing objectives?

Premium pricing (also known as 'skimming the market')
This involves setting a price higher than competition to reflect the high level of product quality. This approach also provides a means of differentiating the product and is a sound strategy for products manufactured to cater for very clearly defined target markets. In the case of a new product, where there is little or no competition, the firm can skim the market by setting a high price in the know-ledge that it will attract customers from a distinct segment of the market. Premium (or skimming) allows the company to maintain higher contribution margins.

On the Internet, as in conventional markets, a high price can be read by consumers as a signal of quality. Indeed some products would sell less well if the price was reduced ('exclusive' industry analysis, or the 'best' business education both use high prices as a quality signal). To sustain high prices, a supportive style, brand, packaging or guaran-tees are necessary, and can create a lucrative business.

Penetration pricing
This involves setting a price below competition in order to stimu-late an increase in demand and to achieve high market share in the short term. A product should be of equal or better quality than the competition to attract buyers. Traditionally, companies operating this policy could only sustain growth if:

(a) market is price sensitive, for example video recorders, personal computers and compact disc players;
(b) the company's price advantage over competition is at least 10 per cent. A much higher price difference will make the customer suspi-cious of the product quality;
(c) the company has a technical or material advantage which earns at least equal gross margins to the rest of the industry, despite the lower price. The Japanese, for example, adopt penetration pricing on most of the products exported to the UK and Europe. They ensure high quality products at medium price ranges and gain a foothold in the local markets from which they grow by dominating the markets.

However, on the Internet penetration pricing has been widely used by service providers to build market share and secure a first mover advantage. In the UK, Freeserve (a pioneer free Internet service provider) is a classic example of this approach. The same tactic has been used by digital television firms to win viewers. The approach can only work if the advantage gained by winning users is sustainable, and customers are unlikely to switch having been lured to the service.

These approaches to price setting operate within a series of constraints:

- The relationship between demand and price is often unclear. This problem can be tackled in a number of ways: conduct willingness-to-pay surveys with your target audience; ensure you mine any data your firm has concerning prices and sales, and ensure new data is stored to make this sort of information accessible; analyse your competitors' pricing policy and notice how one firm responds to another's price movements (if they generally respond quickly, the market is probably highly price sensitive).
- Government legislative controls. European and national government measures aimed at fair trade and free competition are an important limitation in many markets. Legislation has become a primary price consideration in specific industries such as water, gas, transport, electricity and communications. You should ask yourself whether your industry is likely to come under government price scrutiny in the period of your product business plan, and build this into your calculations.

Price takers

There are three main ways in which price takers receive prices.

5. Contract or tender pricing

Here, the firm sells its goods or services by contract, and to win business it must set the price lower than other competing firms. Because the price set cannot be lower than operating cost, the contract is priced around expected profit level. The Internet enabled an expansion in this sort of contract auction. The government uses the Internet for tendering and Japan Airlines uses the Internet to run bidding for contracts for consumable items like plastic cups and rubbish bags. GE, the industrial conglomorate, also uses the Internet to run bids for supply contracts. By definition, successful firms selling into these markets find themselves taking the market price, often with tight quality criteria attached. These firms will experience downward pressure on prices.

6. Auction pricing

The Internet has seen a growing number of auctions and markets online. Many of these are not run directly by purchasers, but by independent market makers. The stock market is the best known example of this approach. Similarly, online firms like Fast Parts operate a market for overstocked electronic equipment by matching buyers and sellers. Firms selling goods into these markets simply have to decide which offers they are prepared to accept.

7. Going rate pricing

In offline markets, going rate pricing is a popular way to price, especially on entry into an existing market. The company adopts the market price on the basis that it represents the collective wisdom of the industry and will yield a fair return. This type of conformity will preserve industry harmony and is advantageous for all concerned. The same approach can be adopted online. The classic examples of this are petrol, steel, and opticians. In these oligopoly type industries, the products and services on offer are very similar in appearance, function and quality. The main concern of the firm is price stability and target return on capital employed, with steady long-term growth.

Pricing – channel conflict

We have already identified the potential of the Internet to cause conflict between different marketing channels. This is one of the most pressing practical problems you will face as you start to take products from an offline firm online, particularly if you face challenges from online-only retailers with lower cost bases. Creating online versions of products and services has been highlighted as one approach to reducing the problem. New online brand creation is another solution. A third complementary approach is to differentiate your online offers by the pricing packages that you offer. The techniques you can use are:

- Cash discount (when buying direct from the Internet you may require immediate payment whereas offline you may offer credit).

- Volume discounts (cases of wine online could be sold more cheaply pro rata than bottles in stores).
- Quality discounts (e.g. sell 'seconds' online, or offer cheap online banking which excludes customers from branch services, justifying lower charges. An example of this is the tactic used by a US retailer of outdoor leisure goods. The Internet site offers overstocked, discontinued, or out-of-season products. Prices are 'radically reduced' and only apply to Internet orders).
- Sales or return policy (variation between online and offline outlets can reduce channel conflict).
- Cumulative discounts (where previous purchases are taken into consideration for calculating discount).

Pricing – new products

There is no established pattern for pricing new products and companies adopt a variety of strategies. The choice generally is between entering the market at high price (skimming) to recoup the development and promotional costs early in the launch and to make successive price reductions in response to long-term competitive reactions; or entering the market at low prices to discourage competition from following (loss leading). This can help the company to build a significant volume share of the market which competition will find difficult to attack.

It is often argued that considerable benefits accrue by several companies introducing a new product idea simultaneously, since promotional costs are shared and volume share is more easily acquired in the short term. This gives directory providers, brokers and agents the marketing opportunity of putting a trade directory or supplier index on the Internet. The benefits to all are the reduced costs of climbing up the learning curve independently of one another and the reduced cost of providing only one website.

Pricing in summary

Pricing policy is one of the key marketing tools and must be established in the context of a company's overall marketing strategy. It requires a systematic planned approach and should not simply be based on the cost-plus method or posing the questions:

- What do competitors charge?
- What does it cost to make?
- What can we get away with?

The rational process of setting prices should involve:

1 Having a clearly defined target market for the product.
2 Establishing clear pricing objectives in relation to company objectives.
3 Having a clearly defined business model within which to locate prices.
4 Analysing price elasticity, competition and the product's profitability, taking pricing constraints into account.
5 Having an agreed model for price setting that links detailed decision making to wider company strategy.

Once a method of setting prices has been fixed, the overall objectives set, a clear view established of the value offered to customers and the nature of the competition, then you are in a position to set prices for your products and services.

It is exactly this approach which will enable a marketer to create a strong and robust position on the Internet just as in their traditional marketplace. Without this thinking and careful planning, the organization is in danger of being sucked into price wars, damaging the brand image and potentially ruining the profitability of the company.

You can go out of business easier, quicker and more effectively than ever before.

Place

The concept of 'place' on the Internet might seem like a contradiction in terms. After all, the Internet has no geography. However, by breaking down the idea into its component parts, this traditional marketing concept provides an essential component of your marketing mix.

Place is shorthand for two concepts – the *location* of sale, and the structure and location of your *distribution* system. Taken together with 'promotion' these are three crucial elements of the marketing process, and they need to be planned carefully. With the advent of the Internet, the marketer faces new issues with regard to 'place'. This section will help you resolve them successfully.

Before the Internet, all promotion, selling and distribution inevitably happened offline. For local shops, all three activities took place on the same site. Other firms used billboards, for example, and press adverts to promote themselves, telephones for transactions and direct mail for distribution. With the Internet each one of these elements – promotion, sale and distribution – may move wholly or in part online, and it is likely that most medium and large businesses will soon use the Internet to support one of these activities at the very least.

Any combination of on- and offline promotion, selling and distribution is possible. For example, Amazon uses online and offline promotions to win online sales of products distributed from (offline) warehouses. Schuh, the footwear company, uses on- and offline promotion to win offline sales in shops where goods are distributed. *The Financial Times* and *The Economist* use offline and online promotion to win online subscription sales of products carried out and delivered online. US college text book publishers use offline promotion to win offline sales of books which come with extra online resources: in this model, the Internet is used primarily as a distribution system. This section will give you the framework to find the right approach to sales and distribution for your product or service.

This section deals with sales first, and then examines distribution.

How the Internet changes sales channels

There is considerable potential for the location of sale to move wholly or in part onto the Internet. This is already happening, and is likely to accelerate as Internet access expands with the growth of

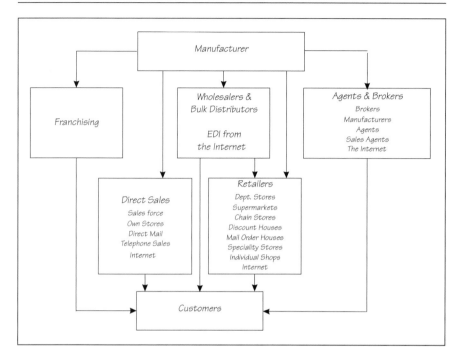

Figure 6.1   Channels of a distribution system

digital TV and mobile telecommunications. We have already seen, however, that the online sales channel suits some products better than others. This section will outline the principles determining the effectiveness of the Internet a sales channel for *different types of products and services*. It will explain how you should decide whether to *sell directly, or to use a third party*. Next, the issues you face concerning *online payment* systems are outlined, which can be an important barrier to selling. Finally, it will be shown that the location of sale has important implications for the *distribution network*.

1. Which products sell best on the net?

All products and services are not equally suited to selling online: the following types of goods are less suited to online selling.

- fragile goods (the customer will be concerned about damage during delivery);
- goods that require physical inspection before purchase for quality, colour, smell, feel;

- goods that are highly perishable;
- more expensive goods are harder to sell online, unless the goods are very predictable in quality, and the customer is very price sensitive;
- goods and services that are highly personalized (bespoke services, tailored goods, individual design).

The common quality of goods and services suitable for Internet selling is 'predictability'. It must be possible to provide all of the information needed for a sale online. Predictability is increased by offering trials, guarantees, warranties, comprehensive no-quibble return policies, independent endorsements (from customers, reputable individuals or professional organizations) and branding. Branding is a very powerful means for increasing the predictability of products sold online. The section on 'Product', above, provides guidance on re-thinking your product to enhance its marketability on the net.

Your decision to use the net for selling must also be guided by the needs, wants, lifestyle and values of your target market. Selling is a social process as well as a technical one, and you must use the channel that provides the best context within which customers can make the buying decision. Only this understanding can allow you to decide if the Internet is relevant to your target audience. For example, the Sinclair C5 personal transporter failed partly because the company used an inappropriate method of distribution when the C5 was launched. The only method of purchase was through direct mail order. This distribution strategy did not take account of customers' needs and buying behaviour. A product like the C5 needs to be seen, 'test driven', demonstrated and actively sold by trained personnel. By contrast, a supermarket's home shopping service (tied to product collection at, for example, the nearest garage) might well suit the lifestyle of a busy professional. Is the direct sales channel through the Internet really going to appeal to your customers' needs and buying behaviour?

If you think your product will not sell well on the net, beware: your competitors may not agree. The car, for example might sound like a heavily branded good which requires personal experience before purchase, and therefore unsuitable to the net. Most customers want to drive a car before purchase. However, it is still possible to sell these goods online. A strong motor brand tells customers that one copy of a Mercedes sports car is going to be as good as the next. Internet retailers can and do capitalize on this fact and capture the business of customers who have experienced the feel of a car in an offline showroom. In effect the Internet firm is converting sales decisions taken offline by tempting customers with more competitive prices. It is likely that customers of the Internet car retailer www.totalise.net, which launched claiming to undercut showrooms by £2600 on popular cars like the Ford Focus, will have made their decisions in ordinary car showrooms. The Internet makes it easier and more tempting for buyers to separate the decision-making and purchasing process, a fact which threatens a wide range of offline traders and dealerships.

This possibility should be borne in mind when considering the appropriateness of the Internet for your products.

2. Which organizations are best at selling on the net?

Having decided that your products can be sold on the Internet, you must decide whether your organization is capable of selling them. The options you face are to sell directly to customers or to sell via other organizations, known as intermediaries.

Direct sales

In traditional marketing, direct sales is often the most costly to instigate and the hardest to maintain. The Internet makes direct selling a more viable option. As such the Internet potentially enables the manufacturer to attract, sell and take orders from the customer direct. By cutting out the middleman, the customer can be offered a more attractive price and the manufacturer gains increased margins. For all but the middleman, it is a win-win deal.

Examples of the benefits of the Internet in the area of direct sales include:

- Artists display their pictures online and selling direct to the art-buyer without paying around 30–50 per cent commission to galleries.
- Contractors offering their services online without having to use agencies.
- Hotels offering online booking without having to use booking reservations agencies.
- Industries creating their own directories online rather than paying a middle agency to create and distribute paper-based directories.
- Theatre and concert bookings direct rather than going through ticket reservations agencies.
- Book publishers selling directly to customers.

Indirect sales

When the Internet was first recognized as a potent commercial medium, it was thought that direct selling would dominate, and that middlemen would be squeezed. The Internet would make their powerful position in the supply chain redundant. The jargon was 'disintermediation', as intermediaries standing between the producer and the market were cut out of the loop. In practice, there has been no clear pattern of disintermediation, and for many producers, the dream of direct selling will remain just that.

Offline, indirect selling is very familiar. Many manufacturers sell products through retailers who take a mark-up, or via agents (e.g. commission-based sales teams) or brokers. These firms can be very powerful (the food retailers now control the whole food supply chain), and they remain powerful online. You may have to use them to market your goods.

There are now thousands of indirect online sales sites. The Gardeners Supply Company, an American gardening retailer, is an online outlet for brands including Birkenstock shoes, and books published by Rodale. The calculation for these firms is that the Internet site will give them more cost-effective access to the gardening audience than they could achieve alone.

Sometimes manufacturers have to go through more than one intermediary to reach their customer. Citizen watches and Swarovski crystal are available online at discount prices. To buy it, many consumers first visit the US jewellery site www.Jewelrymall.com, and then click through to www.eJewelry.com, one of the sites accessible via www.Jewelrymall.com. Only when they get here can they make their purchase. Once again, for the product manufacturers the key issue is whether they have to accept indirect selling like this, or can they draw enough traffic themselves to achieve higher profits.

Using an intermediary is the right policy for your firm if:

- you lack the product range to sell direct;
- your firm lacks the skills to sell direct;
- your range of offers will not be able alone to draw significant Internet traffic;
- your sales do not produce enough revenue to justify an online outlet;
- the online market for your goods is growing only slowly, and you will lose nothing by delaying setting up your own outlet.

For offline indirect sellers themselves, the challenge is to adapt to the online environment. If this has not already been achieved, it must be done very quickly. Online indirect selling has been an area of strong growth, and is now a very competitive area. Retailers offering generic products which can be purchased without sampling are at most risk, and it is unsurprising that Argos, Tescos, Sainsburys and Toys'R'Us, which offer products of this type, are some of the first retailers to take advantage of the Internet. Taking an intermediary business online requires a model that offers value to the consumer and to product manufacturer. This implies establishing strong relationships and partnerships with key product suppliers. But, as the Internet rapidly matures, firms are becoming increasingly committed and new entrants will find it harder to secure a foot-hold.

Setting up the online sales channel must be carefully planned. Chapter 9, 'E-commerce', explores some of the practical issues facing firms seeking to conduct transactions over the Internet.

3. How the Internet changes distribution channels

Once you have achieved your sale, your product or service needs to be distributed to the consumer. This involves the final stage in the channel of distribution, the means by which a product travels from manufacturer to the customer. Most channels of distribution consist of inter-dependent businesses that engage in product movement and availability. The decisions regarding the choice of distribution is as important as the product itself. The efficiency of the distribution channel, and the location of power within it, is critical to profitability. The reliability of the channel is an essential component of service. If delivery is late, goods are damaged or do not arrive at all, the business will quickly collapse.

The Internet has the capacity to change radically the shape of the distribution channel: distribution can be *transferred to the net*; online sales *change the logic of offline distribution systems*; and the *information-sharing capacity* of the net liberates firms to re-think relationships and roles in the distribution chain.

Distribution via the net

The most obvious way in which the net changes distribution channels is by replacing them altogether. We have seen in our review of 'Product' that this is occurring in the music industry, news and information industries, and soon in the television industry as online video begins to spread. These are a limited set of businesses: the Internet's potential as a distribution channel is not confined to them. Whatever your business, you can use the Internet to distribute extra information and support services at very low cost, giving your core products a competitive edge. The channel can also be a means of cost saving by distributing information on the net that is already available offline. These approaches work well for a string of information and service activities that support physical products:

- **Technical support information.** Firms selling machinery could publish maintenance information and answer queries online. This would be more convenient and less expensive than a paper or phone based service.
- **Financial support information.** Details of customer accounts, payment dates, etc. can be accessed through password protected sites.
- **Manufacturing and stock control information.** Levels of inventory, and last-ordering dates can be valuable aids to client planning.
- **Company contact information.** Customers using your firm will want to find out easily whom to contact with problems, ideas and questions. Making it easy to do this helps break down the barriers between your firm and the outside world, improving customer relations.
- **Interactive online learning support.** Firms selling software or offline educational material could use the Internet to provide online, computer generated, interactive tuition.
- **Background product information.** Customers using your products may value very quick and easy access to relevant data. Pharmaceuticals sites could include trial and toxicity data, supermarkets information on product policy decisions (e.g. GM foods). Specific questions can be answered online.
- **Service and manufacturing quality information.** The Fedex online parcel tracking service provides a model that other firms can copy. Opening up your databases in this way emphasizes the quality of your service and helps customers deal with things that do go wrong.

In many areas online information can be supplemented by two-way communication on the net – questions and answers. However, you should make sure that phone contact is encouraged too. Putting too much of the customer interface online can be as limiting as too little. Sites backed with call centres have a 200 per cent increase in customer loyalty.

The impact of the net on offline distribution

If you are selling a significant proportion of your goods online, the entire logic of your distribution system is likely to be *directly* affected by the net, and you will need to re-plan to achieve the most efficient and effective support for your sales. In other words, a key competitive advantage will be the efficiency and responsiveness of your logistical backup. In general, a shift to online selling will have the following impacts:

- Distributed retail outlets will become less important. Their primary purpose is to achieve sales, which are now online. If you own your retail outlets, you will need to plan what to do with them.
- Central warehousing will replace stockholding in retail stores, saving overheads and reducing inventory. If your best selling location is online, your best stockholding location will be next to national and global transport hubs, to achieve efficiency in distribution.
- Transport systems will shift from bulk distribution to shops, to fragmented distribution to individual buyers. These orders might come from anywhere within your currency or language zone, and your business may not have the scale or skills to deliver them efficiently.

These general principles, of course, must be applied with care to particular products. For example, transporting perishable or fragile goods long distances direct to individual consumers can be very expensive, and customers may not trust the system to work. Flowers, a case in point, *are* available by mail order, but the bulk of deliveries are made from a local retail outlet. The centralizing trend outlined above, then, does not apply to all products. Similarly, many firms that sell online will retain retail outlets – although these may not be the most efficient locations from which to organize deliveries.

One of the key areas you must re-consider here is transport. Many firms run their own logistics, with a dedicated transport fleet. The economics change completely when the delivery is direct to the customer. Even if you retain a retail chain, it may not make sense to run deliveries yourself. The cost of providing the service may be greater than outsourcing through an appropriate partnership with a delivery specialist. But these relationships are critical. This is the only time your customer will have direct contact with your firm, and so it is important delivery is on time, the staff are courteous, and that the goods are undamaged. To ensure this happens you must set clear quality standards, which allow you and your customer redress if they are not achieved.

Whatever proportion of sales migrate online, your distribution system will experience *indirect* effects from Internet technology. This is because of the capacity of the Internet to support information sharing between organizations. Prior to the Internet, the difficulty of sharing information between organizations meant that, for many firms, a whole series of relationships had to be handled in house (for example transport, warehousing, parts supply, packaging). The cost of transmitting endless detailed order requests and information about plant capacity was too high to make out-sourcing efficient. The Internet allows firms to reconsider these decisions. It is now very easy to share very detailed, real-time information between businesses, so a key justification of 'doing it in house' is removed.

You will need to examine the relationships in your distribution chain one by one to see whether the Internet makes new, more efficient relationships possible. This may be possible even if you do not sell via the net.

A good example of the way improved communications can re-structure a supply chain more efficiently comes from the timber industry. Once, timber was cut into standard lengths, and stored until sold. Now orders for specific lengths of wood are communicated directly to the machine cutting trees, reducing the need for inventory in the supply chain and so saving money. Secure Internet links are an excellent medium to achieve this sort of communication between firms, and can be a source of efficiency in the distribution chain. The effect can be to reduce demand for warehousing. The Internet can also open up the possibility of out-sourcing, stock-holding and transport. You should consider this option if the key justification of doing these operations in house is the difficulty of information sharing.

These indirect effects also affect franchising, one of the fastest growing forms of distribution. A franchise is a contract – a legal agreement between the franchiser (usually a corporate body) and a franchisee (usually a sole trader or a small business) which allows the franchisee to process, stock and sell the franchiser's products, methods or machinery, and to trade under his name. Another term for franchising is licensing. A manufacturer can grant or sell another business a licence to make and sell its products or services. The Internet makes it easier to both attract interest in a franchise opportunity and ease the contractual process. By improving communication between the franchiser and franchisees, it also enables the franchiser to

- communicate best practice around the group;
- communicate new standards and new product information around the group;
- share training modules among franchisees;
- monitor franchisee financial performance more closely.

The effect is to increase efficiency, making it more realistic to use the franchising model. The Internet also creates another central sales channel which can feed orders out to respective franchisees. Examples of this approach are Pizzahut, Interflora and many hire companies. In this way the Internet reinforces the brand name, adds value to the franchise and provides business for the franchisee in a cost-effective manner.

Selecting the right distribution channel
Re-planning your distribution system, therefore, involves looking at both the direct and indirect effects of the Internet. But deciding upon the best system for your product involves looking at more than how costs are affected by better communications, and the growth of online sales. You must also look at the way the Internet can change the balance of power in a distribution chain. The most powerful firms are likely to capture the most profit, so this is an important factor that affects your business in the long term.

The importance of power in the distribution system is best exemplified by the UK supermarkets. Thirty years ago, the most profitable players in the food chain were companies like Birds Eye, food manufacturers who grew product, froze it, and transported it themselves to small retail outlets. The rise of the supermarkets has shifted the balance of power, and now the big retailers control the supply chain and capture most profit.

The Internet has the capacity to shift the balance of power in the distribution chain. Manufacturers lose power if they have to sell through large Internet retailers instead of small offline outlets. They may also lose their direct contact with the market. A good example of this comes from the UK education sector.

Research Machines sells hardware and online educational materials to UK schools. One of their products is the 'Living Library', a subscription service which provides schools with online dictionaries and reference material. Before the Internet, firms providing the content (like OUP) sold it directly to schools. Now RM is between them and the market. To make things worse, the book publishers going online have to use an American software house, which also captures some of the value generated by the use of the service. From being direct sellers, publishers using this channel now find they have two intermediaries between them and the market. The publisher is in a less powerful position than before the Internet arrived.

By contrast, a firm which can sell directly over the net is cutting out potentially powerful retailers, and so increases its power in the supply chain and thus the profits it can attract.

When selecting your distribution chain, therefore, you should work out:

- Will the number of intermediaries between you and the market increase or fall? More intermediaries generally means a worse deal for the supplier.
- Will you be more important to your online outlets than you are to your offline outlets? The terms you can negotiate will depend on how much you matter to your distributor.
- Can you use the Internet to reduce your dependency on a particularly powerful buyer? If you sell most of your product through one outlet, you will be in a weak negotiating position. You will benefit from diversification which you might achieve online.
- How can you re-engineer the distribution chain to increase the power of your position within it? Can you create an alliance of producers to set up a jointly owned online outlet, or do you have to use a third party intermediary who will be harder to control? Your capacity to do this will depend in large part upon your ability to promote yourself (the focus of Chapter 7).

4. Evaluating and modifying the channel system

The selection and use of a distribution channel system should not be a static activity. Once you have established agreements with the firms in your supply chain, effectiveness and efficiency should be monitored regularly, and evaluated against agreed measures. The measures you should use are:

- cost per unit delivered;
- responsiveness to peaks and troughs in demand, changes in demand;
- market coverage;
- customer reactions;
- quality (breakages, percentage of on-time deliveries, information availability to you and your customers);
- recovery (how do the members of the chain deal with things that go wrong);
- efficiency measures, including appropriateness to your brand identity);
- inventory costs;
- stock-out costs.

It is also important to review the distribution network from a strategic perspective. Subtle changes in the balance of power within a system can soon translate into demands for greater discounts, or reduced responsiveness to your requests for a bespoke service.

Place in summary

'Place' involves reviewing both the location of sale, and the system of distribution in the light of the Internet.

The keynote for selling is to ensure that goods and services are sold in the most conducive and the most efficient medium: this may remain offline, move online, or you may opt for a channel mix. Distribution can be radically affected by the net. Offline goods can be enhanced by support made available online, while some primary products can be distributed online. The offline distribution network might also change, and should be reviewed to reflect the possible impact of information sharing between firms. This will affect outsourcing decisions, the level of efficiency and control achievable through franchising. Whatever you sell, the cost of sale will be a key ingredient in your profitability. By re-planning your sales location and distribution systems to maximize the benefits of the Internet, you can reduce these costs and increase your margins significantly.

Conclusion

We have outlined three of the four elements of the marketing mix – product, price, and place – and provided an overview of the ways the Internet affects each of these at a macro (industry-wide level) as well as at a micro (company specific) level. By following the techniques and analysis outlined in this chapter, you now know:

How integrated your use of the Internet is within your existing marketing strategy.	☐ Yes	☐ No
Why and how your target audience currently buy on the Internet if they do.	☐ Yes	☐ No
How to use your product design and pricing policy to differentiate yourself on the Internet.	☐ Yes	☐ No
How appropriate it would be for you to use the Internet to develop new products.	☐ Yes	☐ No
What impact the Internet is likely to have on the existing pricing structure of your industry.	☐ Yes	☐ No
What impact the Internet is likely to have on the existing pricing structure of your organization.	☐ Yes	☐ No
What impact the Internet is likely to have on the existing distribution channels within your industry.	☐ Yes	☐ No
What impact the Internet is likely to have on the existing distribution channels.	☐ Yes	☐ No

What next?

In Chapter 7 we will cover the final element within the marketing mix – promotion. Many people think that, because the Internet is a communication medium, promotion is the most important part of the Internet marketing mix. We have left it until last to under-line the fact that the best promotion will not make a profitable business unless the product, the price and the place are all properly thought through. Now you have mastered these elements, Chapter 7 will show you how to bring them together with the right promotional strategy for your target market.

Chapter 7

Promoting yourself online

To promote your firm, product or service effectively online, you must understand first why it is that some of the rules governing promotion change on the net. This chapter will explain what makes the Internet different and show you how to develop effective promotions strategies to maximize the benefits of the medium for your product.

But first, remember that lots of things do not change. The Internet may have some special rules but, at heart, it remains a communications medium, not a technical one. Whatever you do, you need a deep understanding of your market, you need to know why people buy, and you need to know what benefits you offer over and above your competitors. It is tempting to get very excited about all of the new things you can do online. Start by remembering the importance of the old!

'You too can have a globally ignored billboard.'

That said, promoting yourself online does involve some different principles to other traditional media. We will begin by explaining what promotion is for, and how it has changed online.

What is promotion?

Promotion is one of the four elements of an organization's marketing mix. Most organizations, large and small, use promotional tools to help them sell goods and services. In the traditional media, the promotional mix is made up of the following main methods of communicating with the marketplace:

- advertising;
- sales promotion;
- merchandising;
- publicity and PR;
- direct marketing and personal selling.

These tools, or methods of communication, have distinct purposes and are interrelated in terms of how and when they should be used. Many organizations invest in advertising and personal selling, but without any sales promotion effort to support the campaign, nor any effort in projecting the company image. In order to achieve some return from such investments, management should understand the capabilities of the different promotional tools and carefully co-ordinate their use to meet specific communication objectives.

In most marketing situations, competitive or differential advantage can be established and communicated through the use of promotional techniques. For example, when a new product such as a chocolate bar is launched, it may have the novelty factor or some other distinctive features through its design or use of technology. But this differential advantage will be lost when competitors launch similar products on the market. Likewise, the new product may be priced lower than competing brands to gain an advantage. But economic pressure may mean that this is only a temporary measure used to promote the product at an early stage of its life. Or a company may decide to use different means of distributing the product. Again, this advantage may only last until the competition follow the same strategy. A company, however, can use the promotional mix to create and communicate lasting differences and advantages in a competitive market. Advertising, sales promotion and merchandising provide a crucial element in the creation of a reputation for a product or organization. Reputation – or brand – is the single most important method of securing long-term competitive advantage, and of achieving higher than average returns for your investment. A brand represents consumer trust that a particular firm can be relied upon to produce goods and services of a certain quality and character. The fact that you can trust the brand means that it is easier to buy a branded good than one with no brand – because you can be confident that it will be of good quality. As a result, branded goods attract higher prices than unbranded goods. Examples of brand differentiation through the use of promotional mix include Guinness (the drink for the thinking person), Green Giant (quality canned vegetables), Volvo (safe cars). If Volvo produce a new car, customers will find it easy to believe that it is safe, making purchase for safety-conscious consumers more likely.

The promotional mix of any organization should have the following aims:

- To create an awareness of the availability of products or services and how they can benefit the customer.
- To encourage sampling of the products or services on offer, or of an organization as a supplier of goods and services.
- To encourage repeat business.
- To establish and maintain positive corporate and product brand values that will help the overall marketing effort.

Figure 7.1 shows how the promotional mix can help achieve these objectives. The three techniques are concerned with persuading retailers, wholesalers (and other marketing intermediaries) and customers to behave as outlined in Figure 7.1.

The result is that your customer:

- buys more of an existing product or service;
- buys more of a new product or service;
- buys a new or modified packet, size or version of a product or service;
- buys at a different frequency level;
- buys from a particular outlet or supplier.

Communication goals	Promotional tool
1. Create an awareness of the availability and benefits of products and services, and existence of suppliers.	Advertising
2. Encourage sampling.	Sales promotion, direct marketing and personal selling, and merchandising
3. Encourage repeat purchase.	Sales promotion, direct marketing and personal selling, and merchandising
4. Establish and maintain good corporate image.	Merchandising and advertising

Figure 7.1 Use of the promotional mix to achieve communication goals

What makes the Internet a unique promotional medium?

Marketing theorists have now developed some clear models to highlight the key differences between the Internet and traditional advertising and promotional media. The most important one is this. Traditional communications media generally involve a 'one-to-many' model. One firm produces one message that travels to many potential consumers. The consumers can watch the message, take it in subliminally, or even choose to avoid it (television viewing often drops off during the advertising breaks). There is little or no opportunity for the consumer to talk back to the advertiser. The consumer, generally, does not have to choose to view the advert.

Online, things can be very different. First, the net is interactive. A tiny banner advertisement will tell the user very little unless they choose to click through it to find out more about a product. A web-site may include the most wonderful corporate promotion or product information, but it will only be noticed if users choose to visit it. Second, the Internet does not operate in real time. Websites don't suddenly switch to commercial breaks, effectively forcing viewers to take in your messages. Viewers choose information they want to access, and don't have it broadcast at them to suit the convenience of advertisers and programme makers. Television adverts, compared to this, give the advertiser a megaphone in the corner of a consumer's living room! The megaphone has been taken away. This is a revolution in communication, and it has a considerable upside for the firm: viewers watching analogue TV cannot flick a button to find out more – or even drop a note to the company asking for personalized extra information.

As with so much else, the change can be summarized in a simple phase. The consumer has more choice and more control. Not surprising, then, that a careful approach is needed to marketing on the new medium. This requires sensitivity to your customer, and a deep appreciation of the unwritten code of online ethics, which defines what is acceptable and what is considered unacceptable. Please see Appendix 4 (Netiquette).

You should think about the implications of this change. You have to understand it to create a distinctive presence on the Internet, one that makes life easier and more rewarding for your customer. Many firms think that online marketing is really very easy. This is not the case and the best analogy is the launch of desktop publishing where users perceived that design of marketing material was suddenly made easy. All that happened was that between 1987 and 1990, there was a proliferation of badly designed marketing materials. On the Internet, there is a proliferation of badly designed websites and advertising material, obviously arising from the IT department with little effective marketing. Sales messages are not translated to this new target audience. Graphics are included that add nothing to the end customer, but only make the process of viewing pages slower and more frustrating than it need be.

The challenge is to be innovative and not replicate your conventional advertising material online. 'Successful Internet marketing involves developing a whole new collection of attitudes and words to accompany them' – a widely used remark that shows how the Internet is revolutionizing our everyday lives.

We have stressed the importance of customer choice in viewing promotional material. The extent to which a customer must choose to view your promotional material clearly varies for each of the three main promotional options open to you online.

If you buy **advertising space** on portals and other popular websites, you are obliging visitors to those sites to see your advert. They can exercise choice by deciding whether to click through the advert to find out more.

But if your promotion is based on your **website**, the customer must choose to visit the site, and then must choose what to read when he or she gets there.

Unsolicited **direct e-mail** to potential customers gives the customer very little choice: they cannot decide whether or not to receive the e-mail, but can decide whether to open it. Opt-in e-mail information services (whereby customers request information on new products) put the customer more in control. They have chosen to receive the e-mail, and choose whether or not to read it.

Each of these three promotional strategies raises different issues. Intuitively you might expect customers who choose to visit your website, and choose to see the information it contains, will have a more positive attitude than those who receive unsolicited e-mails from you. Those who spend time downloading your (unsolicited) adverts might fall somewhere in between. This is an example of the sort of consideration that determines the effectiveness of your promotional strategy online.

Advertising

Advertising can be defined as a one-way, non-personal presentation and promotion of ideas, goods or services. Advertising is an indirect form of communication in that it takes place outside the immediate environment of the product or service. That is, the message is communicated to its target audience through the use of various media, and the receiver is not in contact with the physical product or service. For example, an advertisement for a new motorcar is placed in a quality national newspaper that can reach half a million people representing the company's target market. The advertisement is read in isolation of the physical product. The message is therefore relayed from the manufacturer to the potential customer by an indirect and non-personal means and received outside the immediate environment of the product.

Organizations have to communicate with very large numbers of potential customers who may be geographically dispersed locally, regionally, nationally or internationally. In order to communicate with large numbers of people, organizations cannot use personal and direct contact but have to rely on advertising. Advertising – via the Internet, radio, television, posters, cinema and press – assists the sale of the maximum number of units of product at a minimum cost.

How advertising works

An understanding of how advertising works can help the setting of advertising objectives which then influence the other decisions.

A number of models and theories have been developed to explain the advertising process. Although the number, stages and terminology involved in these models tend to vary, their common theme is concerned with indicating that the influence of advertising is a sequential process.

One simple model is AIDA which stands for:

* attention;
* interest;
* desire;
* action.

This model, also known as the hierarchy of effects model, suggests that advertising must gain consumers' attention, hold the person's interest, arouse desire for the product and stimulate action towards the purchase of the product. This model is useful in design advertisements and web pages.

Another useful aid to advertising management is the more recent and comprehensive flow-model of advertising known as DAGMAR (Defining Advertising Goals for Measured Advertising Results). It was developed on the basis that all commercial communications that aim at the ultimate objective of achieving a sale must carry a potential customer through four levels of understanding or stages as outlined in Figure 7.2.

In this model, the first objective of advertising is to create an awareness amongst the target audience. The advertising may be of a product, service or ideas (e.g. policies of a political party) or an organization. Posting an advert on a busy website will achieve this first objective, in that users of the website will become aware of the

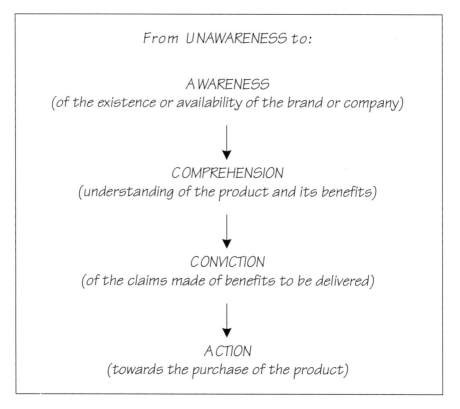

From UNAWARENESS to:

AWARENESS
(of the existence or availability of the brand or company)

COMPREHENSION
(understanding of the product and its benefits)

CONVICTION
(of the claims made of benefits to be delivered)

ACTION
(towards the purchase of the product)

Figure 7.2 The DAGMAR model

advertised product or service. The next step is to ensure that certain attributes of the advertised item are known and understood, for example, brand name, pack size, technical features and benefits and where it is sold. Online, this will involve encouraging the potential customer to 'click though' the advert – which, inevitably, will contain minimal information due to its size – to a page which provides more information, both text and image (sound can be added too). The third stage involves convincing the customer of the claims made in the advertisement. This may take the form of scientific evidence or testimonials from people with credibility. Credibility proof is extremely important on the Internet due to the low cost of producing material and needs careful and thorough design and testing. The action stage of the model occurs when the customer makes some overt move towards the purchase of the product. It may involve a closer inspection of the product, request for sales literature or a demonstration of the product performance, and may result in the purchase of the product. Facilitating purchase – e-commerce – is dealt with in Chapter 8.

Setting advertising objectives

Setting an advertising objective is the most critical but often missing starting point of looking at the use of the Internet. As in the famous words by Lewis Carol, 'The Madhatter said "If you don't know where you are going – you probably won't get there".'

An advertising objective is not the same as a marketing objective and therefore the use of an objective such as 'to increase the company's market share by 5 per cent' is of little use in deciding how advertising should be used. In marketing there is a hierarchy of objectives from which specific communication targets can be derived. For example, a firm may have a corporate objective to increase its share of the computer market by developing computers for the financial services sector (banks and building societies). This corporate objective will help management in setting sub-objectives for the different functions within the business – for R&D, marketing, production, etc. The marketing objective may be to increase sales turnover in a segment of the financial services market by £1m over the next 12 months. The specific advertising objective set to reflect the marketing objective may be to create an awareness and understanding of the firm's range of products, services and reputation.

In using the hierarchical model of advertising, the objective must be:

- capable of being communicated with management and those involved in its execution, in a written form;
- measurable;
- involve a starting point;
- aimed at a defined target audience;
- over a fixed time period.

The most useful information that can guide the setting of objective is that concerning the buying behaviour of the potential market. Effective advertising decisions cannot be made without a thorough understanding of how customers are influenced in their purchasing decisions. In industrial marketing, the decision making unit (DMU) is much more complex than is the case with consumer goods for industrial products. The decision making unit has to decide on what product (the systems choice) will solve the problem and from whom to buy (the brand or supplier choice). The DMU consists of:

Decision maker   The person who makes the financial commitment.
Specifiers   Technical people, engineers, designers, architects,
                     buyers etc.
Influencers   End users of products or services, marketing
                     department, buyers.
Gatekeepers   People who control the flow of information to
                     decision makers, for example, parents,
                     receptionists and secretaries.

An analysis of buying behaviour gives information regarding the target audience that can be useful in setting advertising objectives and also provides a guide for selecting media and designing advertising copy. The setting of advertising objectives helps to integrate the advertising effort with the other ingredients of the marketing mix to form a consistent and a logically developed marketing plan.

Media decisions

Sensible objectives are to do with communicating with actual and potential customers, not with 'getting adverts on the Internet'. Having set your advertising objectives, therefore, you will be able to look coolly at the best medium or media for you message. At this point you should review the fit between your target market segments and the Internet in order to decide whether the Internet is an appropriate channel in which to spend your budget. (Segmentation is covered in Chapter 5.)

Media selection should be guided by a thorough understanding of the buying behaviour and the DMU operating in a particular market. Buying behaviour, and, in particular, the evidence of who act as influencers, specifiers and final decision makers (or financial commitment), aid the process of assessment, evaluation and comparison of the media available to reach various targets for communication. The process of media selection can be further aided by asking four basic questions of each medium available.

- Does it deliver an audience which corresponds to the target audience in the right quantity and at an economical cost?
- Does it offer a particularly valuable form for presentation of the message?
- Does it provide an opportunity to motivate the target audience?
- Has it the correct atmosphere, or will the circumstances in which the message is perceived by the audience help to sell or promote the product or service?

Having reviewed these questions, you may well decide that the Internet should be used alongside advertising in other media. You may even decide that it is worth investing in Internet advertising on an exploratory basis in the short term. It is interesting that in the year when the dotcom businesses really took off – 1999 – American online businesses spent over $770m on advertising in traditional media to promote themselves. These firms buying radio slots and newspaper space were the same dotcom start-ups that saw their share prices go through the roof as investors predicted a big shift to online shopping. What their advertising managers understood was that – whatever your future vision – you spend your advertising budget on the media that will be most effective now. This is not to say online advertising cannot be effective – it can. Indeed, that is why total US online spending in that same year was just over $3bn. The point is that you have a choice, which you should exercise on the basis of your analysis of your target market.

There is further discussion of multi-media campaigns at the end of this chapter.

The use of the Internet as an advertising medium

The first adverts online were posted on busy sites in the hope that users would click on the ad to find out more about the product. More was generally housed on the producing company's own website.

The adverts generally consisted of coloured text, with very simple graphics. Anything more complex would take too long to download. As technology has improved, short animated sequences have been introduced, but the essential aim was the same – to drive customers to a company's website.

Since then, there have been a number of important innovations.

First, some web banner adverts now contain within themselves all of the relevant information a customer needs. For example, clicking on Toyota's Lexus banner-ad allows a customer to order a brochure, see video clips of models and find a dealer without having to navigate their way round a corporate website.

Second, there has been a trend towards service or entertainment delivery via a banner ad. An American insurer provides a banner which calculates the cost of putting a child through university, emphasizing both the skills of the insurance firm, and the potential need of a web-user for their services. Entertainment delivery is increasingly common. Improving compression technology, and faster modems (and lines, in some cases) has allowed more firms to deliver applets containing audio and video via banners. There have been some impressive claims for the effectiveness of these approaches in enticing web users to explore products more fully.

The development of banners reflects the desire of marketers to maintain audience interest by using the latest technology where

possible. New banners containing video sequences, for example, have performed better in terms of user response than traditional, static, text-only devices. This reflects the enthusiasm of Internet users for new, easy-to-use technology. It is likely, however, that each new technical innovation will bring a temporary competitive advantage as net users try out novel applications. Advertisers who use seemingly primitive or out-of-date technology will have worse response rates from browsing Internet users than those who offer a more exciting service.

However this principle does not apply to all adverts. Online advertising has two functions. One may be to entice users to find out more about products. But a second role is simply to help users find a site they may already know about. The widespread adverts for Amazon.com operate primarily as sign posts to connect users to one online bookstore. As such they form part of a strategy to ensure a website is highly visible, and they do not require advanced graphics and enticing software features. British Airways has used online adverts in a similar way, to connect users directly to a booking area for flight offers. This second form of advertising is increasingly common as Internet users see the medium as a source of competitively priced goods and services. Here the key for advertisers is to make sure that the offer can easily be accessed by Internet users – whatever search engine or portal they are using. For this sort of 'signpost' advertising, technical sophistication matters much less than ubiquity.

Measuring results from adverts

There are a number of methods for testing the effectiveness of advertising online. Two common approaches are to measure the number of times an ad is viewed, or to measure the frequency with which users 'click through' a banner ad to view more information about a product or service.

The number of times a page containing an advert is visited is sometimes reflected in the price charged for advertising space. This can be measured as the cost per thousand impressions (known as the CPM). This measurement does tell you the business of the site where the advert is located, but it does not tell you how many visitors to the site took any notice of your ad.

The 'click through rate' (CTR) was designed to provide this extra information. A CTR figure tells you how often visitors click on your advertisement to connect with a source of further information (which is often held on your website). When web ads were a novelty, CTRs were high, but they have fallen dramatically. Common rates today are measured in fractions of a percent of the times an advert is displayed to a viewer. (The percentage represents the number of click-throughs divided by the number of times the page containing the advert is viewed.) This suggests that there has been a shift from browsing – unfocused rooting about on the net to find things of interest – to more deliberative behaviour. It might sound depressing, but it also implies that there has been a change in the quality of viewer represented by each click-through. As CTRs fall, it is likely that those who do click through are more likely to have a serious interest in your product.

A third approach, increasingly common as e-commerce becomes a central focus of web marketing, is to measure the level of sales achieved by web ads. (N.B. e-commerce is dealt with in more detail in Chapter 9.) Measuring the levels of direct sales generated by an online advertising campaign provides the ultimate evidence of the effectiveness of a campaign, and allows you to create figures for the cost of customer acquisition. Of course this measure can only be used for products that are themselves amenable to online selling.

The usefulness of these measures is that they allow you to adapt your advertising tactics as you gather evidence of what works. You must ensure that you get rapid feedback on the effectiveness of different approaches to writing copy and using images. Seemingly small changes can make a big difference. One study, for example, done by Florida State University in 1998, used CTRs to compare the effectiveness of four different copy lines for a banner ad for a dating company.

Copy	Click through frequency
Specializing in finding your soulmate	16
Find your soulmate	33
Click here to find your soulmate	39
Click here	62

The study shows a number of interesting things. First, the web offers quick feedback. It seems that the enigmatic, and seemingly abrupt injunction to 'click here' produced the highest response rate. This sort of copy would be less successful in many traditional media. Given the results, it would be easy to change copy in other adverts to take advantage of the experience gained. It also offers some tricky choices. The marketer faced with the information from a study like the one quoted will need to decide whether viewers clicking through 'to find a soulmate' represent a more targeted (and therefore more valuable) audience than those simply clicking on an enigmatic banner. But the nature of the audience response, and the choices facing the marketer are much clearer online than in less responsive traditional marketing environments.

A number of studies point to a decline in response rates to online adverts as the Internet has matured. This should not be a surprise. Some of the early CTRs were very high, reflecting the curiosity of what was once a new generation of Internet users. As Internet users become more familiar with the medium, they tend to become more focused. They begin to use the net to explore their own interests, and get less pleasure from simply exploring the net for its own sake. In these circumstances, we should expect:

- Users will start to return to sites that they find work well. Why try a new search engine, or news service, when the one you've already found works well?
- Users will click through to advertising sites 'on a whim' less often.
- Users will value the functionality of sites (what they can help you do) more than their appearance: utility – the capacity of an advert to get you quickly to useful information or services – will be valued more and more. Novelty will soon wear off.

In fact, the research shows that all three of these expectations are being fulfilled. The upside for advertisers is that Internet users are starting to look to the net to get things done, and so there is a valuable role for adverts that connect users to clear information about products and services that offer value. When an Internet veteran clicks through to your site, they are doing so for a good reason.

Websites – putting your company on the Internet

A second, very widely used promotional strategy is to create a website for your company. Creating a website requires hard thinking up front. Websites have become key sources of online corporate information and promotion, but many firms have launched them without assessing the importance of a website to their wider business plans, or without thinking through the purchasing and design issues properly. The result is that some very good firms have websites which make them appear less competent than they are. Conversely, some smaller players are able to gain advantage by creating excellent sites online that suggest the firm is much bigger or better established than it really is.

The first question to answer is simple, 'How serious are we?' In traditional promotion terms, do you want a black and white A5 flyer or a 20-page four-colour embossed, pull-out brochure? Budget will be the deciding factor when it comes to designing your website. Again, the decision of how much to spend in reference to the Internet needs to be seen in the overall context of the advertising budget bearing in mind that the Internet presence also needs to be advertised in its own right. It is important to build in ongoing maintenance and updating costs, as well as the initial development costs.

How much you decide to spend will depend on how important your website is to your wider communications strategy, and also how interactive you wish to make your Internet presence. This is, of course, similar to the issues of producing an advert. Too inexpensive and it may cheapen your corporate image in the eyes of your customers, especially if they are used to high quality advertising and marketing materials. Too expensive and it may be costly to warrant and maintain. The key to budgeting is to think through these wider maintenance costs – the costs of replying to e-mails as well as setting up an e-mail facility – as well as the start-up costs.

The stages in setting up an online presence

We have described the elements you will need and the choices that you will face in setting up a website. Whichever option you identify as your goal, you should recognize that getting there involves a process which needs to be managed. Firms generally do not sit down, plan their approach, and simply implement it unchanged. What happens in practice is much more organic. The most common pattern begins with small scale experimentation, during which time there may be sceptics and enthusiasts scattered throughout an organization essentially watching what is going on. The programme may well be IT led – or certainly IT dominated – in the early phases. Then the size of the team may increase, and more senior management may get involved. The goals may change: the initial objective of dipping a toe in the water is discarded (because it's done), and new goals define the desired outputs of a site. Leadership, as well as moving away from IT, might often move up the organization at this stage. The evidence suggests that the sooner this happens the better, and a senior manager should be made responsible for Internet strategy. The web presence of the company should be fully integrated with wider marketing policy.

In other words, the organizational process can seem messy. This is quite natural. Understanding what's going on, recognizing the natural conflicts there may be across the organization and the need for senior leadership will help you deal with the stresses and strains that innovation and change often bring in organizations. There is an upside to this messiness. It allows your organization to learn. It is important to see learning as a key output of the process of experimentation and testing that will inevitably be a key part of going online, and you must make sure that you and your firm maximize the benefits. A second point follows: because you will learn best by experimenting, it is a good idea to get started – even in a small way – as soon as you can!

Locating your website

An important issue online is your address. Every page of marketing material needs to have a reference under which a customer can locate it. This address reveals how much or how little you are spending. For example, **http://www.demon.co.uk/widget** is a page produced under an existing company on the Internet called Demon. You are placing your marketing materials inside their company's area on the Internet. This implies that you have taken a low budget route to the Internet. **http://www.widget.com** on the other hand implies that you have committed to this technology and have created a unique corporate domain name which is registered to your company and are likely to have your own dedicated computer for your customers to access 24 hours a day. This more expensive route also brings with it the advantage that the resulting web address is simple to use and remember – if you can find an identifying name which has not yet been taken! It is not necessary, however to have only one corporate domain name. Companies now use a plethora of domain addresses to entice different target audiences to different offerings within their sites or to satellite sites. www.bbc.co.uk is an example of a site which actively encourages different audiences to subdirectories, e.g. www.bbc.co.uk/food for gourmets.

Increasingly, it is hard to find the web address you would like. There were estimated to be almost one million registered domain names in the UK alone by February 2000! If you're looking to set up something obvious, then you might need to use an un-obvious name. One danger in this area is to use numbers within names. **www.food4U.com** may look good on paper, and might even sound good to say. But imagine telling someone the address over the phone – or on the radio. This is why simple names like **www.news.com**, or **www.health.com** are highly valuable. There is further guidance on the issue of site names later in this chapter.

According to your budget, there are a number of options in setting up a site. You will face decisions over the rental or creation of web space – room on the Internet to store your firm's information – and over design and programming of your site. You can choose to do either in-house or out of house.

Low budget options

I. A directory entry

There are many companies offering this service. They offer web space and design services. These firms offer an easy and cheap way to publish your company's information. They also offer the end customer a 'one-stop' shop. You should investigate this option even if you are considering producing your own web pages in addition. They usually offer the complete service from helping you design your entry all the way through to producing your web pages and maintaining them over time. Additional benefits to your company and your customers is that you may be able to make use of a shared security payment system, a shared enquiry response form or a fulfilment system which would normally be out of your budget threshold. In other words a directory provider may offer a secure credit card payment system which would enable your customers to buy products direct from you online.

The downside of this option is that your are often constrained by the style and amount of pages you wish to publish. You may also find that your pages are costly to change and incur either high monthly maintenance costs or high credit card commission rates.

The best option is to find a provider who specializes by industry type. A good example of this is Dealernet who offer a car dealer directory with specifications of cars and contact addresses. All the big car companies in America are contained within here. Dealernet are commonly cited as a success story but, interestingly, most of their customers also have their own website in addition. Another good example is TRAVELWEB who provide a one-stop shop for hotel bookings across hotel chains.

If you are a consumer marketer, the equivalent to this is the shopping malls. Barclays Square and the London Mall were two of the first in the UK. The downside of this type of promotion is that it fails to provide your customers with a one-stop shop and puts you alongside insurance brokers, chocolate suppliers etc. However, this may be to your advantage if you are wishing to promote a product which is not something that a customer would key into a search engine to look for and you are looking to catch the attention of an existing online purchaser.

Just as the three key issues when buying property are 'location, location and location', the three key issues when looking at placing a directory entry are 'readership, readership and readership'. The only problem is that only the directory provider knows what the readership is and it is in their interest to present you with very favourable figures to encourage you to join. We recommend returning to Chapter 3 on marketing research and asking how your customers might find you online. If directories are a key channel then use them immediately – maybe even all of them! (You may even want to create your own directory. This is not significantly more costly than producing your own website and it can produce a revenue stream to offset the cost. A common approach is to loss-lead for the start-up period and offer listings free and only charge when you become established. It is very competitive business, as many companies are trying to enter this directory market. A list of directories offering listings at a fee is hosted by MMG and referenced on the accompanying web page for this chapter.)

2. Create a company-site using a third-party provider

This is the second most cost-effective way of putting your organization on the Internet. This is the cheapest option if you want control of how your pages look and how the customer can access them. Most of the major Internet providers and Internet marketing agencies in Europe offer this service. Under this arrangement, you rent Internet space from a provider. You do not need to have your company registered as a unique entity (i.e. your own domain name) and the provider names a certain area (or directory) with your company name. Your web address will be: **http://www.yourprovider.com/yourcompany**.

Although this reveals that you do not have your own domain name, you can spend the money you save on creative design of your pages. This is the cheapest way of having carte blanche on your creative design and image. You are also less constrained as to how many pages you can have as compared to a directory entry.

If you want to offer a response form, credit card payments and other services, this is usually provided at an additional cost. We strongly recommend you investigate the cost implications of these options before you commit to publishing with a provider.

First you need to investigate provider prices. These prices vary considerably and it certainly pays to shop around. Ultimately you are paying for the provider's brand image and their technical infrastructure. You also pay more with a brand leader for their technical infrastructure. For example, they may have a backup telecommunication link to America so it is unlikely that you will ever lose your service to America. Some of the cheaper providers may not have such a backup and it is more likely that you will lose your service. The service that your end customer will receive will not vary considerably, speed of access being your chief concern. However, the service that you as an organization receive may vary considerably. Some providers will offer you monthly statistics of how many people are accessing your pages, others won't.

Next, you face a choice over design. Some providers will offer a complete package from design and programming your pages, all the way through to helping you maintain your site. Alternatively, you can create your own pages in-house.

Working in partnership with a provider

This is the equivalent of having your own marketing agency. You brief the provider with your objectives and they create storyboards and design options for you. This is the most preferred route if you need a professional looking website and do not have the resources in-house to dedicate someone full-time on the project.

There are three types of companies in this arena.

1. Technical access

There are the access providers (list provided on the accompanying website referenced under this chapter) who are sometimes focused on the technical side. They often offer a one-stop shop but their designers are often not true marketing designers. Typically these providers are IT focused and your pages will be designed by technical people with minimum marketing creative and design skills. Although the prices may be tempting this alternative can be the online equivalent of having your corporate brochure designed by a printing company.

The difference between an Internet provider & an Internet marketing Co.

2. Marketing companies

Then there are marketing companies who are focused on the professional design, creative input and the marketing impact of their work for you. Make sure that – if you use a marketing firm – they provide good storyboards with a series of options before moving to the programming stage of the project. If they do not, you should ask yourself whether you're using the right company. Professional marketing companies will also spend time investigating your existing marketing materials, your brand, your marketing strategy and your success factors of Internet marketing. Another marked difference, using marketing companies is, of course, price. However, like most marketing projects, investment in planning, design and creative work usually pays off in the long-run. The big question here is do they understand your business?

'Don't ask what the internet can do for you, Sonny-boy, ask what you can do for the internet.'

We would recommend paying for a tender from a few of these marketing companies. State your objectives and include your marketing materials and pay on a time basis for the initial design phase separate from the Internet publishing. This means that you can assess the creative and technical skills of the marketing company and see if you can work creatively with them before you commit yourself to a long-term relationship.

There is much debate whether specialist Internet marketing agencies are better at producing pages than traditional marketing agencies. Some marketers say that PR companies know how to make your website 'newsworthy'; others say that advertising agencies fail to appreciate the interactive nature of the Internet. It is not within the scope of this book to enter into this debate. It is hopefully sufficient to say that any marketing company who can appreciate your business and marketing objectives together with the nature and opportunity the Internet has to offer is likely to be the best choice.

3. Gold-diggers

Then there are the gold-diggers. These are usually one-man bands or small technical companies who are capitalizing on customer naivety, and popularity of the net. They will offer the same as the above on paper (or on the Internet) but are typically technically limited or creatively impaired, usually both. Beware of these.

4. *Doing the design yourself*

This is ideal if you have an internal design and creative team who are also adept at Internet programming (HTML, DHTML, Java etc.) and understand the Internet culture.

One word of warning here. To design and maintain your website yourself, your people must not only have an in-depth understanding of the Internet but enough time to continue to update themselves on this ever-changing new medium. We would recommend at least one full-time person on the project. They also need to have good analytical skills to build a structure to your site and your pages which is intuitive to your customers and will support your future innovations. There are many products on the market to make the process of creating and maintaining your pages easy.

Whichever option you decide to follow, the key is not to get trapped in technology. The technology is only there to help you communicate – and must not dominate the planning and design phase. Before jumping into production, take an analytical step back and involve a good creative team at the conception stage. We recommend you read Chapter 8 on how to produce your promotional materials in the most professional manner.

Whichever of the above, please use our checklist for assessing a provider.

Choosing a provider

We recommend you investigate at least five providers before making a decision. Always test any supplier. It is easy to test out their web-server and look at what they have done for other clients. Things to look for include:

Pricing structure?
Some providers look very attractive by hiding costs by a complex or different pricing structure. Examples of these are:

- per message charges for e-mail;
- per hit charges for your customers' access to your pages;
- hidden costs for transferring your web pages or domain name to another supplier.

Do check out the prices and options for both production and maintenance. Expect to pay between 20 per cent and 50 per cent of production for yearly maintenance updates and hosting. Investigate their ability to get the site promoted in the search engines and across the Internet.

Do they have a sound technical infrastructure?
What is their speed of response? You should try their server at different times of the day and if time permits, spot check it over a number of weeks. What you are looking for is how reliable is their equipment: is it ever offline or running really slowly? Although this is easy to test, this only tells you what their speed of response is today. It is worth investigating their investment plans into new equipment. Particularly if they are good value for money, they will attract a large number of customers and without the right levels of investment, their service will drop off. It is strongly recommended that you pay extra to increase your chances of a sustained good service.

Reliability?
How many connections do they have to the Internet? If they only have one connection, and it goes down, your customers cannot access your pages.

References?
Also ensure that you have a look around at other companies they are 'hosting'. Ask the provider to give you the name and telephone number of an existing customer to talk to. Alternatively e-mail a number of companies that are being hosted by the provider and ask them whether they are satisfied and any response they have received from their customers.

Support?
You need to assess the provider's ability to fix problems and how fast they respond to your needs. Try contacting their

support line and see how long it takes to get through to someone and how customer focused that person is at being able to deal with your question.

Do they have enough people in their company to offer a high quality of service? Do they understand that you are trying to run a business?

Financial security?
This company will be maintaining your domain name and your company image online. Both of these are easily transferable technically but often cause administrative work and stress for you. So to avoid this, it is worth investigating how likely it is that your supplier will go out of business. How long have they been in business? Will they be in business in six months' time?

Do they have professional indemnity in case they make a mistake with your work and you run into a legal battle?

3. Create your own website
This is where you create your own identity independent of your provider. This means that it can be invisible to your customers as to who is 'hosting' or publishing your materials. This is the preferred option if you are concerned about corporate image but want to keep your costs to a minimum.

High budget options

At this point, you will have appreciated the relevance of the Internet as being an effective communication medium for your target market. This section describes how you may go further and really commit to promoting your company on the Internet. It assumes you can afford to have control of your own means of production, i.e. a web-server – the computer that stores your promotional materials and enables your customers to access them 24 hours a day.

There are three choices here: rent a shared server; rent a dedicated server or have your own server in-house.

Rent a shared server

This is charged to you on an annual or monthly basis. The computer is located and maintained at the provider's premises. The provider bears all the set-up and administrative costs, together with paying for the telephone connection which provides 24 hour access for your customers.

This is the cheapest alternative but the downside is that at least one other organization will be publishing their information on the same machine. Because the computer can only serve up one page at a time, your customers will have to compete to access your information. It is important to find out who you will be sharing with and set up some guaranteed service levels on access speed for your customers.

Likewise, because you are sharing, you are likely to have constraints put on you as to what services you are able to offer your customers. The more impressive and customer-focused initiatives like response forms and customer database enquiries require extra computer processing and therefore may be restricted with this option.

This option is ideal if the majority of your site is HTML or image-based application.

Rent a dedicated server

Again this is charged to you on an annual or monthly basis and is located and maintained at the provider's. This is identical to having your own computer but it is maintained and checked for you by the provider. As before, the provider bears all the set-up and administrative costs, together with paying for the telephone connection which provides 24 hour access for your customers.

It is more expensive than a shared server but your customers do not have to compete with the customers of the other company you are sharing the server with. This option is essential if you want to take advantage of the more powerful features on the Internet like interrogating a customer database, lookup prices from a price database, downloading software, intelligent response forms etc. It also means that you can make the server more secure and give only selected customers access to information. For credit card payments, this is the minimum option that you need to consider. Although we would still recommend that you have an in-house server for high security payment integrated into your in-house systems.

The advantage of both the above options is that you can be closer to the core of the Internet. If you decide to select an American provider, you could even be on the 'backbone' of the Internet. This is the core structure which was historically based in the US and funded by the government. The 'backbone' now spreads across the major countries of the world. In the last two years, global telecommunications companies like MCI and AT&T have started to replace the core structure and are investing heavily. These companies are using extremely high-capacity networks. You cannot get a direct link to this core but an access provider may have such a direct link. It is the role of the access provider to concentrate all the small links to individual companies so that there is enough information traffic to justify a link on to the core. The closer you are to the core, the less links there are between you and your customer and this can improve the response rate of your information online.

Your own server located and maintained in-house

This is where you buy your own computer, load some software onto it, attach it to a 24 hour telephone link (usually a leased line connection) and away you go. We exaggerate about the simplicity but it is not as technically challenging as some of the access providers like you to think. It is often in their best interest not to encourage you to go this route. But once the initial headache of setting it up is all over, maintenance and upkeep are relatively simple.

One disadvantage of having your own server in-house rather than maintained for you by an access provider is that you are one stage removed from the Internet. In other words you are connected through a provider, which is one step away from having a machine maintained for you on the provider's premises. The speed differential does not have to be significant especially if you choose a provider who has a good response rate to start with.

For external marketing, this option gives you the most flexibility. Publish as much as your machine can store, use the most advanced functionality of the Internet to your heart's content and update your information easily at the touch of a button. You can set up as much or as little security as you feel fit. This option also means a fast acceleration up the Internet learning curve which will put you in good stead when you want to leverage it further for competitive advantage: you develop skills in-house, which can help you keep up with changes in technology without relying on third party advice.

What do you need?

(a) IT skills to maintain the machine and provide technical support when needed

This person or team need to be knowledgeable about the Internet in order to be able to receive and send information to and from the provider's machine – skills which are becoming increasingly common. They also need to be able to invest time in learning how the software on the server works and is configured. They will need this knowledge base if or when you decide to make use of the advanced functionality of the Internet like clickable maps, sound, video, response forms feeding direct into databases etc. It is wise to regard running your website entirely in-house as a goal, and not the means to going online if your firm does not already have substantial IT skills. You should use outside advice and learn from it before you go it alone.

(b) A computer

The first decision you need to make is which operating system you wish to use. This will depend on what IT infrastructure and skill set you have existing in your organization. This will then define which computer you need and how much you need to spend.

Windows 3.1, or Windows 95 do not make good Internet operating systems because they are not multi-user, not secure and are not robust enough to stand up to the pressure of 24-hour accessing day in, day out. These are ideal for web page creation but not for publishing these pages on the world wide web.

The most popular options you have are UNIX or Windows NT. The most popular operating system for use on the Internet is UNIX. This is because the Internet was built from a UNIX base. The benefit of UNIX for an Internet server is that it is very well tried and tested. All the software you will possibly need for the Internet is available on this operating system. The other attractive benefit is that UNIX scales up from small to very large computers easily. Smaller UNIX systems can be based on PCs but IBM, Hewlett Packard, Digital and Sun offer a range of UNIX machines from the small to the extremely large mainframe type systems. In general, UNIX compatible computers are available from a wide range of suppliers although because there are slight differences between each one, it is better to stick with a single supplier. The downside of UNIX is that it is technically sophisticated and can be quite a challenge to set up and administrate.

Windows NT is becoming a popular alternative to UNIX because of its friendly administration and ease of installation. This is an ideal starting point for a quick and easy installation of a web-server. However, it is still relatively new and a number of companies we have worked with have found that the performance has not been up to their expectations. The other downside is that it does not scale as far up into the large computers as UNIX; instead you buy more NT servers.

The operating system will define the computer you need to buy. Obtain quotes from a variety of different vendors before you decide on the most suitable and ensure that you obtain reference sites of customers who have set up a web-server using the hardware platform that you have chosen.

(The state of the server software market is extremely volatile and much will depend on what you are trying to achieve, so we are deliberately avoiding in-depth discussions on this subject.)

(c) A provider to link your server with the Internet
Again you need to use the provider checklist outlined in the previous section. One other consideration here is how much the provider will support you in the early days of setting it up. Will they configure it for you and train your people? Will they give a good support response time if you run into difficulties?

(d) A telecommunication connection
There are two alternatives here: a leased line or an ISDN link. The leased line is the most expensive to set up but has the lowest running costs. This is provided by your telecommunications company or through your access provider who can arrange it more simply for you. A dedicated telephone line is then installed at your organization where you may have a yearly cost (in the thousands) irrespective of how many telephone calls you make out or in using this line.

The alternative is an ISDN link which is less but you have to pay for the telephone calls in and out on it. This means that the more customers you attract to your website and the more people you have in your organization using your web-server as a gateway to the Internet, the more you pay. You therefore have little control on the variable costs, so this makes this alternative quite unattractive.

You also need what is called a 'router'. This is a device which handles the dataflow to and from your Internet connection. Any messages that come from the Internet will be passed to you by your access provider. They will do this by sending the information down your link to the router which is located in your premises and is usually rented to you and maintained by the access provider. This is usually because the access provider needs to have the same make and configuration of routers.

Once the router receives the messages from the access provider, its task is to pass it on to the correct computer inside your organization. Simply, there is a table of computer identities held within the router that allows it to decide where to pass the data.

The router also has the ability to recognize any messages sent within the organization which are destined for somewhere outside. When the router detects one of these, it passes it on to the access provider as the first step to reaching its destination somewhere in the world.

A router can be used to prevent outside access to your company's computers. But this alone is not adequate for complete security because it is quite possible for someone to falsify their 'sender's address'. This is where the router will think the message has come from a trustworthy source and do its job and pass it straight on. This brings us neatly to the bigger issue of security.

(e) A security system

The decisions involved in deciding the best security system are complex and really outside the scope of this book. There are whole books dedicated to this subject alone. There are also products coming on the market daily to make the complexity in this area easier to understand and act upon.

What we can explain in general terms is what security issues you need to be concerned with, so that you can professionally brief either your internal IT department, your access provider or your IT supplier as to your needs and your concerns.

I want to protect my web pages from being deleted or defaced.

You need to protect yourself from the hacker who may benignly or maliciously use your server and modify your setup and your web pages. You need to ensure that customers can read your web pages but not modify them.

This basic security comes from within your web-server machine. Again, this is dependent on your IT people configuring your web pages securely. With any computer connected to the Internet, it is important to maintain high standards of administration. This includes mandating the use of passwords and keeping the software up to date because this ensures you get the most up-to-date security enhancements.

The best form of security is to have your dedicated web-server as a stand-alone system unconnected to any other computer in your building.

This by-passes the need for any further security beyond the router. However you do not get the benefits of offering the whole organization Internet access.

I want to offer my company Internet access but protect my company information from unwanted intrusion. And I want to restrict Internet services within the organization.

Filters in

You need some sort of filter system on your server which enables your customers to get into your web pages but not go careering around areas that you don't wish them to access.

Filters out

You also need a mechanism to allow the people inside your organization to access the world wide web and send their e-mail out. This may be used in addition to restrict times of people using the server; restrict pornographic areas of the Internet or restrict access to the Internet to certain types of use e.g. e-mail only, no downloading of software, etc.

This filter mechanism for both internal and external data flow is constructed from either a software program, a router or a combination of the two. A filter looks at each packet of information as it passes through. Depending on the type of filter, it will perform various checks, preventing unwanted access by removing packets that do not conform to the rules programmed.

It is worth paying extra for a good router because it will include the ability to filter. If you do not have one of these sophisticated routers, you will need additional filter software and probably an extra computer to run this software on. This extra computer will have to handle all the information in and out of your company. Therefore it will have to be a fast and expensive one.

If you are going to connect your web-server with any other computer in your organization you must take security very seriously. This is critical especially if you wish to take online credit card orders because these need to be stored on a separate machine to your server. You need to investigate 'firewalls'. This is a conceptual term for a set of routers, computers and software which puts up a barrier between your web-server and your internal network. There are numerous configuration options here and we recommend that you read *Firewalls and Internet Security* in the References at the end of this chapter.

A firewall works in both directions and is set to allow only 'safe' transactions across the wall. It acts a bit like a checkpoint where every request is carefully screened. You place this firewall between your web-server and your network. If correctly set up this will make it extremely difficult for external people to access your internal network.

(f) Server software

Now you have got your computer connected to the Internet securely. However you still have to make some more choices. You need to run a piece of software that will turn your computer into a web-server. In essence the software will sit and wait for your customers to make contact. It will take their requests for information, find it on the server and send it to them. It can send many different types of information: formatted text; graphics; sound, video and software programs. Alone, all the web-server software does is find files and pass them back to the user.

For a more dynamic interaction with the customer, you need your web-server to play a more active role. It does this by taking the information from your customer, processing it and returning a response to the enquiry. The processing is done through a set of software programs sitting on the web-server. Some of these programs will come with your web-server, others you may need to source elsewhere.

There are two choices on web-server software. You either buy it packaged from a supplier or you obtain it direct from the Internet. Buying it provides you with manuals and technical support and a certain peace of mind. Unless you have advanced technical skills, this approach is strongly recommended.

Before you select which software to buy, you need to decide what facilities you will require:

I want response forms to ask for my customer's details, check if they are an existing customer, feed back answers to questions they may have and/or thank them for filling in the form.

Some web-server software has the ability to process forms built inside them. This is the most convenient because otherwise you will need to have programming skills within your organization to offer this to your customers.

I want to have several addresses on the same server (e.g. widget.com, widgetx.com, widgety.com).

Check that the web-server does this. You will still have to register these names with your provider.

I want to measure statistics of customers accessing our web pages.

This is the marketer's dream, you can see what pages of marketing material each customer looks at for how long and in what order. This information will help you improve your information and evolve your Internet site in tune with customer needs. Not all web-server software offers this – so do check.

I want to offer different information to different people.

For example, you may wish to offer different information to internal people and to subsets of customers. Flexible security systems with password protection are key features of some web-server software and this is definitely worth investigating.

(g) An uninterruptible power supply (UPS)
A UPS box enables you to ensure that your server stays accessible 24 hours a day even if there is a power cut. You pay more depending on how long you want the UPS box to maintain the machine in the event of a power cut. Your choice will depend on how likely power cuts are to happen and how important the web-server will be to your business.

What domain name can I choose?

Online, you can have what is called a 'domain name'. This is like a name and address in the 'real' world. Like lots of things online, you are free from the physical limitations of the real world. Your domain name or address could be: the name of your company; the name of your product; the name of the service you provide; your product category or in fact anything you want.

Online, all the domains are grouped together, so for example if you are an academic institute, your domain name has '.edu' added to the end. If you are an international commercial organization or in the USA, you have '.com' added to the end.

Each domain name has to be unique. So the domains have been further grouped by country. Anyone in the UK can have '.co.uk' on the end of their domain name.

For a full glossary of international domain names and their meaning please see Appendix 6.

The Internet is pretty anarchic but it wouldn't work if anyone could just choose a domain name. In the UK, Nominet acts as a monopoly registration company, which holds a master list of all the domain names and which computer they are to be found on. This organization processes thousands of requests for domain names every day on a first-come, first-served basis (in the latter part of 1999, 3000 names were registered daily). There is a huge queue of requests for new domain names, so even if you choose a name that you know is not being used, it may be just your luck that someone in the queue has just requested it. It can take many weeks to get to the front of the queue. During this time, all you can do is cross your fingers and hope.

You do not personally apply for this registration, your provider will do this for you. You can include your full name, address and e-mail which will be centrally held so that people can look up your domain name and obtain your full name and address. This can be quite useful if you want to get in touch with someone and you only have their domain.

'http://' is always the first part of your domain name because this indicates that you are on the world wide web. This stands for 'hypertext transfer protocol' and it indicates that it is a 'web page' rather than a file or a newsgroup etc. 'www' is not always necessary but is the syntax stating it is the world wide web. The next bit is where you need to make a decision.

Option 1: http://www.widget.co.uk

You would register 'widget.co.uk' as your domain name and decide on what you would like to call the sub-directory after this domain name, i.e. 'widget'. This indicates that you are a company based in the UK.

Option 2: http://www.widget.com

You would register widget.com as your domain name. This indicates that you are an international company and unless you state you are based in the UK on your pages, your customer has no idea where in the world you are based. This is great if you want to globalize your customer base or give the impression that you are bigger than you really are.

Option 3: Both www.widget.co.uk and www.widget.com

This is our recommended solution because it prevents another organization using and exploiting the alternative name. Passing off (companies trading off the reputation of another) actions are harder to implement on the Internet so this solution prevents later disputes. However, we recognize that it may be extremely difficult to acquire both country and international domains.

How to structure your website

The structure of your website needs to be carefully designed: there is no point in publishing exciting and helpful content unless visitors to your site can find the pages they want to view. Reducing the 'friction' users experience while online is vital. If they find that entering your site is like going into a maze, they are unlikely to come back if one of your rivals offers a less tiresome solution.

There are a number of approaches you should bear in mind while designing your site architecture.

Provide a search form on the front of your site

Provide a keyword search where the customer types in a target word or phrase, and is presented with items that match. This offers visitors a single step straight to the product that they desire. It is notoriously difficult for the customer to choose the correct keyword if they don't have a precise product name in mind, and this can be a cause of frustration for customers. This can make search engines very frustrating and you can risk losing a potential customer because you are making it too difficult for them to find what they want. Only use a search engine when the customer can clearly identify the product that they are interested in (e.g. CD). Make sure your search box is easy to see, is big enough to click on, and is visible without scrolling the page down to find it.

Provide a decision tree for the customer to navigate through

The second approach is to produce a decision tree presenting broad categories for which the customer chooses to follow a number of steps leading them to a product or set of products which are suitable for them. These trees are often presented as a navigation bar, which reveals text lists of options on following pages. This overcomes the disadvantages of the search engine because it enables the customer to select from a list selected. It also offers the advantage to you of being able to entertain and interest your customer longer on their trip around your site and therefore have a great chance of capturing their heart and mind!

This style has the disadvantage that it will take your customer a number of steps to get to the information they require. So decision trees should not be made too deep or this will frustrate your customer who is ultimately paying for the experience of visiting your site. This approach can appeal to the browsing visitor, and is helpful if your site offers a wide variety of content and services which would be hard to access via a search box.

You should aim to make all corners of your site accessible within four clicks from the home page. This will require listing many options on one page, using text instead of images. Ease of navigation is critical.

It is now common approach to use both search engines and decision trees. Often you will find that the visitor who arrives at your site with a narrow focus – to look at a particular product or piece of information – can be enticed to broaden his or her search once they have seen the page they came to view. For example, when you visit *CDnow* you might search and go direct to the CD in which you are interested. Once there, at the top of the page describing the CD, there are links to other offers like Top 100 CDs and special offers. With the clever use of graphics and simple linking it is often possible to encourage even a focused visitor to look at other wares you have on sale.

When designing your site, consider the following tips:

- Ensure there is a home page button, and a top of page button on every page in your site. It is important that visitors can get back to the start very quickly.
- Ensure that there is a navigation bar on every page in the site. You cannot predict what each customer will want to do, and you must ensure that all routes are easy to take.
- Minimize scrolling on pages. Scrolling is another form of friction, which makes the experience of using your site more frustrating and difficult for visitors. Given that a key justification of Internet communication is the ease with which it can be achieved, friction must be avoided as much as possible.

Website content

The content of your website will depend on the nature of your organization, whom the site is aimed at, and how it will be used. A site aimed at regular professional users (such as Pro-Quest, the online journals service) will be cut down, un-fussy and will offer users maximal functionality and minimal extraneous copy. A site aimed at occasional visitors will include more explanation, more imagery and a greater attempt to entice. The key content guideline, therefore, is to focus on *your* stakeholders and customers, and their method of using the net. Websites can serve a variety of purposes.

They might:

- provide **corporate information** to investors (financial performance, strategy, press releases, product development news);
- provide **employment information** to potential staff;
- provide **product information** (range, prices, functionality, availability, compatibility, history, manufacturing location) – this will include communication and development of brand values;
- allow product sampling (downloads of music, text, video);
- provide a **communication channel** with consumers (frequently asked questions, e-mail information response service);
- provide **retail sale outlet**;
- provide **locations of stores**, and company contact information;
- provide **links** to related businesses, organizations, and publications.

The first point to notice about this list is that a website can address different audiences and extend far beyond simple product information and ordering. The entire structure, design and style of the website will tell your stakeholders and customers a great deal about the sort of company they are dealing with. Small firms have a potential advantage here, as relatively small companies can produce sites that are better designed and easier to use than big firms, allowing them to 'punch above their weight' online. The quality of the site, therefore, will influence the user's perception of your brand values as well as allow them to gather more information about your products and services.

The second point to note is that a website will require considerable maintenance and updating. This is necessary to ensure the site keeps pace with technology (a firm selling up-to-date products cannot do so from an old-fashioned looking site), but also to ensure that returning visitors have something new to look at. This can be problematic for sites which invest heavily in graphic-intensive images. For example, a site including impressive flash sequences cannot be changed very regularly, and users returning frequently will find they become familiar with the material on offer. By contrast, magazine-based websites have a ready supply of new editorial copy and images to ensure the site remains fresh.

The detail of the content you should develop will be very specific. However a few general principles should be considered.

Think about your stakeholders. Who will use your site? This may be shareholders, rivals, suppliers, customers, employees (actual and potential) or the wider community. What do you want them to know?

Provide frequently asked questions for target users. Provide an e-mail address for personalized responses. (These can be pre-prepared, if questions are likely to fall into predictable categories.)

Remember – long web pages and lots of images take a long time to download. Ask yourself whether this will irritate your customers. Make sure your design will make things easier for customers, and not simply show off your technical expertise.

If you use landscape page design, make sure it fits on the screen. A home page which requires the user to scroll across to the right each time they want to jump sections sends a bad message about the firm's ability to think about the consumer.

Make as much use as you can of the chance to build customer relationships. Invite feedback, post questions, invite return visits. Consider an opt-in e-mail information service (more on this below).

If you have returning visitors, remember it is important to make sure you've always got something new to offer them. Research shows that changing copy is positively related to the number of web-page hits.

For the web marketer, a website offers the chance to:

- attract customers;
- stimulate desire;
- convert desire into buying action.

Design is a key element in achieving this result. There are endless choices:

1. Creating a company feel online

Many of the car companies make their Internet site feel like a physical location. In this way the customer feels that they are being invited around the organization in a physical way. It can project any message that you wish to convey. For example a large automotive site wanted to project the feeling of innovation and so has references to innovations departments, R&D, etc.

This approach gives the customer a visual, spatial model to remember you by. It also enables you to develop a corporate image and brand in a more subtle way than merely posting your logo on your site.

Remember that this is a visual projection of the company and its abilities and therefore professional design and image is critical. Intelligent use of your company logo integrated with complementary colour, themes, backgrounds and other multi-media devices (like sound) can project the strongest visual messages about the company and its products.

2. Corporate identity

Do not be tempted to redesign your corporate image for the Internet. This will confuse your customers and you will not benefit from the existing goodwill and reputation surrounding your image.

Whatever method is selected for projecting the image of an organization, it must be used consistently and with strict regulations in terms of the logo design, colour, type face, positioning and size. It might be necessary to use only the key graphical features of your corporate identity on the Internet because of its technical limitations (graphic downloading is slow) but you should not apply this rule too vigorously.

Leading-edge companies are producing ECIs. These are Electronic Corporate Identity standards and include page templates, colour and navigation systems. If you have more than one content development team worldwide, it is becoming an absolute necessity.

3. Product display and packaging

Product display and packaging are the aspects most people usually associate with the term merchandising, a key element in the promotional mix. This is because manufacturers employ merchandisers to display their products in distribution outlets and also it is a stage when potential customers are physically confronted with the product. An effective product display is a means of encouraging customers to handle the product in order to understand its benefits. However on the Internet, with only a few exceptions, you cannot handle the goods. However the same underlying theories and techniques are just as relevant.

The factors that constitute an effective display in traditional merchandising environments and the Internet include making:

Full use of customer traffic flow

Just as in a retail store it is possible to measure traffic flow on the Internet using hit rates and make sure that the maximum number of visitors see your key offers. You then monitor and manage this flow.

Full use of product packaging

Packaging is an integral part of the product. Often it is the only method of communicating the promise and benefits of the product to potential customers. Packaging decisions are a key aspect of the product planning process, and an important part of merchandising. However, the role played by packaging changes online where the physical packaging arrives *after* the purchase has been made, if at all. As a result, the issue of online packaging is an interesting one. Packaging is heavily dependent on the type of product that you are merchandising and it is not true to say that you necessarily have to show the product as it looks physically. You can for example have great Internet packaging which has the added advantages of being practically free, easily changeable where you can see how it appeals to your target audience through the comparative hit rate through your website. With the Internet you can use sound, video and animation as part of this packaging. This is the pioneering edge of merchandising on the Internet. If you can't pick it up and feel the quality – maybe you can make it sound like a quality product?

Price advantage clearly visible

For retail environments this is quite obvious but essential. On the Internet, the desire by consumers to find a bargain is a key driver of online shopping, and so price advantages – where you have them – must be made very clear. At the same time, you do need to be careful of triggering damaging price wars. You also need to be careful of the global shopping front where you stand next to shops who may have a better currency rate and therefore cheaper products. However, no-one will buy without knowing the price. Employ all the usual tricks used in a retail environment like:

- Use 0.99 rather than 1.00.
- Use the word 'Only' a great deal.
- Have prices crossed out and reduced ones next to them.
- Use special offer closing dates.
- Compare your price with the RRP (recommended retail price).
- Ensure your main offers are heavily flagged.

Product accessible to all potential customers

In a retail environment, this is about making sure that children's products are put at the correct height, etc. On the Internet, this may be more of an issue enabling international customers to buy from you. Can you reduce the price of postage? Can you take international credit cards without having to absorb a huge credit risk, etc.?

Available technical and other sales support

The best merchandising factor on the Internet is the amount of pre-sale and post-sale support you can offer. The customer has only got a screen to know and understand you. If you can offer a human interface built into the price, this is often the trigger for purchase.

Point-of-sale material

Point-of-sale (or purchase) material is an essential element of communicating particular benefits or incentives of buying the product. It is used in promoting new or modified products and is very useful in gaining shelf space in distribution outlets. The main aim of using point-of-sale material is to encourage customers to sample it for the first time. It is normally closely integrated with a company's advertising and sales promotion campaign and must be designed to complement the image of the product. The type of material used has to be designed with due regard to the target market and type of distribution outlet. Bright colours may be appropriate to promote household items, but much more subtle design is necessary for fashion, consumer durables and industrial products.

Point-of-sales material is particularly useful when customers do not have a brand in mind, but are looking for a product to solve their problems. For example, a person looking for carpet may only have colour, size and quality in mind when in an outlet. The use of point-of-sale material can influence the customer's brand choice by communicating benefits and/or other incentives that can be derived from purchasing a particular brand. The same applies to many industrial purchases that take place in wholesaling or distribution outlets. For example, a customer wishing to purchase electrical cable for plant maintenance may not have a brand in mind but can be influenced by point-of-sale material in the outlet.

On the Internet, this is very powerful and many organizations have been successful at selling additional products at the end of the online sales process. Insurance companies sell legal cover for a small incremental amount at the end of applying for insurance (see www.eaglestar.co.uk).

There is further guidance on website content and structure in Chapter 8, Producing your promotional materials online.

How to make your website visible

Having set a website budget, chosen a technical strategy and developed your content in a clearly structured and appropriate manner, you must now make sure people visit your new site. This is crucial. Achieving a good level of traffic does not depend only on the quality of your site and your products. It also depends on the capacity of potential users to find you.

The adverts you have posted on the Internet will act as direct links to your site, and so are one potential source of traffic.

Research from the Michigan Business School also shows a positive link between the number of site links you offer, and web page hits. So it appears there is a benefit from being generally well linked in to other sites in your field. You must make sure your site is listed on related sites, and that you list them. This involves lots of e-mails and phone calls, and you will find that some popular sites will charge to include your address in their useful contacts section.

Campaigns mounted in the traditional media can also help. Make sure that:

- All promotional and advertising copy contains your website address. Everything, from letter paper and business cards to adverts and flyers should show your address. Promote your web address – and people will not need to find you on search engines.
- You use conventional PR skills to publicize your site. Where possible, make it newsworthy. The Guinness screen saver achieved this, but similar results can be gained even in specialist markets. If you offer a new service online, make sure it is publicized in the offline media. Being the first to do something will ensure publicity if it is of real value to the general public.
- Have a sales promotion or competition contained within the site that is only available to the Internet community. Nothing works better than thinking you are in a privileged position.
- Build links between your site and well known people and brands. Choose a celebrity who is aspirational to your target audience.
- Consider if you can give anything away free. People love getting something for nothing. Many marketers frown at this but ensuring that the give-away is connected to your product means that you can gain traffic, and improve brand awareness at the same time.
- Write personally to newspaper section editors and Internet magazines requesting a review. Alternatively pay for an advert in Internet magazines launching your site to the Internet community.
- Be controversial – be different – be attention-seeking but don't break the code of netiquette in the process because the short-term PR will soon be replaced by long-term disapproval among a growing and affluent Internet userbase.

Make sure you consider all these approaches. But much of your effort must be technical. You need to ensure that your website is listed in all the search engines.

Getting listed on search engines – the issues

To most Internet users, the way a search engine works is something of a mystery. You type in a search word, and get a list of results. Often one of the top ten is good enough for your needs, and you then jump to the site in question. For a business the search engine mystery can be absolutely critical. If your firm comes up number 11 on the search engine (or number 100!), you will not get much traffic.

Getting listed high up the search engines is a constantly changing and increasingly scientific business. You will need to find out what the rules are when your site goes live, and keep track of how they change. This section cannot tell you what those rules will be. But it will explain what some of the issues and key terms are.

In early 2000 there were six main Internet search engines in operation – excluding Yahoo, which is really a directory. The key engines were Infoseek, HotBot, WebCrawler, Excite, Lycos and AltaVista. Most search engines house a database which contains addresses and information about sites that have been submitted by site developers, but which have been expanded by the site's own search facility. Most sites publish rules for entry, although these rules are constantly changing. Making sure your text key words are going to secure high placings when a search is submitted – and keeping them up to date – is key. Given that some search engines store over 30 million pages, you will realize the extent of the problem.

The search engine will look at a combination of three categories of information – title, description and keywords. This information may be searched in the form of a series of 'tags' (called 'metatags') attached to the pages of your sites. In the case of Lycos, the search is carried out on the home page itself. The key information includes:

- <Title> This gives the titles of the organization hosting the website.
- <META NAME – description> This provides a detailed description of what the company offers – for example 'CONTENT = "publishers specializing in reprinting early Victorian British short stories for the American market"'.
- <META NAME – keywords> This section gives a list of likely search words. For example, 'CONTENT = "short story, Victorian, unpublished, literature, story, American, publisher, British, Victoria, early Victorian, book"'.

Having a good 'title' is especially important to ensuring you get a good position on search engines – the search engines consider the <title> html tag of a page to be the most important description of the content, so it is vital that you prepare this carefully. The title will appear as a clickable link when your address is listed by the engine, so try to make it read as an inviting description of your site rather than a dull list of keywords. Also, keep it to about 150 characters (including spaces) so that it will be displayed in its entirety. Some search engines will penalize repetition in your title tag, so try to avoid it.

The detail of the algorithms used by each engine are constantly changing, and one engine may penalize the use of METAtags, while others may search them directly. One engine may be case sensitive, another not. And what happens if you're an American jeweler, and British jewellery buyers come to your site? Simple differences in spellings can lock you out of a whole market. Make sure you read the guidance issued by search engines for entry very carefully. Include the spellings and versions of your key words that your customers are likely to use – think yourself into the customer's mind. Include plurals as well as singulars, and try to make sure you cover all the versions of search strings that are likely to be used by your customers.

Unfortunately you can only find out exactly how search engines make their priority decisions retrospectively, and as a result your use of tags and text will have to be kept up to date if you hope to attract significant traffic through the search engines. Some firms will write a web page to suit each search engine, so different can the algorithms be.

You will need to ensure you either employ someone with current familiarity with these systems, or you must hire the service from an outside firm. This can be a significant expense and you should investigate this early on. Second, you must monitor rankings by keeping track of where your site comes on the various search engines. You will be able to spot erosions in the site's position, and ensure that action is taken to regain lost ground. This is a crucial aspect of maintaining Internet visibility, and you should ensure that a named individual on the Internet management team takes responsibility for this task.

The way to think about ensuring your visibility on search engines is as an advertising expense. The rational approach is to compare the traffic you would expect from an Internet advertising campaign (measured in cost per click-through) with the traffic you would get by employing experts to tailor your pages to secure hits through the search engines. It is quite likely that you will get more traffic from search engine positioning than you would through a comparable investment in advertising.

Usenet newsgroups

These are areas of the web patronized by regular users who have an interest in a specific subject, activity, etc. Many will accept any entry, allowing you direct access to a target community easily. However, before you start to advertise your site, read the charter for each group to ensure that they will not discriminate against commercial entries. Also, word your entry sensitively to make sure that it is not too overbearing. By going in too strong you may alienate the very audience you wish to attract to your site. (This is covered in full in Appendix 7.)

Directories (Galaxy, Yellow Pages)

Another tactic you can use to make sure people find you is to list your site on Internet directories. These are lists generated from submitted information only: the onus is firmly on you to spend time inputting all your data. Sites are stored and displayed by category, so it is important to choose the right one, and to make your copy as enticing as you can. Choosing the right category can be difficult: if you run a luxury hotel do you list yourself under hotels, accommodation or luxury hotels/accommodation? Try to think as your customers might, and use any market research results that you have. For example, potential Ritz Hotel visitors will probably look specifically for luxury hotels and not wish to search through vast accommodation listings.

Targeted search engines

Specialist search engines cater for particular interest groups – specific regions, business sectors or interests. The same cautionary advice applies as for newsgroups, although there is no need to tone down the sales pitch of your entries in these databases.

Yahoo!

Yahoo! is a particular case that demands its own subheading. Yahoo! is a directory service, and getting listed is difficult and time-consuming. However, the Yahoo! service also brings potentially large audiences. Some research suggests that nearly three quarters of all online orders arrive at the site via Yahoo!

The engine was set up in the early 1970s and still runs a procedure whereby each entry is verified by members of Yahoo! staff who know the Internet intimately and are employed to ensure that the database is made up of high quality sites that pass all the necessary tests and regulations. You won't get a listing with Yahoo! unless you understand what they are looking for and do your best to provide it. The fact that humans are judging each and every entry also means that it can take a relatively long period of time for your site to show, even if you make the perfect entry.

To pass the Yahoo! test your site must be a useful and comprehensive piece of quality web design. An amateur one-page advert that takes an age to download is not going to be accepted, but a ten-page interactive guide to your organization will provide a quality addition to the database. Your site should provide some value to the user and look professional and well executed. You must also take care to request a listing in an appropriate category. It is also important that you get your entry right first time as the 'Change URL' form rarely succeeds. Also, do not submit your site before it is complete and fully live on the Internet. 'Under construction' sites will not be listed.

Yahoo! are also likely to reduce the length of your title and your description, so plan these carefully and be as frugal as possible in what you say. Keep the description to one sentence and try to avoid lengthening punctuation or any form of tautology: don't repeat any words or ideas in your title or description, they will only be removed. Make sure that your description is a sentence that makes sense and adequately sums up the contents of the site. Lists of keywords may risk not being listed. You can try to enter sub-directories of your site individually, but the Yahoo! team will probably spot repeated domain names and you risk having your site penalized.

Measuring traffic at your website

Just as it is easy to measure the effectiveness of advertising, so can you monitor the levels of traffic at your website. There are many suppliers of data on Internet traffic (for example, the Netscape 'hitometer' service). These firms offer a choice in levels of data which typically includes site visitor numbers on one day, in the last week, in the last month, and total since records began. Visitor numbers can be broken down by day of the week, and it is possible to get printouts of, for example, the range of search engines used by visitors and the environments they come from (e.g. are they from universities, companies, or are they private). The traffic figures are useful in two ways. First they give you an indication of the number of eyeballs you are getting for your investment – a key measure of the value you are getting from your site. Second, the data on search engine utilization is very important in telling you where to prioritize your efforts in making sure your website is seen. If you have made efforts to ensure you are very visible on the Infoseek search engine, you would clearly like to know if all of your traffic is actually coming from Yahoo!

Watching traffic trends gives you real-time feedback on the effectiveness of your wider communication strategy. Interpreting these figures, however, requires some care.

Although useful, the best source of traffic monitoring is software residing on your webserver, which monitors the number of users using your site (e.g. NetGenesis, Webtrends, Rent-a-guru). However, many of your customers will access your site via a third party Internet service provider – BT Internet, or AOL for example. Most Internet service providers use computers called 'proxy servers' to help improve the speed of service they can offer their customers. These servers sit between the individual user and the server on which each site is hosted. When someone downloads a page from a particular site, the proxy server stores a copy of the pages. Then, when the next user selects the same site, the proxy server checks whether it holds a copy of the page selected, and sends this copy to the user. The consequence of this is that the servers hosting those sites do not count a hit every time someone looks at their pages. As a result, hit rates for websites can underestimate the true level of readership. If you think of the millions of people using an Internet provider like AOL who may all be accessing the same copy of a popular site, the true number of users is likely to be much higher than the figures revealed by site hit counts.

Therefore, it would be unwise to define the quality of your Internet development simply by the number of hits it appears to get. A more sensible approach would be to use hit rate figures alongside records of the number of inquiries you receive from the net, via e-mail or from response forms on the site. These should give you some indication of how much business the site is generating.

Direct marketing by e-mail

The Internet offers a marketer a very cost-effective route to direct marketing. You can now send thousands of letters out at the touch of a button. The challenge in using this channel is to avoid – where possible – alienating potential customers by sending unsolicited mailshots. While this approach can be effective (particularly if you're giving them a really good offer!) it can also annoy. Pressing delete is actually easier than reading your message, and you want to avoid as many delete requests as possible. This section will describe ways of developing a mailing list development, and then explore some innovative ways to avoid having to resort to the unsolicited mailshot.

How do I build up my direct marketing database?

There are seven ways of doing this. The first four are designed to build in your customers' acceptance that you might send them some information, while the last three have no audience consent built in.

1. Collect your customers' e-mail direct from your website

You must put a response mechanism on your website. We have stated this throughout the book and although obvious to every marketer, you would be amazed at the number of sites not offering this.

Preferably use a response or order form which then enables you to capture the respondent's full postal address, full name, company details (if appropriate) and other demographic and segmentation identifications. You may need to offer an incentive to obtain this information but a free report or bulletin can often be all that is needed.

If you don't put a response or order form on your site, be sure to have an e-mail address for your organization which is checked and replied to at least twice a day.

2. Create a mailing list

You can create electronic lists where your prospects and customers can add and remove themselves to your database. They do this to receive useful information which you regularly send out. This is just like customers subscribing to your in-house magazine.

There are a number of Internet magazines and news services that run on this basis. Subscribers to these free publications receive weekly (or even daily) news digests. Subscription begins when an interested customer sends a blank e-mail to the provider company. They are then added to the mailing list and start receiving the newsletter. Each newsletter sent out contains the instruction on how to unsubscribe. To unsubscribe, all the customer has to do is send another blank e-mail message to an 'unsubscribe' e-mail address.

The ease with which a customer can unsubscribe prevents their getting annoyed with your direct mail. The automation of the system means you do not have the cost of taking them off your mailing list. In this way, once this mailing list is set up, it is very easy and economical to maintain. Your only challenge it to attract and maintain interest for your subscribers. Done well it is one of the most fantastic ways of creating a dialogue with your customer base and has been used especially well in regard to loyalty clubs. (N.B. It can also be an excellent way of informing people that your website has changed.)

3. Create an automatic responder

This is identical to the process outlined in (2) but rather than having a regular newsletter, your customer e-mails a certain address to receive a flyer about a product, some information etc. This is heavily used in America but not so much in Europe at present. Many authors of Internet books promote this technique as a good promotion tool. Alfred and Emily Glossbrenner (1995) comment 'Ladies and gentlemen, that is the way to market on the Internet. Set up an autoresponder so that only those users who want your information will see it – which is to say, you will not be forcing your information on someone via e-mail or news group'.

4. Ask your customers

If you want to find someone's e-mail address, the quickest way will be to just to ask them. Ensure that all response forms issued in any promotion or advertising ask specifically for the e-mail address.

Although there are a variety of 'white pages' services available on the Internet, they are far from complete most people are simply not listed. Major e-mail providers are working on a universal directory system, but that could be some time away.

5. Look up people's e-mail accounts from news groups

This is a little on the edge of breaking etiquette, but so long as you use their names with discretion and tell them that this is where you obtained their name and offer them an easy way to disassociate themselves from you, you should get away with it. Not many companies use this promotion mechanism but so long as you are offering the respondent something which you believe will be of genuine value, it is an ideal way of building your database.

6. Mail to existing websites

Many individuals try to generate business by e-mailing the 'webmaster', or contact point on an existing website. Again you have to be very careful because this is cold calling, but with targeted mailings with a good benefits statement up front and a polite explanation of where you obtained the e-mail address, this can be an effective starting point.

7. Buy an e-mail list

Just as you can buy names and addresses of potential prospects, more and more companies are offering e-mail address lists. To all intents and purposes, it is identical to buying postal mailing lists. The e-mail list is usually seeded so that the provider of the list can police the number of times you use it.

What do I do with my long list of e-mails now that I have collected them?

When you do receive their e-mail addresses you then transfer them into what is called a 'Listserver'. It is a piece of software very like an Internet mailing house which then automatically sends a given e-mail message (your direct mailshot) to all the people on your database. This software can be downloaded free from the Internet if you have your own web-server or alternatively there are some commercial versions which you can purchase.

For more sophisticated targeted direct mail by product type, interest area or by customer type, work closely with an Internet marketing company. Most good Internet marketing companies will offer you the services of database classification, segmentation and targeted direct mail.

Carefully categorized enquiries with electronic follow-up can be extremely powerful. Recently one of the authors requested an evaluation copy of a piece of software. He did this by sending an e-mail to the software company in question. A reply was automatically generated which included instructions to get the software and a password to use it. After following the instructions, the author decided that the software was not relevant, deleted it from his computer and left it at that. Two weeks later the author received an e-mail from the software company who said 'Sorry to hear that you haven't registered our evaluation software. Would you be so kind as to help us find out why'. It then gave a list of possible reasons which could easily be ticked and sent back to the company. Although the author did not purchase this time, he was left feeling positive and excited about the company in question. The company also gained from the interaction because they know why the purchase wasn't made and have the author's e-mail address ready for when they announce a new improved version.

The major disadvantage of direct mailshots in the traditional world is that over 90 per cent of direct mail communications tend to be wasted or thrown away by the receiver. In the Internet, you as a recipient of direct mail can easily put up filters which stop unwanted e-mails from being downloaded onto your machine. This takes little effort and therefore you are much less likely to anger customers in the same way as direct postal mail can often do. Also, customers filtering off your direct mail shots do not cost you anything.

The overall aim of any direct mail campaign should be to encourage the receiver to take some immediate action, such as to return to the website for further information. All this can be measured by hit rates and there are great opportunities to learn what works best. Just like traditional marketing where in most instances the high wastage of direct mail effort can be explained by the lack of proper targeting of the receiver, so too is a great deal of e-mail being ignored for the same reasons.

Direct mail has a number of advantages:

• Provides a direct contact between the company and individuals by name, status, job function and their role in the decision making unit.
• Can be personalized by pre-selection of the target audience.

- Allows considerable flexibility in presentation (with the aim of immediate action and filing), frequency and geographical distribution.
- Your message is not simultaneously competing for the reader's attention as in press advertising. Your reader reads the message when they have made a conscious decision to spend time doing it – therefore they are more receptive to the message.
- Helps to keep potential customers 'warm' and informed.
- Allows opportunities for use with other sales production and merchandising incentives.
- Commercial availability of lists of names and addresses of specific target audiences and availability of complete direct mail services, including preparation of lists, letter writing, brochure design, dispatch and response handling.
- Loyalty building especially through the circulation of a company magazine. This is widely used and extremely powerful when the magazine or newsletter gives the reader valuable information and the feeling of exclusivity.

Other routes to direct marketing

The widespread existence of newsgroups and discussion forums create further opportunities to engage with customers for direct selling. You can:

1 Find out about your customers' needs.
2 Offer advice and consultancy.
3 Identify new customers.
4 Sell your products and services.
5 Gathering market intelligence.
6 Suppressing rumours.
7 Provide after-sales service

1. Find out about your customers' needs

By simply listening, observing, and by asking right questions, you can cost effectively market research your customers' needs. Have a look back at Chapter 3 for more information on how to do this.

2. Offer advice and consultancy

Offer advice and consultancy in response to your customer's needs. You can then help the customer decide on the combination of products and specifications that satisfy their needs. The role of the salesperson, therefore, is that of an expert or a consultant – interested in solving the customer's problems.

3. Identify new customers
Some people attend conferences and exhibitions for the sole purpose of networking and building a prospect list. The Internet is another mechanism to do that with the enormous benefits that you can network from your office or home at a time to suit your work commitments.

4. Sell your products and services
Selling is about finding a need and proving that your product solves that need. The Internet collects together people with similar interests to enable a discussion to occur. By taking part in a conversation, you will be able to identify people's needs and then offer to solve them. This can only be an effective sales and marketing tool when you have a credible presence within the discussion group and are seen as an insider.

There is a significant difference between receiving a comment from someone online against meeting them and speaking to them face to face. This is particularly important to appreciate when selling on the Internet. Anyone can send a message online and when you receive it you need little additional information in order to assess its credibility. The mechanisms to gain credibility are:

- professional input or contribution to the discussions in the newsgroups;
- invite people from the newsgroups to visit your website to provide customer testimonials, financial information and other credibility gaining information;
- take care and attention when writing e-mails and newsgroup messages. Although the Internet has a very casual style, spelling mistakes and bad grammar indicate lack of professionalism.

The process by which someone uses newsgroups and forums for selling has to be very subtle. The analogy is that you can meet someone at a conference, take a business card and sell to them six months down the line. You meet people in forums where the conversation is broadcast to anyone who is interested. This is similar to a conversation over a large table at a conference. People who respond will give you their e-mail address just as they might give you their business card at the conference.

You can then use private e-mail conversations to develop the personal relationship and the sales process further. It is as likely for you to be able to do business directly within a newsgroup or forum, as it is to sell your products in the coffee break at a conference. It is much more likely that you invite them to visit your website which, whilst not trying to stretch the analogy too far, is like inviting them to visit your organization on a sales appointment.

A typical online sales process is shown in Table 7.1.

Table 7.1 A typical online sales process

Sales process	Mechanism	Example
Stage 1 – Enquiry	Newsgroup or forum	How do I get a really good frying pan, my problem is that size is a big problem in my small boat.
Stage 2 – Information provision	Combination of one or more of the following: newsgroup or forum, visit to website or e-mail communication	My own company make a special range of pans just for small boat owners.
Stage 3 – Assessment of need compared to product benefits	E-mail or traditional communication	You can find out more on our website http://www.boatpans.com
Stage 4 – Objection handling	E-mail or traditional communication	'What did you think about our website? If price is an issue – we offer the best price in the industry and we can even improve on this if you buy in quantity!'
Stage 5 – Close of sale	Traditional means or online through website	'Can I take your order?'

This is the best way of building your customer database, selling online and promoting your website and cannot be underestimated as a cost-effective promotion tool. Innovative sales managers insist on their sales people becoming well known and respected in appropriate forums for exactly this reason.

A good case study of this approach is *Marketing Guild,* who proactively promoted their Internet marketing seminars in forums, SIGs and newsgroups, inviting people to visit their website. As a result they obtained several bookings which generated £7000 of direct profit and relationships with new companies which has the potential of generating ten times this initial sale.

5. Gathering market intelligence

The other main attraction of putting your whole sales team online is the huge amount of market intelligence that you can gather about competitors, market demand and changes happening in the industry as a whole. Sales representatives are the people closest to the marketplace. They interact with existing and potential customers, come into contact with competitors' products and sales forces and can observe the changes in end user requirements. Information gathered by sales forces on such matters can be more reliable than marketing research data that relies on asking customers direct questions. Many new product ideas and recommendations for product line modifications come from sales force reports to a company's marketing information system.

6. Suppressing rumours

Some companies dedicate one person to scan all forums for potential rumours about their company and their products and services. The impact of bad PR can be very damaging for an organization and being aware and able to suppress such negativity early on can save the organization a great deal of money. Jokes about the Pentium chip having a mathematical error gave Intel some bad press for some time on the Internet.

7. Provide after-sales service

Creating a relationship inside a forum and being dominant over a significant time period will give members some reassurance that on purchasing from your website, they can easily obtain after-sales support. It would not be in your interest if they were to complain about your products and therefore you would be able to give them privileged support. This could act as a further guarantee or warranty on their purchase from you. For you, being able to demonstrate that you have sold only through the forum or newsgroup, but supported people who have bought, adds to your personal credibility and the brand awareness of your organization.

Links with offline promotion strategies

So far in this review of promotion on the net we have focused on net-only approaches. It is important to realize that the Internet **must** be integrated with traditional media. This is the best way to maximize the benefit of the Internet, and will ensure your firm is getting best value for its advertising spend.

The alternative five other mass media are:

- Press – national dailies, national Sundays, local morning, evening and weekly, general interest magazines, magazines and journals.
- Cinema – gives flexibility to targeting local or national markets.
- Radio – national and local independent radio stations.
- Outdoor advertising – posters or hoardings.
- Television – local and national network of independent television companies. Now includes satellite television with possibilities of reaching international markets.

We would strongly recommend that you consider using at least one of these other mass media in addition to your use of the Internet. There are many reasons for this. Most important is the increasingly crowded nature of the net. It is getting hard – and will become harder – for firms without massive budgets to get noticed online unless they have a clever marketing strategy. A key element of a marketing strategy, then, must be to make good use of traditional media. If your website address is printed in a monthly magazine, for example, it may be one of only a few in your category in that edition. You can combine text and quality images, and the potential user can read your address as they go online.

Second, offline media do not rely on users electing to view adverts. If a newspaper is opened at random, adverts will be on view even to those who don't want to see them. Offline, therefore, you may have more chance of attracting people to sample your wares than you do online. When the e-commerce site boo.com was launched in the UK, for example, it relied heavily on billboards to win new users, some of whom it hoped would be fairly new to the net. It is doubtful that those who clicked to the boo.com site would have elected to do so had the campaign been entirely online. In effect, you need an advertising budget to promote your Internet site. Once people find you online, you must ensure that you satisfy their needs so they return and remain loyal.

Third, an offline strategy by-passes the difficulties of search engine listings which many firms will find challenging when they first go online. It is important to get started, and a traditional campaign can help you do that in an effective way.

If you do adopt a mixed media approach as we recommend, then follow the following advice:

- **Integrate your advertising themes across media.** The theme of advertising helps to give the product a personality that helps communicate an understandable message. By making sure your messages online and offline are the same, you can reinforce this process of character/personality development in a powerful way. Often the result is more than the sum of the parts as advertising across medias reinforce, support and enhance each other.
- **Do not make your spend too diffuse.** Many organizations make the mistake of excessive dispersal of the advertising budget by using too many different media. It is far better to opt for concentration, in terms of size and frequency, in a limited number of media, than to risk limited exposure to a larger audience by advertising in many media.
- **Ensure you can dominate at least one medium for a period.** Any advertising should dominate at least for some of the time and in relation to some of the target audience. In the long term, the budget available determines the amount of advertising that is possible, but to outspend the competition is the only way to achieve domination of the selected media. In some cases, a different creative approach from the competition can achieve domination of the media for a short period of time. On the Internet, you can dominate more effectively and cheaper than on any other media. However, dominating an advertising media is only relevant if the whole of your target audience reads that media. Do not invest in domination of the Internet if your target audience is not present yet – learn, experiment and wait for the best time to invest heavily.

- **Ensure you can repeat your message.** Awareness and comprehension of product benefits and attributes can only be communicated to large target audiences by repetitive exposure to the advertisements. Research suggests that advertising effectiveness requires at least three exposures to its target audience. On the Internet this is also true, as you need to encourage your customers to come back three times before they will buy. In order to reach a substantial number of your target audience, invest in repetitive advertising.

The considerations of *repetition, domination* and *concentration* will help you formulate an appropriate budget and channel choice strategy for your product or service.

Conclusion

This chapter has explained the key differences between the Internet and traditional media, and has highlighted the key promotional strategies you have at your disposal. These involve a careful use of advertising, and developing a website that is easy to use, and easy to find. We have also covered the different ways in which direct marketing can be developed using e-mail, and shown that there are very real opportunities to develop relationships with potential customers using one-to-one e-mail communication. Finally we have seen that promotion on the Internet must be integrated with your offline promotional strategies to ensure maximum effectiveness. Many firms blunder onto the net and do not step back to look at the issues. By thinking through the points addressed in this chapter and applying the lessons to your own circumstances, you have an opportunity to realize the full potential of the net.

Checklist

You now know:

What promotion is.	☐ Yes	☐ No
How the use of promotion can act as a differential advantage for you.	☐ Yes	☐ No

What makes up the tools and techniques within this element of the marketing mix.	☐ Yes	☐ No
Which tools and techniques are used to achieve your communication goals.	☐ Yes	☐ No
How to set advertising objectives.	☐ Yes	☐ No
How to decide which media to use.	☐ Yes	☐ No
How appropriate the Internet is as a media choice.	☐ Yes	☐ No
Where the Internet is today.	☐ Yes	☐ No
How it differs from traditional medias.	☐ Yes	☐ No
What choices there are for putting your organization on the Internet.	☐ Yes	☐ No
How to merchandise your products and services on the Internet.	☐ Yes	☐ No
How you can use the Internet for direct marketing.	☐ Yes	☐ No
How you can use 'personal selling' on the Internet.	☐ Yes	☐ No
How promotion is not the only issue you need to consider when you think about 'marketing on the Internet'.	☐ Yes	☐ No

What next?

Having appreciated the various communication goals and approaches to promotion, you may have decided to launch a presence on the web. We have introduced some of the issues you will face as you prepare to create Internet materials and build a site. Chapter 8 develops these ideas in much more detail, and provides a step-by-step guide to solving the practical challenges you face in building a winning presence on the web.

References

Cheswick, W. and Bellovin, S. (1994) *Firewalls and Internet Security: Repelling the Wily Hacker*, Addison-Wesley, London.

Glossbrenner, A. and Glossbrenner, E. (1995) *Making Money on the Internet*, McGraw-Hill Inc.

Chapter 8

Producing your promotional materials online

If you haven't produced promotional material for the net before, you should start by comparing what you can do on the net with other media. In many areas, the Internet offers additional functionality over and above traditional promotion mechanisms.

- Internet promotional materials can be **used more flexibly** than other media: each customer might take a different route through your site.
- Internet promotional materials can be changed and **re-published more cheaply** than materials in other media.
- They allow **greater interaction**, allowing customers to talk to each other, or to a company when it suits them. Firms can post messages, and customers pick them up and reply exactly when it suits them. Promotional materials can also allow customers to post questions and request inspection copies. Websites offer the potential to create community centres, meeting points where experts, customers and suppliers in the same field can gather to discuss and debate issues affecting their common interests.
- Companies hosting websites can enjoy **more rapid learning** than firms operating in other media. It is possible to measure site traffic, find out which pages are most popular, and conduct experiments in which results come back very quickly indeed. Customer databases can be built up online, and surveys conducted at very low cost.

To make use of this powerful added functionality, you must decide who *your* customers are and what will entertain and involve them.

The difference between an Internet magazine reviewer and your customer

If you get this right they will come to you. Don't do what so many organizations do, which is to try to involve and entertain 30 million people. The likelihood is that you will fail to impress anyone including your existing customers. You may even damage your company image by bad reviews in the press.

The real test of a good website is the extent to which it drives traffic and builds the relationships and channels that support sales. If your target audience is prepared to spend time and money clicking around, you have succeeded. You may still get some bad site reviews from reviewers with a different value set to your intended target audience. This is OK because you then have a valid comeback which is that it was not intended to impress them!

A good analogy is to compare creating a website to the process of building an exhibition stand. Do you really want to draw in every visitor to the exhibition? You put in great plants, free coffee and ice-cream. You give away free products, you entertain everyone. It costs you a fortune. You build up a database of everyone at the exhibition. But you then spend another fortune after the exhibition trying to identify who is actually interested in your products and another fortune trying to convince them that you have the solution to their needs.

We recommend that you set up a totally targeted exhibition stand (online) which is geared around meeting the needs of your intended target audience. Taking the analogy a little further, you only offer free coffee if this is what your intended customers hanker for. You offer entertainment which only your customers will find entertaining. You give freebies that are only of interest to your target audience. Your stand only looks of interest to your intended audience. Then you wait. Yes, lots of people will look and walk on – but that's great, you haven't wasted money giving them your promotion material. At the end of the exhibition, you have only 200 names and addresses but these are people who are likely to buy.

You know your exhibition stand has really worked if you find the customers you most want to contact start meeting there to talk to each other: you know that your company is seen as an integral part of their community. The parallel applies online, where the best websites try to become the natural home for the community of people who are interested in one sector/product range/issue.

This does seem so obvious to existing marketing managers and business professionals as it complies with traditional marketing think. But this knowledge and know-how is often not applied to the Internet. Hardened marketing people hanker after huge 'hit rates' (people accessing their pages), fail to offer response devices and fail to leverage the true business potential of the Internet.

How do you go about it?

This book is not about how to produce interesting and exciting web pages. There is a plethora of books on the market doing exactly that. What you really need to know is that the secret of writing a good website is the same secret you already know about producing a good brochure, i.e. appealing to your target audience. The plethora of books about 'Marketing On The Internet' are often IT professionals helping other IT professionals understand what promotional devices do work and don't work.

So what are the stages involved in making your Internet presence professional and leading edge and most importantly effective as a marketing device? We recommend that you plan for three distinct stages: a planning and preparation stage, a design stage, a launch stage and lastly a maintenance stage. So many companies jump straight into design and then spend little time launching effectively. Even if you are a relatively small company, spending time planning and launching effectively can double the effectiveness of your Internet marketing. Equally, it is important to be aware of the maintenance costs of your site. So many companies put their presence up and forget it after two or three months – this communicates to your customers that you don't really care about them.

Getting ready to go live

Brainstorming and creative input

Involve people as early as possible in the project; they will feel more committed to making it a success. Involve people closest to your customer to ensure that the Internet site is most likely to win the hearts and minds of your target audience. Involve front-line business people alongside the marketing team to brainstorm out all the possibilities. Capture them in any format that you desire but documentation is critical here because it sets the scene to your website and is a good reference to return to three or six months into the project or when you have sufficient resources to move onto other ideas.

Constrain the creative process as little as possible but do take some of the learning from the book to guide the creative input. Two of the most valuable inputs are: who are we targeting with this website and what value are we offering these people in exchange for reading our promotional materials.

Decide your objectives and your budget

Be realistic. In our experience, companies want to conquer the world for as little money as possible, as fast as possible. This is feasible but only with an extraordinary creative exchange between your target customer and yourself. As the Internet becomes increasingly popular, the chances that you can come up with a unique creative concept like this becomes less – another good reason for going live sooner rather than later.

We recommend that you focus on a phased implementation strategy. Here you would set up phased objectives:

- Phase 1: Getting yourself known – register your company and/or brand names; produce some initial promotional materials using existing proven concepts.
- Phase 2: Start to interact with customers – create an interactive dialogue with your target audience to test various concepts.
- Phase 3: Start to experiment – take orders off the Internet to create a revenue stream; use it as a sales promotion tool, etc.

The main reason we recommend this approach is that Internet customers like to be wooed. Evolving your site over time, adding value as you go, leaving on-line ordering until later, will create a certain amount of goodwill. Typically a user needs to visit a site three times before they buy anything, so you need to create good reasons for them to come back again and again.

Internal 'buy-in'

The sooner you can involve key decision makers, product managers and sales people the better. They will be critical to the success or failure of your Internet promotion. A good communications strategy up front will save a huge amount of time and effort justifying your pages after you go live.

Financial commitment

Don't attempt an Internet site on a shoestring if you need a credible and professional presence. Obtain quotes from Internet marketing companies and ensure that you have the financial commitment to this level of investment. The Internet is packed with half-baked sites which could have been success stories with the correct level of investment. We have already recommended that you ask, 'Are we serious?' If you've done that and find money is a major constraint, you need to rethink the objectives.

Remember – the more content you decide to include on your site, the higher the ongoing maintenance costs will be. Content needs to be kept up to date, and this must be built in to your plans.

Designing your site

The three rules to website design are:

1 Understand your target audience.
2 Understand your target audience.
3 Understand your target audience.

We cannot stress this enough and the **only** difference between a good site and a bad site is in their understanding of their target audience.

Your target audience are Internet users, so you do need to see the Internet from their perspective. Never think of becoming involved in the design phase unless you have visited at least twenty sites. You should make especially sure that you are familiar with all of the key sites in your sector. Do not forget to include sites based overseas, as these can often be a good source of inspiration and ideas: if you're not looking at them, don't forget that your rivals almost certainly are!

In general your target audience has similar needs to every Internet user so there are some basic rules that you need to abide by:

General rules for all Internet sites

Do not use graphics for their own sake

We know that you are proud of your logo and you want it big and bold but, remember, downloading your logo takes time. For your user, this is a cost both in terms of convenience and phone bills! If your graphics don't add value to your site, you risk making your potential customer feel negative towards the very imagery that was designed to generate positive feelings. Use graphics only when they give the customer something they will value – you do not want them to switch their graphics display button off when they visit your site. If they do, they will associate you with dull and unimaginative presentation.

However, a strong visual idea can often communicate more convincingly than half a page of factual information. So the best compromise is to use graphics when they give something to the reader: a picture of your product, the packaging, etc.

Alternatively, design your website such that your visitors can read some great benefits statements about what you are just about to offer or show them – while they are waiting for the graphic to be downloaded. One example of this is the recipe pages within J Sainsbury plc. You can read all the ingredients and instructions for cooking and just as you finish you are rewarded with a wonderful picture of the dish.

The best way to reduce the problem of graphics is to reduce the number of colours used. Some sites get round the issue by using only line art images which download fast and can still look very effective.

Most browsers keep the picture stored in memory for a certain amount of time after it has been viewed. So if you have a graphic on the home page and your reader has downloaded it fully, on all subsequent pages that display the same graphics, it appears almost instantly. Therefore re-use graphics to make your site appear even faster than it is.

This all sounds so obvious but so many sites that you go to force you to wait for their graphics before you can see anything or make any decision about whether it holds any information of value for you.

Use exciting copy

You have less than four seconds to attract, captivate and absorb your Internet reader. So do remember the two models, AIDA and DAGMAR, covered in Chapter 7. Use all the traditional techniques that you use in direct mail, PR, advertising and promotional literature. Tell them what is of interest for them, not about you. If you excite them, interest them about what your products or services can do to make them happy, rich or successful – don't worry, they'll find out more about you!! They'll respond immediately.

'A bore is someone who talks more about themselves than they do about you' – the same goes for a website.

The exceptions to this rule are the 'metatags' described in the previous chapter. The search engines will only display these tags when customers search to find you. It is therefore imperative that these achieve the following objectives:

- Describe your organization and what you offer.
- Describe what value your pages are offering.
- Make it attractive for the person seeing your listing in a search engine to investigate your sight further.
- Declare your geographic boundaries if you only want to attract customers inside them.

Use a good copywriter on this task and ensure that the metatags change throughout your site so that you can attract different target audiences into different areas, i.e. investors to share and financial information, etc.

The other area of strategic importance is that the style of copy will differ greatly on the Internet because it is a less formal medium for talking to your customers. Some companies fail to appreciate this and alienate their customers by making it appear too much like their corporate brochure. This is similar to turning up on your first date with your best work suit on! So many sites make simple mistakes like having an icon saying 'Our products and services'. Innovative sites use less formal language and more of a direct marketing approach such as 'Find out how to increase your productivity by 20 per cent'; 'Special offer ONLY to Internet readers'. 'Discover what we can offer you'.

Hot copy tips

- Make it 'newsy'. People love to feel they have privileged, state of the art information, so make like a news bulletin. This will appeal to the global workers, the knowledge traders and the get-aheads (Chapter 5) who are trying to keep their fingers on the pulse.
- Make it 'verby'. To convey an interactive and dynamic feel to the website use verbs to indicate what action you wish the reader to perform: 'Read our exciting newsletter'; 'Fill in our response form to receive our free report'. This will appeal to the global surfer but also maintain the attention of your reader, whichever target audience you are appealing to. Remember you are trying to persuade them to explore your site as much as possible.
- Make it short. Don't use large sentences or long paragraphs – people tire and frustrate easily. Convey your message as quickly as possible in the most exciting way. Remember that your customers are reading from a screen.
- Give them the option to read it offline. People don't find it easy to read off a computer screen – so offer the option of sending printed copy by direct mail or autoresponding to their e-mail.
- Make it intimate. You can afford to be more personal with this new medium. Use the word 'you' more than you would in a brochure. If you fail to convey an intimacy, people will think that you are stand-offish and using the Internet purely as an advertising medium, not as an opportunity to talk to the 'common person'. Even if you are a blue-chip multinational company – this is your chance to present yourself as a caring, interested and real entity. Body Shop in the UK has gone so far as not to promote their products and services but to sponsor and publicize ethically sound projects, inviting their customers to become involved. Here their customers can join them in a common project and in doing so become intimate with the organization.
- Make it memorable. Your readers will read so many sales messages that you need to differentiate yourself. Good copy can do this and is worth paying for (see Chapter 7 on direct marketing). Another

option is make sections of the website downloadable in file format, which users can save onto their computer and read offline. This saves their telephone bill and shows that you understand their needs. It also means that when they do read it, they are likely to be more relaxed and interested in what you have to offer. The Adobe Acrobat Reader™, a product widely distributed on the Internet, will allow you to do this. What you put on an Acrobat document appears exactly the same including fonts, columns, layouts etc. Your customer downloads this file in 'pdf' format, and they save it on their hard disk. Customers would then print out your document and read off paper. An important advantage of this approach is that customers see your reports and publications in the layout you designed, and not as text files that might appear on a word processor. For publishers and others concerned with the appearance of quality, this can be a major advantage.

Enable people to respond and interact with you

Rather than displaying every product and service your company provides, use forms or clickable graphics to enable the Internet reader to choose what interests them. Enabling your customer to see the benefits and giving them options of what most appeals to them means that you are creating an interactive conversation with them. The more like a conversation you make it, the more response and information you will elicit. You then create a dialogue which is documented in the hit rate comparison of your pages. You will be able to find out how many people see your home page and then as a response what percentage decided to take the various paths forward that you offer. For example, how many take you up on your special offers (page 2) or look at your special marketing report (page 3). If you find that people are not attracted to your page 4, which is all about Product X, you can conclude that either your copy about Product X is not exciting enough or that this product does not appeal to your target audience. In order to assess this, change the copy for the link into these pages: make it look more appealing and see if this affects the hit rate. In this way you are truly interacting with your customer because you are evolving your website in tune with their response. It is now essential to monitor hit rates and redesign accordingly. As soon as your customers appreciate the dynamic nature of your website, they will return to it regularly (e.g. they bookmark you).

Prove your credibility

An Internet site is as easy to produce as a business card. Just as you would not think to invest in someone solely because they had a business card, neither can you expect customers who don't know you to invest in you solely because you have a website. The question is how do you prove credibility on a website? Client lists, company financial information, PR articles are used frequently. Having a secure website (i.e. Netscape's Security feature) helps because it proves that you have afforded this option and therefore are unlikely to be a gold-digger. However, people will still be reluctant to part with their money unless you can demonstrate your credibility in real terms. We would recommend that you publish basic information to make this as easy as possible. Your address, your telephone number and your company registration number. This is especially important for any website where you are asking the Internet reader to purchase anything.

Offer guarantees and warranties with any product you sell online, ensuring that you explain your ordering and refund policy clearly.

Don't expect too much from your Internet reader

Just as we highlighted in the preface to our book. The Internet is a courting tool allowing you to woo your customers to build a lasting relationship. We argue that this will help you understand your market well enough to adapt to its needs in order to achieve business profit. Our advice is to ensure that your site conveys the courting ritual approach rather than the one-night stand. Yes, you want the business so it is very tempting to publish a glorified order form. Unfortunately, this is a little bit like going on a first date with a tooth-brush sticking out of your pocket. Some sites offer a list of products which, when you click to find out more, takes you straight into an enquiry form, e.g. Lawnet. Whilst it is good that they offer you a means of communicating and responding with them, it fails to convey that they are interested in a dialogue or a relationship with you.

The classic example of expecting too much from their readers is companies asking for orders of high priced products. It is too much of a high risk for a user to pay serious amounts of money direct on the Internet to a company that they may not even know. Instead, entice your reader to buy a small item of reasonably low value from you. Deliver it efficiently and then the next higher-value sell will be easier.

Enable your customer to respond to you
So many sites offer no way of responding for their customers. Sometimes they have a bizarre reference to their 'webmaster' at the bottom of the screen but this is not designed to elicit customer feedback. It is usually intended for the customer to comment on the design of the Internet site.

Response from your customers must be one of your main driving forces behind having a website. Just posting a website with no response mechanism is similar to a sales call where you do not ask for the customer's opinion of your products.

So why doesn't every Internet site offer a response mechanism?

Some companies misunderstand the Internet and see it purely as an advertising medium. They are wasting their time on the Internet. It damages their brand image as it reinforces the point that they are not a responsive organization. It may even convey the impression that they are not a caring organization. Large accountancy companies are the worst culprits of this approach.

Most commonly, the lack of a response mechanism is due to the fear of the amount of work needed to respond to the variety of questions a customer may ask, or worry about the number of brochures or information packs that may be requested. Our answer to this is to offer a tailored response form which helps the customer identify their interest area and what information they need and then provide 'autoresponders' (see the direct marketing section in Chapter 7). Alternatively, if you are looking to send samples or product, why not use a fulfilment response handling agency who will collect your responses directly from the Internet and dispatch them for you immediately. Most direct marketing agencies offer this service.

Ensure the consistent quality of your website
It is not possible for you to control exactly what your web-page looks like. The world wide web is based on a page layout system called HTML (Hypertext Mark-up Language). The basic concept is that this language provides a set of formatting commands such as

bold, italic, heading and flashing, to name but a few. These describe your intention as to what the format of the text and graphics should look like. The actual display of these instructions will be dependent on the decisions made by your customers and the browser that they use. You usually have little control of the font that is displayed as the user can define this in their browser options. The user can also define how small or large they like the browser window to appear and this will mean that large blocks of text will automatically position themselves to fit the window. This language is evolving rapidly with new features being added all the time, and there are signs that XML might take over from HTML for some sites, allowing the site publisher to control layout and appearance much more closely. Until transition to this or a similar protocol takes place, you do need to be aware of this limitation. To solve these issues, it is essential to recognize the limitations of the language you have to use to code your pages. HTML does not support complex layouts. Graphs for example need to be written as 'objects', embedded in text which means they take longer to download than would otherwise be necessary. While it is likely that coding will improve, it would be rash to jump ahead of the commonly held technology. To do so would exclude potential visitors and readers.

That said, the browser market itself has simplified since the Internet began, with MS Explorer and Netscape Navigator taking an overwhelming share of the market. This at least means you can guess what sort of software your customers are likely to be using to read your pages, so it is now possible to test your site against customers' software fairly easily. When the browser market was more fragmented, this was considerably more difficult.

Key points

- HTML does not allow you to control layout fully. Browsers will lay out the page based on the customer's screen. Many of your customers choose to have their browser at a reduced screen size, so you should not use very large graphics which span the whole screen but instead use smaller ones that can be adapted to a smaller screen size.
- Some computers display only 256 colours, and what may look wonderful on your desktop publishing system can look coarse and grainy on your customer's computer.

The best advice we can give you is:

- Always test your pages on a cheap computer, with a cheap monitor with a cheap modem with an early version of a standard browser – with the window reduced in size. Most good Internet marketing companies will provide this testing service for you free of charge if they are designing your web pages.
- You should also use this test to review download times. You finest animated applets and flash sequences will actually be a negative point to users with slow modems and slow processors! It's frustrating, but you must accept that the best innovations only work if they work for your customers as well as your designers.

Guide your reader around the site

Your customer cannot read your mind and although it may be obvious to you that they must scroll down the page, it may not be obvious to them. It may be obvious to experienced Internet users that they can click on graphics, but it may not be obvious to all. Helping people navigate around your site with instructions may ruin the design of your site – but we have some ideas.

A common mistake is to fill the top of the home page (your first page) with lovely graphics and lots of copy – leaving all the links to other pages until further down. This will result in customers reading your home page, thinking you only have one page and moving on. Instead, use graphics that lead the reader's eyes down to the second page or put the links on the first screen of the home page.

Another common mistake is to make the home page say it all. It is a misconception that you have to show everything you have got to offer on the first page. The home page should be the invitation in to your website. Give the reader the benefits of reading on; tell them what you have to offer them; excite them about wanting to know more; then invite them into the core of your website. Make it inviting and your customer will make a decision to come into your further pages. Once they have made the decision to find out more, they have demonstrated an interest and are more likely to be receptive to your messages. Cognitive dissonance is overcome and they may even actively search to find something of value to them – making your job easier.

If you are appealing to different target audiences, the home page is the ideal switching device that enables you to cater for their differing needs. Enable the customer to select what kind of person they are or what kind of product they are interested in and from then on you can design and target the further pages to suit the style and appearance which will most attract them.

A UK business school was a fine example of this. The home page gave a list of a variety of different products: MBA, executive programmes, doctoral programmes. As you selected each, the design, graphics and copy style changed dramatically. The MBA programme page was fun and innovative with a conversation style of copy. The executive programmes showed a much more serious granite background with a cleaner use of design with a dramatic change in copy style.

Provide obvious navigation buttons to help your customer return to where they have gone and progress forward easily. If your pages are long (and each web-page can scroll almost infinitely down the page) ensure that you give the reader the ability to return to the top of the page, and provide an index of headers at the start so that the reader can choose which place to start reading from.

Always provide a site map and search engine as back-up navigational tools.

Provide added value to your reader by providing links
Most websites provide links to other sites which their target audience would be interested in. This is a convention but is also very important for two reasons.

1 It is an essential part of the Internet. It is how the Internet has grown as popular as it has in a relatively short period of time. It is critical to its long-term success. Its success is also the success of your website, so do follow this convention by enabling your reader to travel from you to another website which complements yours.
2 It provides a free-of-charge service which adds value to your end customer. Your customer knows this and will be disappointed if you don't offer this service.

To provide a link to another website is very easy and also free. All you need to do is to programme the URL into your web page. You do not need to gain the permission of the website owner. However, there is a protocol which is that if someone references your website, and they attract similar volume of traffic, you will return the gesture and reference theirs. To do this all you have to do is to e-mail the website owner stating that you wish them to reference you, stating why you have referenced them on your website; request that they follow suit and leave your URL. This joint bundling can add value to both parties and is practically free.

You do need to publish a disclaimer if you are to offer these links. This will protect to you to some degree if any of your hyperlinks act in an offensive manner but . . .

A word of warning. There have been cases in America where websites providing hyperlinks to disreputable websites have been incriminated. No real precedent has been set in European law but our advice to you would be to only reference highly credible sites which you would be happy to have your organization associated with. We would not advise you to link to personal web-pages unless you really have to. Lastly, always check your links regularly and keep them up to date. URLs change and it is frustrating for your customers if you lead them up a blind alleyway.

Provide the customer with some other helpful information

Internet users love 'FAQs' or frequently asked questions. These are in effect like 'problem pages' but enable customers to sift through what questions other customers have asked before posting their own. People love to eavesdrop and it is basically a little like this. You create a page with some customers' questions and answer them in a friendly, informative way. Ensure that you date the questions to give the feel of how dynamic the interaction is. Encourage your customers to post you new questions by providing an e-mail address at the bottom and top of the FAQ page. Be sure to update the page regularly. Done well this provides a customer forum for your customers and will add great value to your site – it might even be the highest value part of it. It also prevents you from having to answer the same questions over and over again.

Do be a little careful with this. A FAQ full of acknowledged problems with your products can give a very negative image.

Market test, market test and last of all market test

The true test of a good design is that it has been market tested. No company would even contemplate selling a product which has not been tested, yet very few companies really market test the acceptability of their website.

Invite a selection of your customers to visit a URL, which you have not published on any of the search engines, but published just to elicit feedback. Make it worth their while with a free prize for the most useful feedback and ask them what they liked and didn't like. Be open to suggestions because many people will only visit your site the first time it is launched and you need to get it memorable from the start.

Launching your site

So you have tested your pages, adapted accordingly and you are now ready to launch. The steps we recommend that you take are:

1 List on all search engines – we reference a one-stop site to do this on the web page that accompanies this chapter.
2 Announce it in mailing lists (see Chapter 7 under direct marketing).
3 Announce it in all newsgroups that would find it of interest and abide by the specific etiquette of that particular newsgroup.
4 Promote with classified adds inside the Internet and printed materials.
5 Press release it to journalists worldwide ensuring that all Internet magazines and publications are aware of the site.
6 Ensure that your website is referenced on all your own advertising and promotion materials, especially free product give-aways, e.g. pencils and pens advertise websites well.
7 Get your salespeople to mention it at every sales appointment and within every telephone conversation. Ensure that salespeople use newsgroups to attract people to your website.
8 Show your website at every exhibition and in your customer reception area (running off the computer rather than permanently connected to the Internet).

Keeping it going

This is the hardest stage. The bright lights have faded. The initial excitement is over and you now have to think about how to improve it. It feels like you have just finished decorating your whole house and you are asked to completely redecorate it. However, this is the bit which ensures a long-term dialogue with your customers. Fail here and you fail your customers forever and the whole process has been a total waste of time.

This is in fact the main reason why companies choose Internet marketing companies to work with. They can often provide the inspiration and ideas that will keep the momentum going when your organization has moved on to the next exciting project or campaign.

To monitor the effectiveness of your website you need to compare two ratios of information provided by your web-server or the company who is hosting your web-pages.

Enquiry/hit conversion ratio

The number of enquiries are the number of actual names of people who have approached you as a result of your Internet presence. Typically this is the number of people who have responded electronically through your response or e-mail form but you may need to include here telephone enquiries if you have promoted telephone access on your web-page.

The hit rate is a loose measurement pertaining to the number of people visiting your site. We say that it is loose because it actually refers to the number of requests users have made whilst on your pages. If they click on a graphic, this is also considered to be a hit, so it is not an accurate number but does give you an indication of the activity inspired by your pages.

Again do not get obsessed by a low hit rate of say 300 per week. This may mean that you have hit your target audience effectively and you have X potential buyers looking at your site per week. What is important is how effective your pages are at pulling in your enquiries: No enquiries in your first month after a good launch means that your pages need redesigning.

Order/enquiry conversion

This is the true test of how effective your website is, but only if it has been designed with this sole purpose in mind. Many sites are after brand awareness and so this may not be applicable.

If these ratios indicate a redesign return to the drawing board, conduct some market research to find out why they were a disaster and follow all the steps outlined in this chapter, paying particular attention to market testing and the launch initiative; this was obviously not done thoroughly enough.

When you do launch again, make sure you present the world with your website just as though it was a new one, re-registering it as a new entry with different text in all the search engines. You may even want to reference that it has been redesigned.

The real test of an effective website is that it meets with your marketing objective. If brand awareness has been your desired intention then a good hit rate will be your primary concern.

Conclusion

Our last words are good luck. It is a bit like trying to pass your driving test – it all seems so daunting and frightening at first but once you pick it up, it all seems so obvious! Unlike producing a corporate brochure, making a mistake is an essential part of learning about this new medium and will not result in a stock room tragedy!

Checklist

You now know:

Why knowledge about the target audience is essential to web-page design.	☐ Yes	☐ No
How to go about producing your Internet materials.	☐ Yes	☐ No
How to design your site.	☐ Yes	☐ No
How to launch your site.	☐ Yes	☐ No
How to keep it going.	☐ Yes	☐ No
How to measure if it is working.	☐ Yes	☐ No
The importance of experimentation.	☐ Yes	☐ No

What next?

So far we have focused on the way websites impact on the marketing mix – promotion, product, price and place. But the Internet is also an increasingly powerful medium for commerce, transacting sales directly online. Chapter 9 looks at some of the issues facing companies seeking to set up an e-commerce outlet on the net.

Chapter 9

E-commerce – selling online

Many websites were first set up to provide corporate information and to promote products. Sales were expected to take place in shops, on the telephone, by mail order. The growth in e-commerce indicates that this has changed. The web is seen, more and more, as primarily a direct selling medium, and online selling has grown dramatically. A KPMG study of European companies using the Internet for selling in 1999 showed that the channel accounted for 2 per cent of their total sales. This was forecast to grow to 12 per cent in three years. By 2005, Internet sales were forecast to be 16 per cent of total sales of all companies in Europe – an extraordinary shift in the location of the sales transaction. It is vital, therefore, to consider whether your products and services can be sold over the net, and to understand how to set up an e-commerce facility. This chapter will explain why e-commerce has spread so quickly, and show how you can establish a sales outlet online.

Why sell online?

You may think you know why firms sell online. They can make profitable sales to a wider public than ever before, at relatively low cost. They can achieve competitive advantage over bricks and mortar retail outlets. It sounds obvious. But for the customer-focused marketer, this answer is not good enough. What really matters is why people buy. Firms sell because people buy. So, why do people buy? There has been a great deal of recent research asking exactly that question. The findings should guide your approach to e-commerce.

The top three motivators for online shopping are (in this order):

- saving money;
- saving time and travel;
- getting a wider choice.

Saving money is way out in front as a motivator for online purchase, but around half of online shoppers also rate convenience and choice as very important. Each one of these three factors should influence the way you set up your e-commerce outlet. If customers see the net as a way to save money, then you have to offer them value when they come online. In Chapter 6 we saw that the Internet offers consumers more information and better choice. This means they have greater power, and they expect to be able to use it to get more for their money.

It's also important to take to heart the importance that consumers attach to saving time and effort. In part, the Internet itself will deliver savings in effort. Customers don't have to travel to go online. But if saving effort is so important, then you have to make sure that you e-commerce outlet is easy to use. You must avoid designs and software that force customers to wait while images download or unnecessary action sequences unfold. Everything must be as easy and quick to use as possible – including making the purchase itself. Later in this chapter you will see that the technical choices you make (e.g. over supplier of server space) will influence speed and ease of use.

As well as value and convenience, you must also think about choice. For small firms hoping to sell their own goods via their own sites, this presents a challenge. After all, the choice one firm can offer is smaller than the market, and so there's little incentive for a buyer to come to a single firm's site if the same goods (at similar price) can be bought via a larger site pooling other firms' goods. For some firms this means there is a dilemma. Which approach is best?

- Undercut other third-party sales outlets. The danger here is that you drive a price war in your own goods, which is not a good idea!
- Provide a better service and more information than rivals at the same price. Although costs are higher, this allows you to preserve prices.

- Join up with other producers to make an e-commerce site that does offer choice and so attracts heavier traffic. It is this principle which encourages shops of similar types to cluster together in the same area: the Bond Street art dealers know that each individual retailer will benefit from the greater traffic generated by the draw of many dealers in one location. The same principle applies on the net.
- Sell entirely through third-party sales outlets (using a website hot link to connect your visitors to a sales point). This saves the cost and effort of setting up a site. The approach has been tried by Psion who connect visitors to a vast list of firms which sell their products. The downside here is that the customer faces a hard task in choosing whom to buy from, and finds it hard to know that they really have got the best deal. The re-sellers also may not have any particular incentive to sell your products ahead of anyone else's.

It is important to consider all of the options before setting up your own e-commerce outlet. In the end, you will need to choose the option which produces maximum revenue at minimum cost, while still securing your market position and brand reputation. You may find that it's cheaper to let someone else sell for you, but relying on this may damage your image. Visitors to your website who expect to be able to buy direct may be very un-impressed if they have to switch to a badly designed third-party sales outlet, particularly if your products are high-tech or are heavily branded. Your image is likely to be damaged, whereas selling direct allows you to control the way your products and services are presented.

We have begun this chapter with the customer's perspective deliberately – because many firms facing technical decisions forget they are making them to serve their customers better. When facing a technical issue, don't forget to start with your customer's viewpoint when you're deciding what to do.

How to promote online sales

The research evidence on customers' motivations for buying should guide you in designing a successful selling environment. But the process of buying itself also has to be promoted. There are a number of ways you can do this by allowing potential customers to sample your goods, creating incentives to buy them, and thinking through the tools you can use to encourage re-purchase.

Sales promotion should be used as a deliberate policy to achieve defined objectives rather than as a catch-up response to your competitors. Sales promotion is an integral part of the marketing mix. As such it requires proper planning and effective implementation. Sales promotion activity falls into two main types:

• strategic sales promotion; and
• tactical sales promotion.

Strategic sales promotion

Sales promotion should be incorporated in your organization's annual marketing plan to support new product launches, growth in distribution outlets, increase in branch use or simply to encourage sampling and changes in frequency of repeat purchase.

An example of this may be a decision to adopt a two-tier pricing strategy, one for the Internet and/or mail order and one for retail or traditional distribution channels. Software companies often choose to have a different (reduced) pricing strategy for the Internet. This reflects in part a response to the competitive dynamics of the net, where costs are lower. But it is also an integral part of a sales promotion strategy in which the importance of sampling is recognized. Firms offer a stripped down version of software at a much reduced cost, in order to encourage the customer to buy. It is low cost and low risk for the consumer and practically free to the supplier. Persuading a customer to buy a basic version of their goods is a major step towards purchase of the full product. This sort of sales promotion needs to be approached in a strategic way, and must be considered in the context of the overall business and marketing plan of the organization.

Tactical sales promotion

The second type of sales promotion is shorter-term, and more tactical in approach. These tactical moves may be in response to the actions of competitors, or derive from changing expectations of consumer buying behaviour. This sort of sales promotion is used to ensure that the firm continues to meet specific needs of the product in order to achieve the overall marketing objectives in terms of market share or sales turnover.

Encouraging sampling is the main tactical sales promotion tool used on the Internet. The easier and quicker it is for a customer to sample your product live from the comfort of their home, the more likely they are to buy and return regularly. Examples of effective sales promotion to encourage sampling on the Internet are:

• Free chapters of books which you can download and read at your leisure and later purchase the book directly from the Internet.
• Samples of music which, although not long in duration, can help you decide if this is the CD for you.
• Downloadable full working copies of a given piece of software. Here the software has a flashing message which constantly reminds you that you have not paid for it. If the message is extremely annoying and the benefits of the software can be appreciated quickly, conversion to purchase can be as high as 70 per cent of the people who download it.
• Market research reports where only the executive summary is given.
• Financial assessments or health checks can be automatically generated for you online. This customer service also allows users to sample the expertise of the provider organization, and so promotes relationships which lead to sales.

Encouraging repeat purchases is easier and cheaper than ever before because you can talk to those customers who have bought from you through e-mail. Examples and suggestions of how to encourage repeat purchase on the Internet are:

• Ensure that when you do receive an order that you take your customer's e-mail account. In this way you can:

(a) Thank them for purchasing from you and offer them an immediate incentive to re-order. You can even tailor this e-mail to look very personal. The best example of this we have seen was a message saying: 'Thank you for buying "Elton John's Top Hits". We hoped it arrived safely on the 24 September. Remember, if you don't like it, you can return it within 20 days for your no-quibble money back guarantee.'
(b) Send direct mail to previous purchasers about new products and any special offers that you are carrying.

- Whenever they purchase from you, ensure that when the product arrives, either direct from the Internet or through traditional means, that it contains information on how to purchase again, plus an incentive to do so. The authors have purchased many items from the Internet and very few companies offer any incentive to repeat purchase – even though repeat business is the lifeblood of any consumer business.
- Ask the customer to create an account with your online shop. It is a simple way to obtain their credit card details without having to pay for a secure web-server. It is also a proven way to encourage repeat purchase. If your customer just has to remember an account name, password or number and select their products, they are more likely to purchase again. To encourage account opening, ensure that you offer an incentive and make it as easy as possible. Once they have opened an account with you and purchased, ensure that you send them a membership card which they will want to keep.
- Use a membership club concept so that once a member has purchased more than X amount of products from you, they are entitled to a free Y. The authors have purchased over 20 CDs from an online CD shop in America and were disappointed not to have received any incentive or recognition for doing so.

Sales promotions can help organizations penetrate new markets, and can be an important adjunct to efficient stock management. Sales promotions are an important aspect of launching new or redefined products, and building customer loyalty: offers aimed exclusively at previous purchasers, for example, will encourage your customers to recognize that you value your relationship with them (while also shifting stock). Sales promotion techniques directed at buyers include competitions, coupons, premium offers, reduced-price offers, special demonstrations, free samples and trade stamps. Each of these incentives is designed to achieve specific buyer actions such as to obtain customer loyalty, encourage sampling, reduce stock by increased turnover and gain repeat purchases. Sales promotion techniques should not be used in an ad hoc manner but should be linked with your advertising and merchandising activities. It should not be forgotten that these techniques are equally applicable to the promotion of services and industrial products, where managers can use their expert understanding of customer relationships to encourage product sampling and repeat business.

How to set up an e-commerce outlet

To set up an e-commerce outlet, you will need:

- a **server**, to house your e-commerce site. This may or may not be the same as your website;
- a **catalogue** and **shopping cart**;
- a **payment processing facility** (which needs to be secure, and which offers choices);
- an **order fulfilment system** (warehousing, inventory management, delivery);
- a **customer service system**.

In practice these procurement decisions must be taken together, and are most simply described as a series of outsourcing choices. At one extreme you can write your own e-commerce site, run it on your own server and accept payments directly into your own bank account. At the other, you can outsource the whole job, using a third-party provider of server space who also provides the e-commerce facility, processes the orders and handles the cash. There are many positions in between. For example, you may have your own website on your own server, but you can link users from your site to the 'shop' which is in fact run by a third-party provider on their server, delivering payments to your account.

The decisions you must take, therefore, are heavily interrelated and are influenced by your current position, your objectives and your budget. Your current state of web-readiness is particularly important. Do you have IT skills, and have you established a website? If you don't have your own site, and want to get started, you will be likely to lean towards the outsourcing options all the way down the line. If you do have a website and have a confident IT facility, then your choices are wider.

For each decision, you will need to get quotes from suppliers – for e-commerce software (catalogues and shopping carts), server space, payment processing services (credit card, electronic cash and electronic cheque processing companies) and order fulfilment services (warehousing, mailing, customer service provision). You will need to specify exactly what you need, and then treat the problem as a series of 'make or buy' decisions. Compare the costs of going out-of-house to the cost of going it alone, and use the in-house option as a benchmark of both price and fit with your ideal specifications. If you do outsource, we recommend you tender to at least five different providers to get the best balance between price and quality of service.

The following sections outline some of the issues you should be aware of when drawing up your specifications to go to the market to find the best route to setting up your system.

The server

You need a server simply to store the data that is in your catalogue. If you do not already have a website, the easiest option may be to look at one of the 'all-in-one' service providers, who will host your website and set up an online sales outlet for you. These 'Commerce Service Providers' (CSPs) will also offer to design the pages, run the site and process the orders. If you already have a site, you face a choice. You can:

• Include the e-commerce site within your existing website, on your existing server.
• Use an HTML link on your website to take customers to an e-commerce site which is run and housed by a third party. This solution is increasingly common, and should not cause any interference for your customers who simply push on a 'go to the shop' button.

To make this decision, you must assess your budget and your IT skills. A small budget and low skills means you're likely to outsource. If you locate your site within your existing website, you will be faced with a wide variety of software products which use different computer languages. Very simple solutions may only use custom-made HTML pages, but more complex offers might include code written in Java. You must be sure that your server – or your provider's server – will cope with the language used to write your e-commerce system. Similarly, some complex products are sensitive to the operating system the server uses (e.g. some require a UNIX operating system). Check for technical compatibility.

If you do use a CSP, then be sure that their site will offer your customers the speed they want. If the CSP is also a local Internet service provider, with resources that are stretched between many users, then the result may be a slow service. It is important both to ask your potential suppliers about their capacity and speeds, and to check their existing sites for yourself to see how they measure up. Just as telephone sales are lost when customers don't get through first time, so too Internet purchases are deterred by slow purchasing systems.

External providers will offer a range of pricing models. Some will charge per transaction, while others will charge a flat monthly rate for the service.

Security

One of the most important issues you will face is security. Security is a critical issue. If most online buying decisions are motivated by 'value for money', then the commonest barrier to buying online identified in the studies is the perception that the Internet is not a secure medium. Many potential customers think that sending their credit card details over the net simply saves criminals the trouble of stealing the card! Providing real security, and making sure your customers know it's there, is an essential aspect of Internet selling. There is some sign that attitudes are changing, driven by the increasing number of word-of-mouth reports of successful experiences of online purchasing, and this can be expected to continue. The fact that so many major banks have gone online also suggests that security concerns surrounding payments will diminish. However public timidity is an important barrier, and there are ways you can help overcome it.

There are two major protocols to secure transactions on the Internet – 'Secure Sockets Layers' SSL and 'Secure Electronic Transactions' protocol (SET). Increasingly, the SSL protocol is regarded by consumers as a minimum standard, and potential buyers recognize the system as a good source of reassurance. There are signs that in some sectors the SET standard, which offers even higher security, might become more common. Make sure your server and system can provide good security, and that you explain to your customers exactly what steps you have taken to ensure the site is safe.

Online security 1 – SSL

The most common protocol is the 'Secure Sockets Layers' protocol (SSL), which is supported by Netscape and Microsoft browsers. When a transaction is conducted using the SSL protocol, a customer transmits credit card details over the Internet to a merchant. The technology creates a secure 'session' between the parties, and scrambles the information that is passed between them. Consumers can check that the system is being used – the merchant's URL should change from 'http' to 'https' when processing secure transactions. Outsiders cannot break in. A significant proportion of your customers will be familiar with this protocol and be reassured by it. You may also find that the bank you wish to use to collect online payments will not allow you to open an account without using SSL as a minimum level of security.

If you are using Secure Sockets, you should realize that the system does not allow the merchant to verify the cardholder's identity. The consumer will know that the merchant has received an electronic certificate from a third party who will have undertaken some simple checks. These checks provide some assurance that the merchant is a legitimate organization. (See www.verisign.com for the market leader in this area.) Consumers, however, still feel insecure, although the evidence suggests that businesses take more of the sting (consumers repudiating bills is a bigger problem than business-driven fraud).

You should understand risks, but focus your communications on explaining to your customer how you would resolve problems. There are many good examples of this. One is the American New Age retail site 'Just Wingin' It', which addresses security concerns very directly. The site offers a 'safe shopping guarantee', claiming that every transaction will be 100 per cent safe. It explains how the company will deal with problems, promising customers will pay nothing if unauthorized charges are made to their cards. The contrast with the tone of the marketing copy is marked. The site seriously explains the law in this area (in the US, the Fair Credit Billing Act), which limits customer credit card liability to $50, and Just Wingin' It promises to cover this liability if the loss was accidental and occurred while using the secure server. It is important that your site answers customers' doubts in a clear, non-threatening, but serious way.

Online security 2 – SET

The SET protocol is being developed by VISA and Mastercard. The 'Secure Electronic Transactions' protocol differs from SSL in that it includes a system to check that the merchant is authorized to accept payments on a card, and that the customer is authorized to use it. This client side authentication is only available in a limited number of SSL applications (mainly home banking) and offers a significant protection against fraud. There are three downsides to SET. First, the consumer needs an SET-Wallet (a plug-in for their browser, like a virtual purse) and a valid certificate to use the technology. Obtaining this requires extra effort on the buyers' behalf, although this can be expected to get easier. Second, the technology is thought to be slower to use, although it appears these fears have been exaggerated. Third, very heavy use of SET requires marginally higher server capacity than SSL. The level of comfort offered by the system, however, is higher than SSL and the challenge for SET is to break SSL dominance, a goal that is closer in Europe than the US.

It is likely that you will adopt the SSL system, but watch for developments in SET and ask yourself whether it would be appropriate for your market, particularly if you operate in the business-to-business market. Whatever system you use, from a marketing perspective, the key point is to sell the virtues of the system you are using. Many firms using SET in the early days failed to capitalize on the upside, by providing information in too technical a way, and by relying on links to other firms' sites (e.g. VISA). The following checklist will help you plan your communications effectively:

- Include a link to the third party that provides your SSL electronic certificate.
- Use an appropriate tone to explain payments. This may differ from other areas of your site (serious, clear, but not technical).
- Explain the benefits of the security system you operate.
- Explain very clearly what would happen if things go wrong (what liabilities you will accept).
- Answer all of the key questions on your own site (don't rely on links to partners' sites, as they will not be designed to deal with your customers, and they will impose 'search costs' on your customers, encouraging them to log off. Your URL link to their site might also become obsolete as they change and update their site).
- Make use of external assessments and recommendations to support your choice of payment system (if a well known brand uses the same system, say so; if the system has been evaluated by a trade magazine, arrange to publish the article). Properly located, this information will not clutter your site, but reassure users.

The catalogue and shopping cart

As well as server space, you also need a shopping cart and catalogue software. This allows you to display your goods, and lets your customers choose to buy, and send you an electronic order including their credit card number. By far the cheapest approach to getting this software is to buy it in. There are now hundreds of firms offering software solutions for businesses seeking to set up online shopping facilities, and you can easily review dozens of rival products to get the best value for money. In deciding which firms to consider, make sure you look at and try out the program they have already had installed.

There a number of key design points to look for:

- The catalogue must be easy to use. Look again at the advice on structuring website content, in Chapter 7. Your catalogue must be very simple to navigate, there should not be too many layers and there must be a home page button on every page. What is the search facility like? Does it allow customers to find what they're looking for? Making the order system as accessible as possible throughout the site is important to ensure that numerous paths lead to it and users always have the option to quickly and easily make a purchase. Most sites achieve this by having a permanent navigation bar on every page that allows users to plot an individual way through a site without having to progress through numerous pages to reach particular areas.
- The catalogue must be quick and glitch free. Remember who your customer is: someone who wants an easy, trouble-free experience, but who doesn't really trust the security of the net. If things go wrong, not only is the experience not 'easy', but it also increases the consumer's doubts about net security. The rule is 'no glitches'.
- The software must allow you to create an information-rich environment in which to sell your goods. Good quality, credible product information will help overcome possible barriers to sale. It is possible to publish testimonials from other clients, technical information, guarantee information, manufacture details, reviews, advice on how to use the product, and evidence of the efficiency and effectiveness of the product. In effect the capacity of users to search Internet text allows you to create a virtual sales assistant, who can supply information to overcome barriers to a sale. It is easier to buy a computer knowing that the latest edition of your favourite PC magazine has given it a five-star write up, than if you don't know that. Online, this information can be included right next to the 'buy now' button – but you will need the right architecture to display it.
- Remember as well the importance of choice. If the catalogue is well designed, it is easy to offer customers maximum choice from your own stock. Does the product you're looking at offer the space for

the information you need to include? A key determinant of the software purchasing decision is the number of items you want to include on your site, and this has a significant impact on the price you will have to invest. If you have a big back-list of products and see the Internet as a good channel to give the whole range proper exposure, you must be prepared to pay to achieve your goal. Many of the providers you initially look at will be ruled out because they do not operate at the correct scale for your business. Once again, clear objectives and parameters make the buying decision much easier.

- Look for a solution which will work for your customer. Does it automatically enable you to e-mail your customer to say the order's been processed and is on its way? Once a customer has decided to make a purchase, is the updated shopping cart kept in view? Is it easy for the customer to 'un-buy' a ticked item? Can they always see what's in the cart, and what it'll cost as they go along? Does it make postage prices clear (if they're not clear, they'll put people off).

Off-the-peg programs are always going to be less expensive than a bespoke solution. But when you have to adapt your site to a ready-made product, you will lose some of the functionality you might need. There is a clear trade-off of costs and benefits. Sometimes the cheapest solution is not the best, and you should consider the option of getting a tailor-made program to suit your business. The Amazon site, for example, capitalizes on its bespoke architecture which allows it to present the reviews and comments that make the service distinctive. A customized system will cost twenty times more than a ready-made one, but may also be the difference between success and failure.

If you do buy a ready-made product, make sure you know what you are getting for your money. What will servicing and updating cost? Will you get any intellectual property rights, allowing you to redevelop and reuse the software? Will you have to pay royalties, and if so on what basis? Look at the hidden, ongoing costs as well as the up-front purchase expense before making a decision.

The payment processing system

When the order is sent from the shopping cart, you need a system in place to process it. You will need to decide what sort of payments you are prepared to accept, and to work out what sort of account to use to take the money.

Payment options

There are a number of payment options. You can choose to accept:

- credit cards;
- electronic cash;
- electronic cheques.

Credit cards have become the dominant payment mechanism for the Internet. In the early days of the net, most sites have operated on the basis that it is impossible to offer e-commerce facilities without offering credit card payments. Your presumption should be that credit cards are a necessary fact of life. But you should also realize that there are markets in which this is not true. Credit cards can also exclude some important buyers who may not be able to access credit cards.

This problem applies to public sector purchasers who often do not have access to business credit cards. In the educational sector, for example, schools do not have credit cards and firms selling online to this market need to develop bespoke payment solutions. If you are targeting this market, it is essential to talk to your customers and create mechanisms which will enable them to use your service (these may involve online credits, or offline billing for transactions that were agreed online). Given the potential for savings through online buying, and the strong political support for Internet technology, it is likely that you will succeed.

A second group hidden behind a credit card payment barrier is the children and youth market. This group, particularly teenagers, includes some of the most active Internet users, and surveys suggest they are willing to use e-commerce. Finding a way to enable them to use the channel, therefore, is potentially important. The most common approach to date has been to hope that children and teenagers will engage their parents' support for purchases, and payment will be delivered from the parent's credit card. This has the disadvantage in that it makes the decision-making unit for the purchase more complex – the product has to please both the user, and his or her parents, potentially a hard task!

Problems like these have driven efforts to create an alternative **Internet currency** – a form of electronic cash or cybercash. Two services in the States, for example, RocketCash and iCanBuy, are designed to allow parents to give their children digital pocket money. It works by creating online accounts for the children, funded by payments from their parents. These credits can then be spent at designated e-commerce sites. The advantage is that the child makes his or her own purchasing decisions, and the range of goods bought should therefore expand. If your goods are targeted at the youth market, you should experiment with these sorts of systems to make payment easier.

But remember, the central question is not, 'Does the technology work?' What matters is, 'Will my customers use it?'

Credit cards are also inefficient for small purchases. The effort of inputting credit card data, and the administrative costs of handling credit card payments, mean that the system works badly for those buying (often repetitively) low value goods. These so-called 'micro-payments' are problematic because credit cards are a very inefficient way to make small payments. There have already been a number of initiatives to overcome this problem, notably e-cash technology which makes it possible to pay very small amounts. This did not, however, take off when it was launched: as well as being technically difficult, some systems were also hard for consumers to understand – a critical success factor on the Internet. If your business relies on repeated small payments, then it will be necessary to explore the current state of technology in this area, as well as consider the potential for advertising, subscription and sponsorships as alternative routes to generate income. Technology is moving quickly in this field. Innovations that are being explored include billing micropayments through telephone accounts. It is clearly easier to establish a micropayment system with clients who are heavy repeat users of a service than it is to capture one-off payments, and this limitation of the Internet needs to be built into your planning.

As more banks and their customers go online, there has been a rapid development in the availability and use of **electronic cheques** (e-cheques). A landmark in the technology came in 1998 when the US government paid GTE $32,000 by e-mail, bringing to popular attention the results of years of technology development by a consortium of mainly American companies. E-cheques are designed particularly for the business-to-business market, and represent an attempt by the banks to reclaim Internet currency from card providers.

E-cheques use a digital certificate system that secures the transfer of payment data between buyers, sellers and banks. The system is designed to be very secure. Each party to the transaction has a piece of software (like an electronic smartcard) which allows them to issue or receive cheques: when a cheque arrives, the technology allows the recipient to test the transmission for integrity before 'opening' it to accept the payment. Both firm's banks, and both firms, need to have opted into the technology, but it is not expensive. Once each side has the software to send and receive cheques, all that's needed is e-mail. The breakthrough the system offers is that it allows e-mail to be used to make and transmit binding payment commitments between trading companies that are then automatically enacted by participating banks.

The system is still developing, but the signs are that it will become more and more pervasive. It is significant that the GTE payment involved the Federal Reserve, traditionally a conservative body. Singapore banks have also started to offer it, and many businesses will be attracted by the potential for security and savings on transaction costs.

The medium term prospect is that businesses may use the technology for online payments. Consumer take-up is likely to be slower. You should analyse your market to decide whether this is an appropriate option to take up. If you have a limited range of business clients, then it may be worth encouraging them to adopt the technology. It should save them money, and should they adopt they would have an extra reason to buy from your firm.

Sales abroad

You should decide whether your site is targeted at home country customers, or whether you are also looking to win sales abroad. Tax and exchange rates vary between countries, making it complex to use one site to target different currency zones. One common solution to this problem is to set up different national websites with their own e-commerce facility. While this is not difficult to do, you must consider the costs of running several parallel sites and compare this carefully to the projected benefits. It may be easier, for example, to redirect overseas customers to traditional selling outlets (telephone, mail order, retail, agent). There is more information on the use of parallel traditional selling outlets at the end of this chapter. It would be easy, for example, to include a printable ordering form on your site, or to offer overseas customers an up-to-date price for a product (including postage) which could be sent via e-mail. This use of the Internet technology would make overseas sales easier without obliging you to set up a dedicated website.

Alternatively you could direct overseas buyers (via an HTML link) to a third-party e-commerce outlet that sells your goods in that market. The discount you have to offer third-party sales outlets may well be less than the costs you would incur in handling small volumes of international trade directly yourself.

Account options

By this stage your customer has visited your website, entered your e-commerce area, looked through the catalogue and entered a purchase in your shopping cart. They have probably decided to use a credit card, and have pushed 'send' to transmit their details to you over the net. If you currently take credit card payments, you could simply take the information from the e-mail and process it in a traditional way. If you do not process credit cards in this way, you will need a merchant account.

Obtaining a merchant account for Internet transactions raises special problems associated with the risks taken by the bank supplying the account. Put simply, the risks are higher, and so the bank will either charge more for the service, or be more careful whom they allow to open an account. Many banks will do both. This is because credit card payments involve the possibility that the customer will not pay the bill. The risk is shared: the card issuer carries risk; the bank supplying the credit carries risk; the bank receiving the credit carries risk; the company selling the goods themselves carries risk. If a credit card holder defaults or denies that they made the transaction in question, then the detail of how the transaction was carried out will determine who will have to carry the ensuing liability. Transactions over the Internet take place without the customer being 'present' – a situation which increases the rights of the customer, and spreads the potential liability should something go wrong more fully onto the other players in the chain. As a result, business start-ups and small businesses can find it hard to get a merchant account for online trading. Firms with offline merchant accounts do not find they automatically get access to an online facility, but they generally have to negotiate a new Internet agreement. The fees charged by the host bank are for the 'customer not present' situation, and so are likely to be relatively high. Sometimes banks will want to see evidence of a year's trading before offering an account, and the financial management systems of the trading company will be carefully scrutinized. Particular attention, unsurprisingly, is paid to the security systems used by the trading company to limit the potential for fraud and default. These systems can sometimes include

- SSL security or better (see above);
- never sending products to a third-party address;
- using secure delivery, with signed receipt;
- retaining all relevant data (card numbers, nature of item sold, expiry date, delivery addresses).

Banks sometimes offer choices concerning the management of payments. Some systems accept a manual re-keying of Internet card details into a conventional credit card terminal, of the sort used by many shops and businesses. The full authorization for payment is given at this re-keying stage. Other systems offer authorization of credits while the customer is at the 'checkout', followed by automatic transfer of credit to the merchant account. In both systems, payment is cleared within three or four working days after the transaction date, as would happen for normal offline credit card purchases.

Be careful to examine the charges you have to pay. Charges vary widely, both in absolute amounts and in the way they are calculated so (as with everything) shop around, and be prepared to switch your account after a few months if a rival comes up with a better deal. As Internet commerce continues to grow, it is highly likely that the banks will have to come up with more and more competitive offers and you should take advantage of these.

The difficulty some firms face in obtaining a merchant account of their own has prompted the growth of third-party payment collection companies. These firms manage the receipt and clearance of Internet revenues, and transfer cleared funds (minus a commission) to the Internet traders who generated them.

These services will cost more than a direct merchant account, but offer a simple route to going online for firms (particularly small firms and start-ups) which cannot get an account of their own. Sometimes middlemen retain a proportion of funds for a period of six months to cover the risk they are carrying in supporting your business. Typical retention figures are around 10 per cent. Charging systems vary, with some firms demanding a monthly minimum fee, and others operating entirely on a percentage basis. Fees can reach 15 per cent, so it is important to get the best deal and build this cost into your e-commerce model.

Legal issues: forming a contract

The issue of when a contract is formed over the Internet has raised much debate but is an essential element in determining liability for potential losses or fraud. Under English law there are four essential elements to a contract: offer, acceptance of the offer, intention to create legal relations and consideration (the purchase price). An advertisement on the Internet is generally treated as an 'invitation to treat' (if worded correctly) rather than an offer, so that the advertiser may be entitled to turn down an application from a potential customer. The application by the potential customer would be treated as the offer which the website owner does not have to accept.

If selling products from a website, it is important that the terms and conditions underpinning the transaction are referred to and available for the customer to read. These may well be distinct from the terms and conditions governing access to the site. Ideally, as with disclaimers and health warnings, the potential customer should be obliged to scroll through the terms and conditions and immediately prior to the finalizing of a transaction confirm that he or she has read them and accepted them. They should, at the very least, be referred to prominently on the first web-page with a hypertext link to the actual terms and conditions. When designing a web-page it is important to ensure that the customer cannot circumvent the 'accept' dialogue box by, for example, bookmarking the final page and going straight to it at a later date and avoiding the 'accept'. This is particularly important if the terms and conditions change in the interim.

The law is currently not settled as to when acceptance of the offer occurs and thus the contract is formed – is it when the offeror sends an e-mail confirming the customers' order or when the customer receives that communication? As the law is unclear, it is advisable it should be made clear in the relevant terms and conditions or by a statement that will be seen by the customer before sending an e-mail, that the contract will not be formed until the website owner has received the e-mail accepting its offer.

Certain types of contract may only be formed once they have been signed. At present, it is likely that the English courts will not recognize a digital signature in those instances where a signature is required by statute or even by rules of self-regulatory organizations (for example the Investment Management Regulating Organisation (IMRO) require that customer agreements must be signed).

Order fulfilment and customer service system

Order fulfilment is an important dimension of your e-commerce system. You've got the money, and it's important that your customer gets their goods quickly, and in good order. Managing the link between an order on the net and the departure of goods from your warehouse presents real opportunities, particularly for larger firms. Given adequate size, it is possible to use sophisticated computerized inventory management software that tracks demand, alerts managers to low stock levels, and ensures customers on the website are kept informed about stock availability. This approach can keep inventory at a minimum efficient level by triggering re-ordering decisions on the basis of demand.

Given that many firms see the Internet as a good channel for selling a wide range of goods (because of the text search facility), inventory management is particularly important. There's no point in winning a sale, only to have to tell the customer the item they want is no longer available. Similarly, there is no point in carrying excess stock simply because you have not sorted out the best balance between demand and inventory.

Inventory management is particularly hard when selling on the net because your potential market is so large. If you have a shop in Leeds, it is unlikely that the whole of the UK will visit it to buy the same thing. Online, the situation is very different, and you may get a surge (or slump) in demand. Planning stock levels and capacity (the numbers of people and machines you have in warehousing, packing and distribution) can be very hard. The difficulties are made worse by the rapid pace of the evolution of the Internet, which means both more competition and more shoppers with unpredictable spending patterns.

You will simply have to learn as you gain experience of your niche. But while demand may be variable and hard to predict, the fact you'll get it wrong from time to time is much more certain. This is something you can, and should plan for. When things go wrong, when you're out of stock or your despatch system breaks down, *let your customer know*. You have their e-mail address. E-mail them to let them know what's happened, what you're doing about it, and when the problem will be fixed. If goods are going to be late, tell the customer when they will arrive. It is amazing how few Internet traders yet use the power of e-mail properly to recover from the problems that inevitably arise. If something goes wrong and you tell your customer how much you care and how you're fixing it, your reputation will survive intact. It may even be enhanced. Do nothing and you've thrown away a great deal of goodwill.

Your transport strategy will also need to be reconsidered. If you're selling through retail shops, you need to be expert in bulk deliveries to relatively few locations. If you're selling direct to the customer online, you need to be able to deliver small quantities of goods to many, very dispersed locations. The infrastructure needed is completely different, and the economics generally require much greater demand. Many firms find that they have to outsource delivery, even if they had been expert in running their own logistics to support a network of shops.

As the Internet becomes better established and (even) more competitive, being expert in service and logistics will become more and more critical to determining which firms will operate profitably, and which hopeful start-ups will go to the wall.

Integrating your online and offline sales channels

It's likely that if you have an offline business as well as an online one, you'll use the offline channels to promote your website and e-commerce facility. You must also make sure you use the net to promote the offline outlets as well. Make sure that potential customers get a proper choice. They may have visited your site to see the range of your goods, but would still like to speak to someone about them, or see them in a shop or showroom. Make sure that your site tells them how to do this. A potential buyer who lives twenty miles from your nearest outlet may find the net more convenient, but you'd also like the customer who's close to you to call in and see your goods face-to-face. To achieve this you must include addresses, phone numbers, maps, and times of opening for your high street outlets. There are no prizes for selling in one medium or another. The best results from the Internet can come from integrating the Internet into your wider marketing strategy. This sounds obvious, but it is amazing how many websites fail to give contact numbers and addresses where customers who need to see goods or speak to someone can make contact.

Conclusion

Setting up your e-commerce site involves dealing with a wide range of potential suppliers of software, server space, banking facilities, warehousing and logistics. Having read this chapter, you should not be daunted by dealing with these firms. The absolute key is to start off with a good understanding of what you need to offer your customers to succeed in your market, and a budget. Until you're clear about these points, you should not talk to the myriad firms who are keen for your business. Then, by following the advice in this chapter, you can be confident of getting good value from the firms competing to supply e-commerce outlets. Then, by taming the technologists and building a facility that really suits your market, you can transform your business performance.

Checklist

You should now know:

What motivates the online shopper.	☐ Yes	☐ No
How to adapt sales promotions techniques to the Internet.	☐ Yes	☐ No
The key elements of an e-commerce site.	☐ Yes	☐ No
How to create a secure sales environment.	☐ Yes	☐ No
The choices for processing credit card transactions.	☐ Yes	☐ No
The legal issues concerning online contracting.	☐ Yes	☐ No
The importance of integrating your online and offline outlets.	☐ Yes	☐ No

What next?

Having launched a site and begun to sell online, you now need to integrate the net into your everyday marketing activities. It is only by using the net yourself that you can get a real feel for the way your customers use it. It also has some huge benefits to offer you as a professional wishing to develop yourself, your team and your organization. Read on for some ideas of how it can help.

Chapter 10

Where is all this taking us?

Much of the Internet culture will seem as quaint to future users of the Information Highway as stories of wagon trains and pioneers on the Oregon Trail do to us today.

Bill Gates, *The Road Ahead*, 1995

It's a sign of how right Bill Gates was back in 1995 when he wrote of the unpredictable future of the Internet that even the language he used then now seems so out of date. No-one today talks of the 'information highway', and the special 'Internet culture' of 1995 has been supplanted by something new, in which selling has a powerful role, big businesses figure large alongside small organizations, and which caters for new mass audiences. But if we stick to Mr Gates' wagon train analogy, the Internet wagon train has still a long way to go before it reaches California. There is a great deal of unpredictable change still to come, and it's worth spending some time thinking through the likely shape of the land that lies ahead.

First, we have identified a shift from an Internet dominated by early technology enthusiasts and highly educated specialists to a mass market. Most Internet users are not IT people, and many access the network from home. This shift is not going to be reversed, and the trends that it has ushered in are only likely to get stronger. In particular, technology is being replaced by marketing and customer service. Internet services are increasingly being built around the needs and desires of the market. In this sense, the maturing Internet is becoming more and more focused on customers – more like any other communications medium, in fact. Throughout this book we have emphasized the importance of using traditional marketing techniques on the net (segmenting your market, developing a clear marketing mix, promoting sales, etc.). This reflects the way the net is going. Customer-focused businesses are going to be the winners on the net just as they are in other media, and the importance of marketing-led approaches is only going to rise.

Second, from a commercial point of view we can see that the Internet is going to become more and more competitive. There has been a dramatic rise in the numbers of Internet users, but the rate of business investment on the net has if anything been faster as firms raced to carve out a strong online identity before their rivals. The pace at which new users are logging on means that – by definition – the point will soon come when there are no more new users to take up the service. As this point approaches, firms will not be able to build business plans around capturing new users, but they will have to fight to take customers from each other. Life will not only become more competitive, but also more unpredictable, especially so in the information/entertainment sector, where the pressures of Internet competition are complicated by the digital revolution. The fact that television, books, music, articles, radio and pictures can be encoded and transmitted digitally means that the boundaries between some firms are being broken down. Suddenly BT or WH Smith might become online publishers, challenging firms that were traditionally in different sectors altogether. There's likely to be plenty of disruptive movement between sectors as one firm uses its IT skills to enter a new business area.

Indeed, there's already evidence of the increasingly competitive nature of the net. Throughout 1999, the volume of advertising space created on Internet websites grew at a faster rate than the number of new Internet users, causing a fall in online advertising prices.

Another trend is also evident. Big global players are putting more and more money into the net, hoping to dominate the new mass market medium. There have been strings of dramatic acquisitions, creating new online giants which seek to dominate in their sectors. This is only likely to continue as the costs of getting noticed and keeping sites up to date start to tell on middle-sized companies who haven't thought through their online offer as well as they might.

We're beginning to get more of an idea about customers on the net. While the big numbers in online shopping are mainly still on the 'projections' graphs, a picture is starting to appear of the way people will operate on the net as they become more familiar with it. They are starting to develop site loyalties, and be more discerning about the sites they'll visit. The net is being used more for a purpose, and less to satisfy simple curiosity. An interesting hint about the growth of site loyalties came in a study which showed that – while the numbers of sites were mushrooming – the number of sites individual net users visited was actually falling! It seems that net users try a few locations, and then discover which places suit them best, and stick with them.

Net technology will also continue to develop. Interactivity is getting easier all the time, and the advent of faster and faster lines to connect up Internet users means that it will get easier to use animated sequences, video clips, and complex software. The advent of ISDN or ADSL lines, which offer much broader bandwidths than conventional telephone links, will make this sort of software much more common. If customers demand more complex software, small firms with low budgets will be squeezed.

There remains one identifiable major uncertainty on the technical horizon – the advent of digital television, which promises some level of Internet access to homes through the TV. Cable users will have highly interactive Internet connections, while digital terrestrial or satellite users may have slightly more limited access. Whatever the level of access, television will revolutionize net access, with the real possibility of creating universal Internet access within ten years. Bill Gates' pioneers on the Oregon Trail are about to be overtaken by a wholesale migration. But how these new migrants will behave is open to question. Internet access feels very different sitting back in the sofa with a remote control in the hand, to the way it feels sitting up at a PC. And then there is mobile phone technology to consider (e.g. WAP). Time horizons have been short on the net, prediction has been hard. But even as the technology matures, it remains impossible to see accurately a long way down the 'Road Ahead'. New technologies promise new disruptions, and businesses planning investments will have to remain flexible and open to change as it occurs.

The result of all this? We can suggest a number of things.

• Getting noticed will become harder as the net becomes more crowded. Customers will face more real choice of service provider, and marketing skills will become more and more important.

- There will be more focus on back office efficiency as the forces of competition start to punish firms who are not able to control costs.
- Customers will become more price sensitive as time goes by. There are some good reasons for this. First, as they get to know their way round the net, they will find it easier to compare prices. In fact software is now available which enables customers to find the best offer for the goods they hope to buy. Second, as the net matures it is likely that the more price-sensitive customers are going to go online. These are the people who have waited (and waited) to buy a PC, and are now able to get a very fast desktop at bargain prices. Once they start shopping, they are going to make sure they get the best deals. It's also inevitably the case that as more firms put their wares on the net, there are more and more offers to choose from. When there are six (or sixteen) online bookstores all selling the same book, it's likely that those setting high prices will be punished. All of the theories suggested that the Internet would drive down prices. It looks as if this is happening.
- Some firms that thrived in the traditional media will fail to adjust to the Internet channel, and will be destroyed. They will be remembered in the same terms as the towns which refused to admit the railway, and soon after died. The successful will see the Internet as an opportunity, and many powerful offline brands will transfer their skills to create a successful online presence. For these firms, the key will be leverage. By using their name and reputation across different media they will become more successful than their rivals which ignore the Internet, or which *only* compete and communicate online.
- The Internet is not the end of the road. Digital television and mobile phone data communication is coming. But the final shape of this particular communication revolution will be determined not by the technologists, but by the choices and needs of consumers, without whom all of the networks in the world are empty and silent.

It's an exciting picture, and not a little daunting. But what we have given you in this book is a key lesson in the importance of real marketing skills in this seemingly technical world. This is the only approach that can offer you a successful future – and it is all the more powerful because so many firms have not yet recognized how important it is.

The net will continue to change. But you are in the privileged position of being in on the process. The medium is still open, and full of opportunity. You are only constrained by your imagination.

And your imagination will be fuelled by technical and creative developments that take place almost every day. You have the advantage that you are not looking at this innovation from a technical perspective and therefore your innovations are marketing focused and by implication more likely to succeed.

We would like to reinforce this in our parting message to you. The Internet and other online services contain a great deal of corporate dribble. A great deal of it is media hype propagated by people with vested interests. It is also heavily dominated by IT people who are not adept at marketing and merchandising. Adopting the methodology suggested in the book and using a good creative team or agency can mean the difference between an overnight wonder and a lasting success. It is important not to be carried along by the hype. You may even decide that the Internet does not fit with your marketing strategy. If so, remember it's OK to pull back and review its relevance over time!

Whatever you decide to do, we hope that you have appreciated the core message of the book, which is that although the technology is new, your approach to it does not have to be. Using traditional marketing concepts will ensure that your message is communicated to your target audience in a meaningful and powerful way. Implementing your Internet marketing plans in this structured way will put you years ahead of your competition, who may have rushed in on the rather wobbly bandwagon.

Conclusion

Mary Cronin (1995) completed her seminal book on Internet commerce with the statement: 'The electronic highway is not merely open for business; it is relocating, restructuring and literally redefining business in America'. *Cybermarketing* has been intended for a European audience, where the same process of relocation and restructuring is going on today. We have attempted to show how the Internet affects the process of marketing as a discipline and how it can be integrated into an organization's overall marketing effort. Throughout this book we have emphasized the central importance, not of technology, but of customers. Success and failure in business depends on customer choices, and marketers are uniquely well qualified to understand what those choices are and how to use the

Internet to ensure that customers choose their products. This involves a holistic approach and, almost without exception, those companies who have been successful in their use of the Internet have been those who have integrated it fully into their marketing and business strategy rather than just simply using it as another advertising medium.

The analogy is similar to the invention of the printing press where marketers ask 'to what business benefit can this technology be used?' The only answer is 'what do you do, what do you want to do and what are you trying to achieve?' Imaginative and integrated marketing is the only answer. We hope that in this book we have outlined the concepts and ideas which can act as a framework for this wider creative process.

We welcome your feedback about any issue discussed in this chapter and indeed this book. We can be contacted via the web-site that accompanies this book. We look forward to hearing from you.

www.marketingnet.com/cybermarketing

References

Bill Gates with Nathan Myhrvold and Peter Rinearson (1995) *The Road Ahead*, Viking.

Mary Cronin (1995) *Doing More Business on the Internet*, Van Nostrand Reinhold, New York.

What is the Internet – give me the background

1956	Sputnik launched by the USSR. The US forms the Advanced Research Projects Agency (ARPA) to gain competitive advantage in science and technology for the military.
1965	Ted Nelson coins the word hypertext.
1967	Andy Van Dam and others build Hypertext Editing System – the core of HTML which is the layout language used on the Internet.
1968	Doug Engelbart demonstrates NLS, a hypertext system.
1969	ARPANET group set up by the DoD for research 'networking'. First ever Internode set up at UCLA. First manned moon landing.
1972	First International Conference on computer communications. ARPANET was demonstrated on 40 machines. E-mail was invented and demonstrated to work where users collected their messages remote from the network.
1973	First international link up. England and Norway connect up and HM the Queen sends her first e-mail message.
1977	THEORYNET created at the University of Wisconsin providing electronic mail to over 100 researchers in computer science.
1978	The Aspen Movie map, the first hypermedia videodisc, shown at MIT.
1979	USENET established, which enables and lists newsgroups. Prestel and MicroNet established in UK. The personal computer is born.

1981   Minitel (Teletel) is established in France by French Telecom. This is then used to organize strikes and blockades in the late 1980s.

           Ted Nelson conceptualizes 'Xandu' a hypertext database encompassing all written information.

1982   First definition of an 'internet' as a connected set of networks. This comes from INWG establishing TCP (Transmission Control Protocol) and IP (Internet Protocol) the core communication of the Internet.

1983   ARPANET split into ARPANET and MILNET. Personal computers become popular as desktop workstations.

1984   Over 1000 host computers. JANET (Joint Application Network) established in UK. Number of computers breaks 1000.

1986   ARPANET bureaucracy prevents it from being used to interconnect centres. NSFNET established by NASA and DoE. This enables connections to grow, especially between universities. MS-DOS 3.0 becomes networkable.

1987   Over 10,000 host computers. Office-based IT revolution comes about. Windows Version 1. released by Microsoft. Apple Computers introduces Hypercard, the first widely available personal hypermedia authoring system.

1989   Over 100,000 host computers. Electronic mail provider CompuServe links up with the Internet through Ohio State University.

1990   ARPANET ceases to exist. Electronic mail provider MCI links up with the Internet.

1991   Commerical Internet Exchange (CIX) Association Inc. formed. WAIS released from Thinking Machines Corporation. Gopher released by University of Minnesota.

1992   Over 1,000,000 host computers – growing exponentially. Internet Society is chartered. World wide web released by CERN. First audio multicast and video multicast. Local area networks are common. Modems fall dramatically in price.

1993   US White House, UK Government, United Nations and the World Bank go online. Internet Talk Radio begins broadcasting. Businesses and media start to take notice of the Internet. Mosaic takes the Internet by storm; WWW proliferates at a 341,634 per cent annual growth.

1994   Communities begin to be connected though local suppliers. Interflora takes flower orders. Shopping malls and mass marketing grow. Mass e-mailing takes place and are correspondingly censored.

1995   Many millions of host computers are now established. Netscape takes the Internet market by storm and gains 80–90 per cent market share of the 'browser' market (i.e. software interface to the WWW). 10,000 businesses go online. Electronic payments systems become practical and widespread, supported by Barclaycard. TV programmes encourage readers to write in using e-mail. Increased interest in the Internet by the general population. More than 30 providers in the UK. Local Points of Presence (PoP) covers 90 per cent of the UK population. Microsoft release Windows '95 and MSN. MSN will enable every Windows '95 user to access the Internet for a monthly subscription. Sun Microsystems release Internet programming language called Java, which radically altered the way applications and information can be retrieved, displayed and used over the Internet. The number of Internet hosts is over 4,000,000.

1996   The number of Internet hosts is over 9,000,0000. More than $1 billion spent at Internet shopping malls. The www browser war, primarily between Netscape and Microsoft, rushed in a new age in software development. Search engine technology takes off.

1997   The number of Internet hosts now over 16,000,000.

1998   La Fete de L'Internet – a countrywide Internet fest held in France. Digital TV launched, the emergence of portals, e-commerce and online auctions.

1999   E-trade, online banking, MP3 music technology and WAP (Wireless Applications Protocol) emerge.

Appendix 2

Get me onto the Internet

'I want to go on-line'

Before you can surf the net, you need to get connected. To do this, you need to have your own identity as an individual on the Internet – your own e-mail address where people can write to you. This is not difficult but it can seem so because of the new language and communication issues. All you need is a reasonable (less than two years old) PC or Mac and a modem and a telephone socket.

A modem translates the output from the computer into a signal for the phone. The faster your modem is at translating and sending the data, the faster your Internet access is going to be. If you are paying for your telephone calls, this can save you money because you can obtain information quicker. It is measured in bits per second, this is called the baud rate. The range is 9600 baud (mobile phones) to 56,000 (modem). The average modem is 28,800 but achieves higher speeds through clever compression techniques. However, most Internet content is already very compressed so the result from a 'high-speed' modem can be disappointing. If greater speed is required then consider using ISDN (Integrated Services Digital Network) which is capable of operating at speeds of 64,000 or 128,000.

You need to be technically quite knowledgeable to add a modem to your computer. So either buy a machine which is pre-configured or make sure your supplier is willing to set it up for you. Alternatively contact your IT department if you have one in your organization.

Next you need the software to get connected. You will get this when you subscribe to an Internet provider. Some of the software that is commonly used with the Internet is free to download once you are connected. On the book's companion website under this chapter, you will find links to various software which will be useful additions or substitutions to the software provided by your Internet provider.

Tell me about e-mail accounts

What do you call yourself online?

Your access provider will issue you with an e-mail account. Depending on the supplier, you may have the option to choose your name online. All e-mail addresses are of a similar structure:

yourname@domain

yourname
Your access provider may give you free choice for the 'yourname' part of the e-mail address. It's popular to use your surname and initials joined together to make one word, e.g. bickertonmj. Your e-mail system will restrict the characters you can use in an e-mail address. In particular, the space character is unacceptable, so it is common practice to use a full stop, '_' or '-' to represent a space.

domain
This is made of two sections: the first is defined by your access provider, the second is fixed by the Internet standards. The first part could be the name of your access provider. Some providers actually allow you to use your own company name. This is usually an additional expense. The second part is one of two types: the original Internet classification '.com'; or alternatively it will be of the form '.co.uk'.

The format of e-mail accounts differs per provider and here are some examples:

Examples of e-mail formats by provider

CIX users	bloggs@cix.compulink.co.uk
Pipex	bloggs@dial.pipex.com
Demon	bloggs@demon.co.uk
or	bloggs@mycompany.demon.co.uk

Companies who have their own Internet connection (see Chapter 7) may have e-mails of the following form:

bloggs@company.co.uk

or   bloggs@company.com

You might also have customer service lines, or help desks as the following:

moreinfo@company.co.uk

helpdesk@company.com

One consideration is the company image of your provider, especially if it is going to appear on your business card. Because you are aligning your company and yourself with a supplier, it is best to ensure they too have an image which is of high quality. Another reason why we recommend choosing an established and high quality supplier as your provider.

When do I get my e-mails?

The way that e-mail works is that messages sent to you will be stored by your access provider, waiting for your collection. When you connect to the Internet and start your e-mail software it will collect your messages, moving them from the access provider's machine onto yours. If you get a lot, you might want to disconnect and read and reply whilst not taking up time on the phone. Then re-connect later to dispatch the messages in one go. It is very difficult for us to give you a step-by-step guide because all mail software works in a slightly different way.

How do people know my e-mail address?

They don't unless you tell them. There are directories of e-mail names but these are usually so user-hostile, time consuming and incomplete, that it is best to assume that there aren't any.

Don't worry about the fact that you have to remember people's e-mail addresses because as soon as you have written to someone once or they have written to you, you can store that message and reuse it at a future time.

How do I manage my e-mail system?

The key to managing your e-mail is to create a structure of folders as soon as possible. Most e-mail systems support this in various ways. We suggest:

> Prospects or Enquiries
> Int_Boss
> Int_Companymemos
> Ext_Customer1
> Ext_Customer2
> Ext_Supplier1
> Ext_Supplier1
> Know_Articles
> Know_Info
> Projects_Campaigns

Where **Int** implies internal to your organization; **Ext** implies from an external source; **Know** implies knowledge and information (typically from news groups etc.).

Used well, e-mail can be an incredibly efficient way of communicating and increasing your productivity by degrees of magnitude. Your correspondent does not need to be there when you wish to communicate. They are more receptive when they read your message because they have chosen a time to collect their communication. You can be shorter and less formal than in conventional communications and people respond faster because it is easier to do.

Warning: e-mails are not secure. People can read your e-mail as it is being passed to the intended recipient – use conventional communication if this is an issue. Encrypted e-mail is possible which will reduce this problem; look for Pretty Good Privacy (PGP) that can be added to your e-mail system.

How often should I check for new e-mail?

People expect you to read your e-mail once a day and reply immediately. This is etiquette and if you do not wish to follow this – we would suggest you tell people how frequently you pick up your messages at the first point of contact (e.g. when you give them your business card) so that you do not disappoint or insult them.

What if I am inundated with e-mail?

Good e-mail packages will allow you to set up rules which act as filters. You can decide that you want to delete every e-mail from a given source automatically. You can decide automatically to store all e-mail from a given source in a certain folder for reading at another point in time. You can also use 'auto-responders'. Here a customer may send a message with a prescribed (by you either on your web-page or promotion materials) subject heading or contents. When this message reaches your access provider, it can be automatically replied to with a reply which you have written. Talk to your access provider about setting this up. Auto-responders can be built into your website (see Chapter 7).

Finding someone's e-mail address

If you want to find out what someone's e-mail address is, the quickest way will be to just pick up the phone, call and ask them! Although there are a variety of 'white pages' services available on the Internet, they are far from complete – but most people are simply not listed. Major e-mail providers are working on a universal directory system, but that could be some time away.

Some 'white pages' services might give you some leads but not much more. If you want to have a go at finding someone on the Internet, then use one of the following:

www.people.yahoo.com
> An online directory service with millions of listings that are free to search and available to anyone with a web browser.

There is a basic search or a more advanced search if you know the area in which the person you are searching for lives.

Also try www.bigfoot.com

Searching Listserver mailing lists
You can ask a Listserver to send you a membership list. To do this, send mail to listserv@host. In the body of your message, include the command 'review list-name', where 'list-name' is the name of the mailing list you wish to search.

E-mail the postmaster
Most sites have an individual responsible for network and mail operations at the site, usually with the user ID of 'postmaster'. Many postmasters will refuse to answer questions about user identification, for reasons of privacy, though they may be willing to forward your address so your intended recipient can write to you.

Appendix 4

Tell me things I need to know – *netiquette*

You can insult people quicker, easier and more effectively than ever before.

The Internet has a culture of its own and when in Rome, do what the Romans do is definitely important. Because you are talking across country, organization and cultural boundaries, there are rules which prevent you from unconsciously insulting people.

When you are writing e-mails, the style is informal. So you are lulled into the sense that you are having a conversation but it is not face to face. A comment face to face comes with a smile, a wink or anger but the same words in an e-mail leave no clue. It is very easy to cause offence.

Emotions					
:-)	Smile	:-D	Big Smile	>:)	Evil grin
;-)	Wink	:-))	Very happy	>:-)	Evil smile
:-X	I'm not telling	}:-)	Devilish	:^)	Tongue in cheek
0:-)	Saint	:-)8	Wearing a bow tie	8:-)	Happy with glasses
%-)	Drunk	:-0	Shocked	:-l	Indecision
:'(	Crying	:-(	Sad	:-{	Sad
>:-(	Very sad	:-###..	Being sick	[:-)	Wearing headphones

You are more informal using e-mail than in a fax or letter. In fact if you do not make the style of your e-mails like this, you can easily appear pompous. At the other extreme, if you use expressions like 'lots of love', this can also be misinterpreted and you can appear too familiar. Never use the word 'love' unless you are talking to your partner.

Never use capital letters in e-mails, (e.g. PLEASE REPLY TO MY MESSAGE) this is very rude on the Internet as it implies shouting. If you want to emphasize something, use * around the word you wish to stress, e.g. *Please* reply to my message. This takes the place of using bold or italic.

When you construct your e-mail message try not to exceed more than 60 characters across because it makes it hard for your correspondent to read it.

When replying to someone, another netiquette rule is never change or delete words within a line of their original message. You can delete lines but not delete or add words into their lines. This means that when you are asking someone a question, it is best to put each question on a separate line so that the responder can just insert an answer.

How do I search for things?

The Internet

The Internet is like a library of books, articles, flyers and waste paper, dropped from 1/2 mile up and left in a huge pile. Therefore, the secret to mastering the Internet is to make use of 'search engines' and other guides. We have given you the easiest way of searching by providing a web-page with all the search engine entry forms on one page. Here you can enter your key search word in a selection of search facilities and we deal with all the different commands that you would otherwise have to learn. This is the most valuable thing the accompanying website offers you and we recommend that bookmarking this site is the first thing you do when you visit this book on-line. Go to:

http:/www.marketingnet.com/cybermarketing/search.htm

Even if you get nothing else from the accompanying website – this will provide you with an easy starting point to explore the world wide web for yourself.

The main ways of searching for things on the Internet are:

Your own bookmarks

Whenever you go to a site that is interesting and you are likely to return to again, all you have to do is 'bookmark' it. This is supported by most Internet software and you usually just make a menu selection when you are on the page that you wish to bookmark. We would recommend that you immediately bookmark:

www.marketingnet.com so you can return to us at any point.

As you become more experienced on the Internet, the fuller this bookmark list becomes, and it then becomes your starting point for searching. We recommend that you follow a structured approach to bookmarking with a hierarchy at the top level similar to the following:

Search tools
Your company website (if you have one)
Competitors
Professional interest
Personal interest
Fun and entertainment
News and general information
Needs sorting out

Magazines

The most popular way to find out what is new on the Internet is to read Internet magazines. They are becoming more and more targeted towards a certain age and interest area so you need to decide the one most suited for your needs. They typically review new and popular websites by subject area and are good for giving you an overview of what is available online.

After you have whetted your appetite with these magazines, you may now want to conduct some searches of your own on a specific subject. Because there is not one centralized search facility on the Internet, we have provided you with a list of search facilities under this chapter on our accompanying website. Below, we explain what the differences are between these and recommend some good starting points.

Robots

There are computers connected to the Internet which spend all of their time following links from web-page to web-page. As they go, they collect information about each page. They are continuously searching and some of the more established machines have absolutely enormous databases containing extracts from a high percentage of all web-pages. They allow you to enter keywords and return lists of possible sites of interest. It is important to remember that the searching is automatic and so you have to accept lots of inappropriate recommendations. For example if you want to understand the concept of the 'world wide web' and you type this in as your search criteria, you will receive a huge list of almost every site as often web-pages say 'on our world wide web page, we can . . . . . .'.

Lycos is one of the most popular robots on the Internet and with a well designed interface is a good starting point. The search results displays the first set of words which appear on that particular page.

Categorized lists

These computers are connected to the Internet but are not actively searching around the Internet but are databases which people submit information. People add entries describing their website which is then updated to appear in a classified list. It is up to the person publishing their pages to define where their entry appears. The extracts held in the database are also specifically defined for entry into this database and as such make for much better reading when you have completed a search.

Again, you can enter keywords and receive lists but the descriptions are usually more intelligible. However, the real strength of this approach is that you can start with a broad category, e.g. travel, and then explore down a decision tree to narrow your search. This is a very good way of assessing how much other related information exists for a particular topic and therefore how popular this topic is.

Yahoo is one of the most popular categorized lists. It is free to make an entry and it's free to search. They sell advertising space to make their money. When you get the results of your search, you will get a panel enticing you to click on it and move to a company's website. Because this service is so popular, they provide the opportunity for advertisers to gain access to a large number of users.

Infoseek is free to add an entry into the database and also free for users to search on a limited basis. For full search functionally they make a small charge. You set up an account giving your credit card number over the phone and then they deduct payments as you use this service. One nice feature is the ability to store your search criteria and return to them at a later point. This is an excellent way of tracking competitors outlined in Chapter 2.

Haystack is free to search but you have to pay to have your website as an entry. There are various levels of charges depending on how much information you want displayed on the search results for your customers to look at.

News group searches

Although news groups are classified into subject areas, it is sometimes difficult to guess where a particular issue will be discussed. Therefore, an excellent way of finding the right way to talk is to use one of the news group search engines.

X is a good example. You enter a key search word and it will report back a list of messages that have been sent recently with this key word in – listed by news groups.

The best of. . .

Particularly loved by the 'global beachcombers' (see Chapter 7), these give you a chef's tour of interesting or new sites to review. The Top 5 per cent is an example of one where sites are nominated by anyone who cares to express an opinion and the top five each year are given a Top 5 per cent Award – this is the equivalent to the Oscar and is a very sought-after award. For the ultimate beachcombing experience there are several sites which will randomly choose a site for you. It is quite incredible what you can see using this approach. We recommend that you do this just to soak up the atmosphere of the Internet.

Links off other sites

It is a common feature of a website to offer links to other relevant websites. What usually happens is that web publishers agree to cross-link their pages in this way.

Advertisements

It is becoming more and more popular to include a website in all your promotional literature. Look out for this in papers, magazines and TV.

Asking people on forums

It is quite acceptable to find the right news group and post a question asking for recommendations. 'Do you know of any websites that do ...?' Many news groups would appreciate if you posted back a summary of your findings for use by other people. This is an extremely good way of coming in on a news group and also of publicizing your website if it is of relevance to your particular news group.

Guessing URLs

This is very desperate, it is a last ditch attempt but quite common. This is where you type in a likely company URL at the bar at the top of the screen. It is very hit-and-miss but try several combinations as follows:

http://www.companyname.co.uk
http://www.companyname.com
http://companyname.co.uk
http://companyname.com

Also try product names in the same way.

This Appendix has given you the basics for searching. Please remember that you are unlikely to find all your needs satisfied by only one search mechanism and it is the combination of the above which can make you a true Internet professional.

Technical terms for the Internet

Agents (also known as Bots, Robots, Worms or Spiders) These are software programs that gather information or perform some other service in your absence at a pre-scheduled time within chosen parameters.

Attached file, Attachment or Enclosure A file or number of files added to an e-mail message. An attachment is not included in the text of the e-mail, but is a file carried with the e-mail. This can prove useful for sending documents with complicated formatting such as Word documents.

Most popular e-mail programs, such as Microsoft Outlook, Notes or Netscape Mail, allow attachments. It is usually done simply by clicking the attach button (often shown as a paperclip), then browsing the files on your computer until you find the one you wish to send.

Banner A banner is a rectangular box with a graphic contained within it. They typically appear in search engines and portal sites and are clickable, taking the user to the site that they are promoting.

BBS (Bulletin Board System) This is the electronic equivalent of a pinboard. The software program allows you to read the notices left by others and respond to or post fresh messages. A series of messages under the same topic is referred to as a 'thread'.

Binary file   A document that contains more than just text, such as an image, or a file with formatting such as a spreadsheet or word-processing document.

Browser   A browser is the program that you use to read information published on the world wide web. The two most popular browsers (used by 98 per cent of all Internet users) are Microsoft Internet Explorer (www.microsoft.com), and Netscape Navigator (www.netscape.com). As Internet technology advances, the browsers are updated and produced in different versions, which are usually numbered, e.g. Netscape Navigator 3.01. Upgrading your browser is free and you simply visit the company website to download the latest release.

Client   A client is the requesting program or user, downloading information from the server. For example, when your browser requests to download web pages from another computer, the browser is the client and the computer holding the web pages is the server.

Cookie   A piece of data that is given to your browser to store in a text file by a web server for later access. Without cookies the server would have no 'memory' of you having visited the web pages it holds. Uses for cookies include shopping baskets and passwords.

Direct access   This is the term commonly used to describe a PC which is permanently connected to the Internet. This is achieved through a permanent telephone line between the PC and the Internet provider. Direct access is required if you wish to publish information on the Internet.

Domain name   The unique URL or address of a website, and also the right-hand side of the @ sign in an e-mail address. They are equivalent to area codes in a telephone system. In general, American addresses end in an organizational suffix, such as '.edu' (which means the site is at a college or university). Other American suffixes include:

.com for businesses
.org for non-profit organizations
.gov and .mil for government and military agencies
.net for companies or organizations that run large networks.

Sites in the rest of the world tend to use a two-letter code that represents their country. For example, .ca for Canadian sites, .ch for Swiss sites, .za for South Africa.

Our domain name at MarketingNet is marketingnet.com or marketingnet.co.uk. To prevent duplication of domain names on the Internet, an organization called InterNIC registers the .com domain names for a small fee and Nominet in the UK manages .co.uk addresses. To check which names have been registered, visit www.netnames.co.uk.

Download	To transfer software from a remote computer to your own machine.
e-mail or Electronic mail	Messages sent via the Internet to a particular individual or group. Files can be sent via e-mail as attachments.
Emoticon	Another name for smileys. A group of characters used to denote intonation and body language. Emoticons are in common usage in e-mail and IRC, e.g.

:-) (smiling/happy)   :-D (surprised)
:-((sad)   :-(((very sad)
:-o (shocked)   8-) (happy person
                         with glasses)

Encryption	The conversion of data into a form that is readable only by the receiver. This form of data

is called a cipher. The process of returning the data to a readable format is called decryption.

Extranet   This is effectively an Internet site, which is secured against the general public but permissible only to individuals given a name and/or password. They are used powerfully for subscription marketing, client only Internet sites or for creating supplier communities.

FAQ   FAQ is an acronym for Frequently Asked Questions. The FAQ (pronounced 'fack') has its roots in newsgroups, whereby the commonly asked questions are listed with their answers in one document to acquaint newcomers to the group with the rules, and to avoid asking the same questions. When joining a newsgroup it is always advisable to read the FAQ.

Finger   This is a utility that will allow you to get some more information about someone. If all you have is their e-mail address, you can run the finger utility and, assuming the owner of the e-mail address has enabled those requests, you will receive back some additional information about them.

Flame, Flame   The questioning of someone's opinion or beliefs, **war and Flamers**   usually on a personal level, often found in newsgroups. A flame war is a number of such messages sent back and forth between two flamers.

Flash   A technology used to make animations on the Internet. It is created using a development application produced by Macromedia Director and can be used for CDs as well as the Internet. At the start of January 2000, 82 per cent of Internet users were capable of viewing this and of the remainder users simply have to download the plug-in.

Freeware   Software available for free on the Internet. However, it does still remain copyrighted and so cannot be incorporated into any other programming. (See also shareware.) A good source of freeware and shareware can be found at www.shareware.com.

FTP (File Transfer Protocol)

An application for the purpose of transferring files across the Internet. FTP is the normal way of sending files to or receiving files from a server. When a designer needs to transfer web pages from their computer to the server they use FTP so that people on the Internet can access their files. Although FTP has a user command interface for the user to login, send, receive or move files, there is software available with a graphical interface, much like that of Windows Explorer. FTP utilities are available for download from the web: CuteFTP, WS_FTP, and FTP Explorer.

Gateway

A type of intermediary device or program that transfers information between networks that would not normally be compatible.

GIF

A format used to save graphics for use on browsers. Specially designed for compression for ease of download.

GUI (Graphical User Interface)

Pronounced goo-ee. An easy-to-use graphical front end to computers. Originally the user interfaces to computers were text-based like that of the DOS operating system.

Hit

A request for a single file to be downloaded from a web server. A request for a single web page with two graphics will be counted as 3 hits, one for the HTML document and 2 for the images. Hit counts are a good measurement of the amount of traffic visiting a site, but can be a misleading indicator as to the number of pages being viewed.

Home page   From a web user's point of view a home page
                       is the first page opened when starting up a
                       browser. For a designer it is the first page
                       shown when visiting a website.

Host   Any computer connected to the Internet which
                       is capable of serving files to users.

HTML (Hypertext   These are the programming commands that
Mark-up   define how your pages look when your
Language)   customers see them. Your browser interprets
                       the HTML in the document describing the web
                       page, and then places the text and images on
                       the page in your browser accordingly. To look
                       at the HTML of a specific web page, use the
                       right-hand mouse button and click 'View
                       Source' (Microsoft Explorer 4+). Notepad will
                       then display the actual code used to make the
                       page look as it does. Some examples of the
                       language are:

                       <H1>   = start of heading 1
                       </H1> = end of heading 1
                       <B>   = bold
                       <I>   = italic

HTTP   Hypertext Transport Protocol. In the early days
                       of the Internet many different standards of
                       software programs were used on the Internet so
                       it became etiquette to reference the protocol to
                       which the code followed. This protocol is the
                       one most commonly used by the world wide
                       web and is no longer needed when referencing
                       Internet sites, e.g. http://www.company.com
                       has become www.company.com.

Hyperlink, Link   A link can be text, an image or other object that
or Hypertext   can be 'clicked on' to take you to another web
link   page, or a new place on the current web page,
                       or to start downloading a file. The most
                       commonly found form of a link is highlighted,

or sometimes underlined, text. It was the hyper-text concept that brought about the invention of the world wide web.

Internet or   The International Network is a worldwide
'the Net'   system of linked computer networks. Its origins lie in the development of the ARPAnet, the Advanced Research Projects Agency network of the US government back in 1969. The intention was to create a system that would still function even if a large part of it was destroyed.

    The Internet utilizes current communications systems such as phone lines to provide remote login, file transfer, electronic mail, newsgroups and other services.

Intranet   A private network in an organization or company, using technology to share information and resources amongst employees.

IP address   Internet Protocol address: a unique number comprising four parts that identifies a computer on the Internet. Because it is hard to remember such numbers, domain names were invented to alias them which also means if your Internet site is moved from one computer to another and therefore the IP number changes, the Internet is still able to reference your site through the alias name.

IRC   Internet Relay Chat: a group of people worldwide talking to each other in real-time over the Internet.

ISDN   Integrated Services Digital Network: a high-speed digital communications system that is intended to eventually replace the telephone system.

ISP   Internet Service Provider: a company that provides Internet connections. To gain access to the Internet you need to open an account with an ISP.

Jargon   The frequently incomprehensible language used to talk about a specialized project.

Java   A programming language designed for the creation of programs that can be downloaded over the Internet and run without fear of harming your computer. Java can also be used to create Java applets – small programs that add functionality to a web page such as calculators, animation and clocks.

JavaScript   A script language, easier and faster to code than compiled languages such as C or C++, used to enhance websites.

JPEG   Joint Photographic Experts Group: the group who defined the compression scheme to reduce the size of images for use on the Internet. The other type of image used on the Internet is the GIF.

kbps   Kilobytes per second. The speed of a modem is calculated by the number of bytes it can transfer per second. It is standard today to measure the speed of a modem in kbps.

Keyword   A word used as a search criterion for an online database or search engine.

Kilobyte, KB   A kilobyte consists of 1024 bytes.
or kbyte

Leased line   A dedicated telephone line rented for a period of time. The pricing is usually such that you do not pay for the amount of usage but simply pay a flat rate.
                      When you describe a leased line you often also describe how much traffic it can carry at one time. A 64k leased line means that two users can

send information through using a 28.800 modem. The third person trying to use the leased line will not receive a connection at the full speed but will instead have to wait for resources to be freed up from the existing two users.

Listserv   A popular and powerful program used to automate mailing lists.

Live   When used in the context of the world wide web, live refers to a site that has been made available for public viewing on the web, instead of being in development.

Logon, Login,   To logon or login is the process of providing
Logoff   identification to a network or system. Usually a username and password are required. Logging off is the process of notifying the network or system that you are ending your interaction.

Mailbomb   The flooding of someone's e-mail address with electronic messages, and sometimes attachments, often in response to a flame war. A mailbomb can overload the recipient's e-mail account, and may even cause the server to cease to function. Mailbombing is antisocial behaviour and is often penalized by system administrators.

Mailing list   A list of people who receive periodical postings from a group by e-mail.

Megabyte, MB   A unit of measurement equal to 1024 kilobytes.

Metatags   Code, which is hidden in the web page code, which the search engines (such as Yahoo, Altavista, Google, Excite) use to find your Internet site. They contain three key elements:

                      1. The **title** carries the most amount of impact in Altavista, Infoseek and Excite. Repeating words and putting the most important

words first makes a huge impact on the positioning within these search engines.

2. The **description** then carries the most amount of weight. This must be no more than 160 characters and this includes commas and dashes. This description is displayed by the search engines so it must be powerfully written to promote the organization, the products and services and the inherent value of the site. The earlier placed words in this sentence carry the most amount of weight as search words. You don't need commas and spaces in the keywords so to save characters, remove the spaces.

3. Most search engines (certainly the top ten) also accept 1000 characters in the **keyword** section. Again the earlier placed words carry the most amount of weight as search words.

Modem   Modulator–demodulator. A device that allows your computer to communicate with other computers using telephone lines.

Netiquette   Etiquette on the Net. The greatest need for netiquette arises when sending e-mail, posting an article to a newsgroup, or when chatting in IRC.

Newsgroups   Online discussion groups dedicated to particular topics. There are thousands of newsgroups covering just about every kind of subject imaginable.

Offline   When a computer is not connected to the Internet or a host system, it is offline.

Online   The state of being connected to the Internet. A frequently-used adjective when describing activities available on the Internet, such as online shopping, online gaming, or online chat.

PGP Pretty Good Privacy, free encryption software that works with 'keys'. The user has a public key, which can be made available to anyone, which will then encrypt the data. When the user receives the encoded data he/she decrypts it using a private key that only he/she knows. More information can be found on the International PGP Page.

Platform This is the term used to describe what operating system is loaded on the computer. It is often prefixed with the actual name of the operating system. You might say, 'we are running our website on a UNIX platform' or 'we are looking for an NT platform'. It does not describe the hardware but most operating systems are designed with certain hardware in mind, therefore it is easy to guess at what the actual computer is.

Plug-in An additional helper application that is easy to install and becomes part of your browser software. Plug-ins enable you to do more through your browser: for example, allow you to view documents as you would in print with Adobe's Acrobat, or view interactive animation with Macromedia's Shockwave for Director.

POP Stands for Point of Presence. The telephone number through which an Internet provider can be reached. This is the number you use to connect to the Internet. POP is also the short form for Post Office Protocol, which is used to store e-mail for you to pick up when dialling in.

Portal A website designed to provide an inventory of links and content designed for a specific target audience. www.handbag.com is an example of one designed for women.

Posting A single message entered into the electronic communications system.

Protocol   Protocols are sets of rules which determine where, when and how information is transmitted on a network

QuickTime   A technology by Apple allowing for the development, storage and playing of multimedia files using text, sound, animation and video. The files can be viewed by using a QuickTime player, which are available with browsers, or can be downloaded from Apple. The file name extensions for QuickTime files are: qt, mov and moov.

RAM   Random Access Memory: the place in your computer's memory that information and programs reside whilst you are working on it.

ROTFL   Roll On The Floor Laughing: shorthand used in online forums and e-mail to show appreciation of a joke or hysterical laughter.

RTM   Read the Manual: shorthand used in online forums and e-mail to tell the user that they are being lazy in asking people to take the time to explain something that is clearly documented in the manual.

Roll-over   The graphic or look of the text changes as your cursor/mouse hovers over the specific item.

Search engines   Search engines act as catalogues of web pages, and attempt to point the users in the right direction for the information they need. This is done by entering keywords, words that you think will appear in the type of pages you are looking for. The most popular search engines are:

- yahoo.com/yahoo.co.uk
- Altavista.com
- Infoseek.com
- Excite.com

- Ask.co.uk
- Google.com
- Hotbot.com
- Lycos.com
- msn.com

Server

In its simplest form, a computer on a network that holds the information or provides the service that you, the client, require. The majority of servers on the Internet are PCs and are no more sophisticated than ones used within the average organization as a server.

SGML

Standard Generalized Mark-up Language, a generic grammar used as the basis for the publication and delivery of electronic information. More information is available from the SGML University.

Shareware

Software that is available for download on a try-before-you-buy basis. If you find that you like the software, you are expected to pay a registration fee in return for documentation, updated versions and technical support.

Snail mail

The standard name used on the Internet to refer to paper mail, as an e-mail can arrive in a matter of seconds, and...well...paper mail just doesn't.

Spam

Sending repetitious e-mails to newsgroups or mailing lists. The emphasis is on multiple. The name is derived from the famous Monty Python spam sketch.

TCP/IP

Transmission Control Protocol/Internet Protocol, the program that all computers on the Internet must run to be able to communicate with each other.

Telnet

Providing that you have permission, Telnet is a way of accessing someone else's computer via a network.

Thread	A group of messages found in a newsgroup that share the same title and topic, so you can choose to read or delete the messages.
Universal Resource Locator (URL)	This is like the location address for a piece of information on the Internet. A URL is the unique address of a web page or file on the web, e.g.www.marketingnet.com/index.htm.
UNIX	This is the generic name for a large number of computer operating systems (its equivalent on your PC is Windows). Unix is a popular operating system for web servers on the Internet.
Upload	To transfer data or files from your own computer to another.
Usenet	Also referred to as newsgroups. Online discussion groups dedicated to particular topics. There are thousands of newsgroups covering just about every kind of subject imaginable.
Virtual	Not real. A simulation of the real thing using modern technology. The Internet is a great source of that which is merely conceptual, such as virtual shopping, virtual sex or virtual server.
Virus	A program that replicates itself by concealing itself within other software, which is passed from machine to machine. Often the intent is malicious.
VRML	Virtual Reality Modelling Language. It is probably easiest to think of VRML as the 3-D version of HTML. Using VRML it is possible to create a three-dimensional world on screen, whereby you navigate by using keys or the mouse to go left, right, up, down, forwards and backwards, and in response to this the images on the screen change to create the illusion of moving through space.

World wide web, the web, WWW, W3	The world wide web is one of the most recent parts of the Internet, and probably the easiest to use. It is also one of the most popular and growing at an incredible rate. It is also the most spectacular, for the web pages contain not only text, but images, sound, video and more. The main reason the WWW has taken off so quickly is that it uses a WIMP (Windows, Icons, Mouse Pointer) system to navigate. This makes it easy: just point and click. The underlying system making this navigation possible is called hypertext, and hypertext links are the parts you click on to take you elsewhere on the web. The language used to create the web pages is called HTML or Hypertext Mark-up Language. These HTML documents can then be stored on any machine connected to the Internet running server software. To view the HTML documents you need to use a browser, which is most likely to be Netscape Navigator or Microsoft Internet Explorer.
Website	A collection of related web pages that have an introductory page called a homepage. The website address will take you to this homepage, and from there the visitor can follow links to the other pages. When a company or person has a website, the address they give out or advertise on literature is that of the homepage. For example, at MarketingNet the address of our homepage is www.marketingnet.com.
Web page	A web page is a single HTML document, a single page that can be viewed in one browser window. A website consists of a group of related web pages.
W3C	The World Wide Web Consortium. The following definition is quoted from their own website: 'The W3C was founded in October 1994 to lead the world wide web to its full potential by

developing common protocols that promote its evolution and ensure its interoperability. We are an international industry consortium, jointly hosted by the Massachusetts Institute of Technology Laboratory for Computer Science [MIT/LCS] in the United States; the Institute National de Recherche en Informatique et en Automatique [INRIA] in Europe; and the Keio University Shonan Fujisawa Campus in Japan. Services provided by the Consortium include: a repository of information about the world wide web for developers and users; reference code implementations to embody and promote standards; and various prototype and sample applications to demonstrate use of new technology. Initially, the W3C was established in collaboration with CERN, where the web originated, with support from DARPA and the European Commission ... The Consortium is led by Tim Berners-Lee, Director and creator of the world wide web, and Jean-François Abramatic, Chairman. W3C is funded by member organizations, and is vendor neutral, working with the global community to produce specifications and reference software that is made freely available throughout the world.' For more information visit the W3C website (www.w3.org).

XML
Extensible Mark-up Language is a new standard for defining data formats that is in development. Like HTML it is a subset of SGML, but HTML is used to define how data is presented, whereas XML is used to define how data is treated. The reason this mark-up language is called extensible is that it will allow the creation of data descriptive tags. For further information visit www.xml.com.

Yahoo!
Yahoo! is a hierarchical directory of websites organized by topics, and is one of the most popular ways to browse the Internet by subject

today. Created by David Filo and Jerry Yang whilst graduate students at Stanford University, Yahoo! was the first of its kind. Beginning as link pages organized by category on a college site, Yahoo! has grown to become a multimillion dollar corporation.

Zip drive

A compact, portable disk drive popular for archiving computer files and transporting data. The zip disks will each hold 100 MB of data, which is approximately the equivalent to 70 floppy disks. It has been said that the zip drive is the floppy drive of the future. More information can be found on the Iomega Corporation website.

Zip file and zipping

Files that are transferred over the Internet are often compressed so that download time can be decreased. One way to compress the files is to zip them. Popular compression software includes: PKZIP for the DOS operating system, WinZip for Windows, and the Stuffit range for the Macintosh. A zipped file is usually denoted by the '.zip' suffix.

Once a zip file has been downloaded it can be extracted and uncompressed. Often the files are self extracting and just need a double click to unpack them. When the file is restored, double-clicking on the setup.exe will install the downloaded software in your operating system (if you're working on a PC, that is).

News groups

News groups are an essential tool for the marketer. They represent discussions on particular topics and as such are a vital market segmentation tool. Used effectively they provide an ideal communication channel with your target audience.

News groups on the Internet are provided by the Usenet system. Unlike e-mail, which is usually 'one-to-one', Usenet is 'many-to-many'. To many people, Usenet *is* the Internet where over 100 million characters a day are entered into the system – nearly an encyclopaedia's worth of writing. These are like conversations with a group of like-minded individuals. It is similar to e-mail in style but unlike e-mail, which is one-to-one, it is one-to-many. Anyone can 'listen in' on the conversation and then make a comment. The comment is composed just like an e-mail and is 'posted' to the news group. The comment is then copied around the world, allowing everyone who is looking at the group to see your comment. A reply can either be sent privately to you via e-mail or publicly by adding a comment to the news group. The news group builds up to be a list of messages and by reading through them it allows you to follow a discussion made up from people posing a sequence of comments on the same subject.

Each group will have a style and culture of its own. Some are open to new comments, with others it can be difficult to make a comment without eliciting a rude reply. The best way to understand the culture of a group is to spend some time acclimatizing to the news group before making your first comments. If you see others posing seemingly well-intentioned comments and getting a negative response, adjust your comments to fit. However, the majority of busy groups welcome new contributors and it can be a very rewarding use of the Internet.

Usenet is made up of over 9000 news groups (on other networks these are called conferences or forums). Each one is dedicated to a particular subject. The news groups distributed worldwide are divided into twelve broad classifications. These are:

bionet   Research biology.
humanities   Professional and amateur topics in the arts and humanities.
bit.listserv   Conferences originating as Bitnet mailing lists.
biz   Business products and services.
comp   Topics of interest to both computer professionals and hobbyists, including topics in computer science, software source, and information on hardware and software systems.
misc   Groups addressing themes not easily classified under any of the other headings or which incorporate themes from multiple categories.
news   News about Usenet itself.
rec   Groups oriented towards the arts, hobbies and recreational activities.
sci   Science other than research biology. These discussions are meant to be marked by special and usually practical knowledge, relating to research in or application of the established sciences.
soc   Groups primarily addressing social issues and socializing, often ethnically related.
talk   Politics and related topics. These groups are largely debate-oriented and tend to feature long discussions without resolution and without appreciable amounts of generally useful information.
alt   Controversial or unusual topics; not carried by all sites.

In addition there may be local news groups such as:

uk   UK related topics.
pipex   Pipex (the access provided) related topics

Clarinet

Usenet 'news groups' is not really the correct name, they are often not news but provide for discussions and questions. However there are several sources of news and sports on the Internet.

One of the largest is Clarinet, a company in Cupertino, California, that distributes wire-service news and columns.

Because Clarinet charges for its service, not all host systems carry its articles. Those that do carry them as Usenet groups starting with 'clari.'. Some of the areas covered include business news (clari.biz); general national and foreign news, politics (clari.news), sports (clari.sports); columns by Mike Royko, Miss Manners, and others (clari.feature); and NewsBytes computer and telecommunications reports (clari.nb). Clari news groups feature stories updated around the clock. There are even a couple of 'bulletin' news groups for breaking stories: clari.news.bulletin and clari.news.urgent. Clarinet also sets up new news groups for breaking stories such as major natural disasters and the like.

News group netiquette

This section[1] describes the Usenet culture and customs that have developed over time. The key to successful marketing with the Usenet news groups is to become adept at becoming 'part of the conversation'. The role you wish to play is up to you but here are some basic rules which will help you improve your performance.

Select your news groups carefully

When you post an article, think about the people you are trying to reach. Try to get the most appropriate audience for your message, not the widest.

Be familiar with the group you are posting to before you post! You shouldn't post to groups you do not read, or post to groups you've only read a few articles from – you may not be familiar with the on-going conventions and themes of the group. One normally does not join a conversation by just walking up and talking. Instead, you listen first and then join in if you have something pertinent to contribute.

Remember that the Usenet news group system is designed to allow readers to choose which messages they see, not to allow

---

[1]Based on the FAQ *'A Primer on How to Work With the Usenet Community'* by Chug Von Rospach.

posters to choose sets of readers to target. When choosing which news group(s) to post in, ask yourself, 'Which news groups contain readers who would want to read my message' rather than 'Which news groups have readers to whom I want to send my message?'

If your message is of interest to a limited geographic area (apartments, car sales, meetings, concerts, etc.), restrict the distribution of the message to your local area. Some areas have special news groups with geographical limitations, and the recent versions of the news software allow you to limit the distribution of material sent to worldwide news groups. Check with your system administrator to see what news groups are available and how to use them.

When you decide to post a message you will need to specify the news group in which it should be sent. However, sometimes you will feel the item should be discussed in more than one group. For example you may feel a question about vegetarian restaurants would be best discussed by participants in both rec.restaurants and rec.vegetarian. Cross-posting is a mechanism within the Usenet that allows this to be done. By sending one message but marking it for both groups you will be able to attract both audiences. The undesirable alternative would be to send two messages, one to each news group, this would result in someone who is registered to both groups seeing your message twice; using the cross posting they will only see it once.

Sending a message that is of no relevance to a news group will cause a lot of consternation. For example posting an advertisement for your services in an unrelated discussion group will do you more harm than good; even if your service is good your audience will see your act as destructive. The Usenet is a workable system only because people attempt to make it work. This is a central tenet of the majority who use the news groups: to attempt to subvert the news classification scheme and filling up people's computers with your unwanted advertising is extremely anti-social.

Avoid spamming

Spamming is the great news group 'crime'. Here you will send a message, of no direct relevance, to many news groups. The aim is to shove your message in front of as many people as possible, the result will be a PR disaster. Although there may seem no problem attracting the wrath of Usenet users, unfortunately the most zealous network of Usenet defenders are the systems operation personnel who manage the underlying computer systems. There is a well practised procedure that has been developed which can result in your connection to the Internet being ruined or cut off. The typical action taken is to send you so many e-mails your e-mail system fills up and you start to miss messages or your web-server is overloaded with automatic requests for information.

Never forget that the person on the other side is human

Because your interaction with the network is through a computer it is easy to forget that there are people 'out there'. Situations arise where emotions erupt into a verbal free-for-all that can lead to hurt feelings.

People all over the world are reading your words. Do not attack people if you cannot persuade them with your presentation of the facts. Screaming, cursing, and abusing others only serves to make people think less of you and be less willing to help you when you need it.

If you are upset at something or someone, wait until you have had a chance to calm down and think about it. Hasty words create more problems than they solve. Try not to say anything to others you would not say to them in person in a room full of people.

Don't blame system administrator for their users' behaviour

Sometimes, you may find it necessary to write to a system administrator about something concerning their site or one of their users. No matter how steamed up you may be, be polite to the system administrator, he or she may not have any idea of what you are going to say, and may not have any part in the incidents involved. By being civil and temperate, you are more likely to obtain their courteous attention and assistance.

Never assume that a person is speaking for their organization

Many people who post to Usenet do so from machines at their place of work. Despite that, never assume that the person is speaking for the organization that they are posting their articles from (unless the person explicitly says so). Some people put explicit disclaimers to this effect in their messages, but this is a good general rule. If you find an article offensive, consider taking it up with the person directly, or ignoring it. Learn about 'kill files' in your news reader software, and other techniques for ignoring people whose postings you find offensive.

Be careful what you say about others

Please remember – you read netnews; so do as many as 3,000,000 other people. This group quite possibly includes your boss, your friend's boss and your girl friend's brother. Information posted on the net can come back to haunt you or the person you are talking about. Think twice before you post personal information about yourself or others.

Be brief

Say it succinctly and it will have a greater impact. Remember that the longer you make your article, the fewer people will bother to read it.

Your postings reflect upon you – be proud of them

Most people on Usenet will know you only by what you say and how well you say it. They may someday be your customers, co-workers or friends. Take some time to make sure each posting is something that will not embarrass you later. Minimize your spelling errors and make sure that the article is easy to read and understand. Much of how people judge you on the net is based on your writing.

Use descriptive titles

The subject line of an article is there to enable a person with a limited amount of time to decide whether or not to read your article. Tell people what the article is about before they read it. A title like 'Car for Sale' to rec.autos does not help as much as '66 MG Midget for sale: Beaverton OR.' Don't expect people to read your article to find out what it is about because many of them won't bother. Some sites truncate the length of the subject line to 40 characters so keep your subjects short and to the point.

Be careful with humour and sarcasm

Without the voice inflections and body language of personal communications, it is easy for a remark meant to be funny to be misinterpreted. Subtle humour tends to get lost, so take steps to make sure that people realize you are trying to be funny. Use smileys. No matter how broad the humour or satire, it is safer to remind people that you are being funny. But also be aware that quite frequently satire is posted without any explicit indications. If an article outrages you strongly, you should ask yourself if it just may have been unmarked satire. Several self-proclaimed connoisseurs refuse to use smiley faces, so take heed or you may make a temporary fool of yourself.

Please rotate messages with questionable content

You may see reference to 'rot13' and a very garbled looking message. This is an indication that the person sending the message has included something they think may offend. If you want to unscramble the message after reading the warnings about its contents your PC mail reader software should offer you the option to unscramble it. These can be quite effective at encouraging people to spend the time reading your message, just like the intriguing 'Don't press this' button.

Summarize what you are following up

When you are following up someone's article, please summarize the parts of the article to which you are responding. This allows readers to appreciate your comments rather than trying to remember what the original article said. It is also possible for your response to get to some sites before the original article. Summarization is best done by including appropriate quotes from the original article. For example:

```
Yes I can help:

> How do I get a really good frying pan, my problem is the
>size is a big problem in my small boat.

My own company make a special range of pans just for small
boat owners. You can find out more on our website
http://www.boatpans.com
```

The convention is to mark quotes from the message you are replying to with a >.

Do not include the entire article since it will irritate the people who have already seen it. Even if you are responding to the entire article, summarize only the major points you are discussing.

When summarizing, summarize!

When you request information from the network, it is common courtesy to report your findings so that others can benefit as well. So if you asked a question and you got lots of personal replies, post a quick summary back to the news group. This is one of the best ways to get on the 'in-crowd'. The best way of doing this is to take all the responses that you received and edit them into a single article that is posted to the places where you originally posted your question. Take the time to strip headers, combine duplicate information, and write a short summary. Try to credit the information to the people that sent it to you, where possible.

Use mail, don't post a follow-up

One of the biggest problems we have on the network is that when someone asks a question, many people send out identical answers. When this happens, dozens of identical answers pour through the net. Mail your answer to the person and suggest that they summarize to the network.

This way the net will only see a single copy of the answers, no matter how many people answer the question. If you post a question, please remind people to send you the answers by mail and at least offer to summarize them to the network.

Read all follow-ups and don't repeat what has already been said

Before you submit a follow-up to a message, read the rest of the messages in the news group to see whether someone has already said what you want to say. If someone has, don't repeat it.

Be careful about copyrights and licences

Once something is posted onto the network, it is in the public domain unless you own the appropriate rights (most notably, if you wrote the thing yourself) and you post it with a valid copyright notice; a court would have to decide the specifics and there are arguments for both sides of the issue. For all practical purposes, assume that you effectively give up the copyright if you don't put in a notice. When posting material to the network, keep in mind that if you post any material published under a copyright this could cause you or your company to be held liable for damages.

Cite appropriate references

If you are using facts to support a cause, state where they came from. Don't take someone else's ideas and use them as your own. You don't want someone pretending that your ideas are theirs; show them the same respect.

Don't overdo signatures

Signatures are nice, and many people can have a signature added to their postings automatically by placing it in a file call '.signature'. Don't overdo it. Signatures can tell the world something about you, but keep them short. A signature that is longer than the message itself is considered to be in bad taste. The main purpose of a signature is to help people locate you, not to tell your life story.

Limit line length and avoid control characters

Try to keep your text in a generic format. Many (if not most) of the people reading Usenet do so from 80 column terminals or from workstations with 80 column terminal windows. Try to keep your lines of text to less than 80 characters for optimal readability. If people quote part of your article in a follow-up, short lines will probably show up better, too. You should also try to avoid the use of tabs, too, since they may also be interpreted differently on terminals other than your own.

Do not use Usenet as an advertising medium

Advertisements on Usenet are rarely appreciated. In general, the louder or more inappropriate the ad is, the more antagonism it will stir up. The accompanying posting 'Rules for posting to Usenet' has more on this in the section about 'Announcement of professional products or services'. Try the biz.* hierarchies instead.

How to create a new Usenet news group

This section outlines how to create a new news group in the comp, news, sci, misc, soc, talk, rec areas. The alt area has a considerably less formal process but follows similar lines. The process will require help and there is a body of volunteers who can be contacted on group-mentors@amdahl.com. They assist people who want to propose new groups with the formation and submission of a good proposal.

The basic process is as follows:

Step 1

A request for discussion on creation of a new news group should be posted to news.announce.newgroups, and all related groups.

Step 2

The name and charter of the proposed group and whether it will be moderated and by whom, will be determined during the discussion period. If there is no general agreement after 30 days, the discussion will stop. In order to proceed a new proposal must be submitted as Step 1.

Step 3 The vote

The Usenet Volunteer Votetakers (UVV) are a group of neutral third-party vote-takers who currently handle vote gathering and counting for all news group proposals. The co-ordinators of the group can be reached at uvv-contact@amdahl.com; contact them to arrange the handling of the vote.

The vote involves sending out a call for votes and for at least 21 days. Those who read the call will be able to vote. It is normal to set up two e-mail addresses – one for 'yes' and one for 'no' votes.

Step 4 The result

After the voting is complete the results must be posted to news.announce.newgroups and any other relevant groups or mailing lists to which the original call for votes was posted. The tally should include a statement of which way each voter voted so that the results can be verified. Next you must wait five days and if there are no serious objections that might invalidate the vote, the results can be calculated.

A news group can be created if 100 more valid 'yes' votes are received than 'no' and at least two thirds of the total number of valid votes received are in favour of creation. The special control message can then be sent and the group started.

A proposal that fails should not then be discussed again for six months.

The news groups

The categorization is somewhat chaotic so you have to resort to scanning through all the groups in order to decide where you might find something of relevance. We have included a list of news groups that are circulated globally. We have only included the comp, news, sci, misc, soc, talk and rec groups. The other main group, alt, is considerably less formal. Although some of the groups are very busy and important there are far too many to list here. You will need to explore the alt group online in order to assess the worth of contributing to one of its groups. For a fuller list, see the web pages which accompany this Appendix.

An M indicates the group is moderated by someone.

News group	Description
alt.building.architecture	Building industry architecture.
alt.building.engineering	Building industry engineering.
alt.building.jobs	Building industry jobs.
alt.building.manufacturing	Building industry manufacturing.
alt.building.realestate	Real estate and the building industry.
alt.business.misc	All aspects of commerce.
alt.business.accountability	Corporate accountability.
alt.business.franchise	Franchising discussions.
alt.business.home.pc	For displaying PC home business plans and services.
alt.business.hospitality	Hotel, resort, tour and restaurant businesses.
alt.business.import-export	Business aspects of international trade.
alt.business.import-export.consumables	Import and export of consumable products.
alt.business.internal-audit	Discussion of internal auditing.
alt.business.multi-level	Multi-level marketing is not pyramid sales, honest!. . .
alt.business.seminars	Discussion and announcements of business seminars.
alt.cad	Computer-aided design.
alt.cad.cadkey	Cadkey, Datacad, and other Cadkey, Inc. products.
alt.calc-reform	Making hardened calcium a productive member of society.
alt.california	The state and the state of mind.
alt.christnet	Equal time.
alt.co-ops	Discussion about co-operatives.
alt.cooking-chat	Food, wine and recipe discussions.
comp.admin.policy	Discussions of site administration policies.
comp.ai	Artificial intelligence discussions.
comp.ai.alife	Research about artificial life.
comp.ai.doc-analysis.misc	General document understanding technologies.
comp.ai.doc-analysis.ocr	OCR research, algorithms and software.
comp.ai.fuzzy	Fuzzy set theory, aka fuzzy logic.
comp.ai.games	Artificial intelligence in games and game-playing.
comp.ai.genetic	Genetic algorithms in computing.
comp.ai.jair.announce	Announcements and abstracts of the Journal of AI Research. M
comp.ai.jair.papers	Papers published by the Journal of AI Research. M
comp.ai.nat-lang	Natural language processing by computers.
comp.ai.neural-nets	All aspects of neural networks.
comp.ai.nlang-know-rep	Natural language and knowledge representation. M
comp.ai.philosophy	Philosophical aspects of artificial intelligence.
comp.ai.shells	Expert systems and other artificial intelligence shells.
comp.answers	Repository for periodic USENET articles. M
comp.apps.spreadsheets	Spreadsheets on various platforms.
comp.arch	Computer architecture.
comp.arch.arithmetic	Implementing arithmetic on computers/digital systems.
comp.arch.bus.vmebus	Hardware and software for VMEbus Systems.
comp.arch.embedded	Embedded computer systems topics.
comp.arch.fpga	Field Programmable Gate Array based computing systems.
comp.arch.storage	Storage system issues, both hardware and software.

comp.archives	Descriptions of public access archives. M
comp.archives.admin	Issues relating to computer archive administration.
comp.archives.msdos.announce	Announcements about MSDOS archives. M
comp.archives.msdos.d	Discussion of materials available in MSDOS archives.
comp.bbs.majorbbs	Support and discussion of the major BBS from Galacticomm.
comp.bbs.misc	All aspects of computer bulletin board systems.
comp.bbs.tbbs	The Bread Board System bulletin board software.
comp.bbs.waffle	The Waffle BBS and USENET system on all platforms.
comp.benchmarks	Discussion of benchmarking techniques and results.
comp.binaries.acorn	Binary-only postings for Acorn machines. M
comp.binaries.amiga	Encoded public domain programs in binary. M
comp.binaries.apple2	Binary-only postings for the Apple II computer.
comp.binaries.atari.st	Binary-only postings for the Atari ST. M
comp.binaries.cbm	For the transfer of 8-bit Commodore binaries. M
comp.binaries.geos	Binaries for the GEOS operating system. M
comp.binaries.ibm.pc	Binary-only postings for IBM PC/MS-DOS. M
comp.binaries.ibm.pc.d	Discussions about IBM/PC binary postings.
comp.binaries.ibm.pc.wanted	Requests for IBM PC and compatible programs.
comp.binaries.mac	Encoded Macintosh programs in binary. M
comp.binaries.ms-windows	Binary programs for Microsoft Windows. M
comp.binaries.newton	Apple Newton binaries, sources, books, etc. M
comp.binaries.os2	Binaries for use under the OS/2 ABI. M
comp.binaries.psion	Binaries for the range of Psion computers. M
comp.bugs.2bsd	Reports of UNIX* version 2BSD related bugs.
comp.bugs.4bsd	Reports of UNIX version 4BSD related bugs.
comp.bugs.4bsd.ucb-fixes	Bug reports/fixes for BSD Unix. M
comp.bugs.misc	General UNIX bug reports and fixes (incl V7, uucp).
comp.bugs.sys5	Reports of USG (System III, V, etc.) bugs.
comp.cad.autocad	AutoDesk's AutoCAD software.
comp.cad.cadence	Users of Cadence Design Systems products.
comp.cad.compass	Compass Design Automation EDA tools.
comp.cad.i-deas	SDRC I-DEAS Masters Series software.
comp.cad.microstation	MicroStation CAD software and related products.
comp.cad.pro-engineer	Parametric Technology's Pro/Engineer design package.
comp.cad.synthesis	Research and production in the field of logic synthesis.
comp.client-server	Topics relating to client/server technology.
comp.cog-eng	Cognitive engineering.
comp.compilers	Compiler construction, theory, etc. M
comp.compilers.tools.pccts	Construction of compilers and tools with PCCTS.
comp.compression	Data compression algorithms and theory.
comp.compression.research	Discussions about data compression research. M
comp.constraints	Constraint processing and related topics.
comp.databases	Database and data management issues and theory.
comp.databases.gupta	Gupta SQLWindows client-server development.
comp.databases.ibm-db2	Problem resolution with DB2 database products.
comp.databases.informix	Informix database management software discussions.
comp.databases.ingres	Issues relating to INGRES products.
comp.databases.ms-access	MS Windows' relational database system, Access.

comp.databases.object	Object-oriented paradigms in database systems.
comp.databases.olap	Analytical Processing, Multidimensional DBMS, EIS, DSS.
comp.databases.oracle	The SQL database products of the Oracle Corporation.
comp.databases.paradox	Borland's database for DOS and MS Windows.
comp.databases.pick	Pick-like, post-relational, database systems.
comp.databases.progress	The Progress 4GL and RDBMS.
comp.databases.rdb	The relational database engine RDB from DEC.
comp.databases.sybase	Implementations of the SQL Server.
comp.databases.theory	Discussing advances in database technology.
comp.databases.xbase.fox	Fox Software's xBase system and compatibles.
comp.databases.xbase.misc	Discussion of xBase (dBASE-like) products.
comp.dcom.cabling	Cabling selection, installation and use.
comp.dcom.cell-relay	Forum for discussion of Cell Relay-based products.
comp.dcom.fax	Fax hardware, software, and protocols.
comp.dcom.frame-relay	Technology and issues regarding frame relay networks.
comp.dcom.isdn	The Integrated Services Digital Network (ISDN).
comp.dcom.lans.ethernet	Discussions of the Ethernet/IEEE 802.3 protocols.
comp.dcom.lans.fddi	Discussions of the FDDI protocol suite.
comp.dcom.lans.misc	Local area network hardware and software.
comp.dcom.lans.token-ring	Installing and using token ring networks.
comp.dcom.modems	Data communications hardware and software.
comp.dcom.net-management	Network management methods and applications.
comp.dcom.servers	Selecting and operating data communications servers.
comp.dcom.sys.cisco	Info on Cisco routers and bridges.
comp.dcom.sys.wellfleet	Wellfleet bridge and router systems hardware and software.
comp.dcom.telecom	Telecommunications digest. M
comp.dcom.telecom.tech	Discussion of technical aspects of telephony.
comp.dcom.videoconf	Video conference technology and applications.
comp.doc	Archived public-domain documentation. M
comp.doc.techreports	Lists of technical reports. M
comp.dsp	Digital Signal Processing using computers.
comp.edu	Computer science education.
comp.edu.languages.natural	Computer assisted languages instruction issues.
comp.emacs	EMACS editors of different flavours.
comp.emacs.xemacs	Bug reports, questions and answers about XEmacs.
comp.emulators.announce	Emulator news, FAQs, announcements. M
comp.emulators.apple2	Emulators of Apple systems.
comp.emulators.cbm	Emulators of C-64, C-128, PET, and VIC-20 systems.
comp.emulators.misc	Emulators of miscellaneous computer systems.
comp.emulators.ms-windows.wine	A free MS-Windows emulator under X.
comp.fonts	Typefonts – design, conversion, use, etc.
comp.graphics.algorithms	Algorithms used in producing computer graphics.
comp.graphics.animation	Technical aspects of computer animation.
comp.graphics.api.inventor	Object-oriented 3D graphics in Inventor.
comp.graphics.api.misc	Application Programmer Interface issues, methods.
comp.graphics.api.opengl	The OpenGL 3D application programming interface.
comp.graphics.api.pexlib	The PEXlib application programming interface.
comp.graphics.apps.alias	3D graphics software from Alias Research.

comp.graphics.apps.avs	The Application Visualization System.
comp.graphics.apps.data-explorer	IBM's Visualization Data Explorer (DX).
comp.graphics.apps.gnuplot	The gnuplot interactive function plotter.
comp.graphics.apps.iris-explorer	The IRIS Explorer, aka MVE.
comp.graphics.apps.lightwave	NewTek's Lightwave3D and related topics.
comp.graphics.apps.pagemaker	Question, answers, tips and suggestions.
comp.graphics.apps.photoshop	Adobe Photoshop techniques and help.
comp.graphics.apps.softimage	Softimage applications and products.
comp.graphics.apps.wavefront	Wavefront software products, problems, etc.
comp.graphics.misc	Computer graphics miscellany.
comp.graphics.packages.3dstudio	Autodesk's 3D Studio software.
comp.graphics.rendering.misc	Rendering comparisons, approaches, methods.
comp.graphics.rendering.raytracing	Raytracing software, tools and methods.
comp.graphics.rendering.renderman	RenderMan interface and shading language.
comp.graphics.visualization	Info on scientific visualization.
comp.groupware	Software and hardware for shared interactive environments.
comp.groupware.lotus-notes.misc	Lotus Notes related discussions.
comp.home.automation	Home automation devices, setup, sources, etc.
comp.home.misc	Media, technology and information in domestic spaces. M
comp.human-factors	Issues related to human-computer interaction (HCI).
comp.infosystems	Any discussion about information systems.
comp.infosystems.announce	Announcements of internet information services. M
comp.infosystems.gis	All aspects of geographic information systems.
comp.infosystems.gopher	Discussion of the Gopher information service.
comp.infosystems.harvest	Harvest information discovery and access system.
comp.infosystems.interpedia	The Internet Encyclopedia.
comp.infosystems.kiosks	Informational and transactional kiosks. M
comp.infosystems.wais	The Z39.50-based WAIS full-text search system.
comp.infosystems.www.advocacy	Comments and arguments over the best and worst.
comp.infosystems.www.announce	World-Wide Web announcements. M
comp.infosystems.www.authoring.cgi	Writing CGI scripts for the Web.
comp.infosystems.www.authoring.html	Writing HTML for the Web.
comp.infosystems.www.authoring.images	Using images, imagemaps on the web.
comp.infosystems.www.authoring.misc	Miscellaneous web authoring issues.
comp.infosystems.www.browsers.mac	Web browsers for the Macintosh platform.
comp.infosystems.www.browsers.misc	Web browsers for other platforms.
comp.infosystems.www.browsers.ms-windows	Web browsers for MS Windows.
comp.infosystems.www.browsers.x	Web browsers for the X-Window system.
comp.infosystems.www.misc	Miscellaneous world wide web discussion.
comp.infosystems.www.servers.mac	Web-servers for the Macintosh platform.
comp.infosystems.www.servers.misc	Web-servers for other platforms.
comp.infosystems.www.servers.ms-windows	Web-servers for MS Windows and NT.
comp.infosystems.www.servers.unix	Web-servers for UNIX platforms.
comp.internet.library	Discussing electronic libraries. M
comp.internet.net-happenings	Announcements of network happenings. M
comp.ividiscodisc	Interactive videodiscs – uses, potential, etc.
comp.lang.ada	Discussion about Ada*.
comp.lang.apl	Discussion about APL.
comp.lang.asm.x86	General 80x86 assembly language programming.
comp.lang.awk	The AWK programming language.

comp.lang.basic.misc	Other dialects and aspects of BASIC.
comp.lang.basic.visual	3rd party add-ins for Visual Basic.
comp.lang.basic.visual.announce	Official information on Visual Basic. M
comp.lang.basic.visual.database	Database aspects of Visual Basic.
comp.lang.basic.visual.misc	Visual Basic in general.
comp.lang.beta	The object-oriented programming language BETA.
comp.lang.c	Discussion about C.
comp.lang.c++	The object-oriented C++ language.
comp.lang.c++.leda	All aspects of the LEDA library.
comp.lang.c.moderated	The C programming language. M
comp.lang.clipper	Clipper and Visual Objects programming languages.
comp.lang.clos	Common Lisp Object System discussions.
comp.lang.cobol	The COBOL language and software.
comp.lang.dylan	For discussion of the Dylan language.
comp.lang.eiffel	The object-oriented Eiffel language.
comp.lang.forth	Discussion about Forth.
comp.lang.fortran	Discussion about FORTRAN.
comp.lang.functional	Discussion about functional languages.
comp.lang.hermes	The Hermes language for distributed applications.
comp.lang.idl-pvwave	IDL and PV-Wave language discussions.
comp.lang.lisp	Discussion about LISP.
comp.lang.lisp.mcl	Discussing Apple Macintosh Common Lisp.
comp.lang.logo	The Logo teaching and learning language.
comp.lang.misc	Different computer languages not specifically listed.
comp.lang.ml	ML languages including Standard ML, CAML, Lazy ML, etc. M
comp.lang.modula2	Discussion about Modula-2.
comp.lang.modula3	Discussion about the Modula-3 language.
comp.lang.mumps	The M (MUMPS) language and technology, in general.
comp.lang.oberon	The Oberon language and system.
comp.lang.objective-c	The Objective-C language and environment.
comp.lang.pascal.ansi-iso	Pascal according to ANSI and ISO standards.
comp.lang.pascal.borland	Borland's Pascal.
comp.lang.pascal.delphi.components	Writing components in Borland Delphi.
comp.lang.pascal.delphi.databases	Database aspects of Borland Delphi.
comp.lang.pascal.delphi.misc	General issues with Borland Delphi.
comp.lang.pascal.mac	Macintosh based Pascals.
comp.lang.pascal.misc	Pascal in general and ungrouped Pascals.
comp.lang.perl.announce	Announcements about Perl. M
comp.lang.perl.misc	The Perl language in general.
comp.lang.pop	Pop11 and the Plug user group.
comp.lang.postscript	The PostScript page description language.
comp.lang.prograph	Prograph, a visual object-oriented dataflow language.
comp.lang.prolog	Discussion about PROLOG.
comp.lang.python	The Python computer language.
comp.lang.sather	The object-oriented computer language Sather.
comp.lang.scheme	The Scheme Programming language.
comp.lang.sigplan	Info and announcements from ACM SIGPLAN. M
comp.lang.smalltalk	Discussion about Smalltalk 80.
comp.lang.tcl	The Tcl programming language and related tools.
comp.lang.verilog	Discussing Verilog and PLI.

comp.lang.vhdl	VHSIC Hardware Description Language, IEEE 1076/87.
comp.lang.visual	General discussion of visual programming languages. M
comp.laser-printers	Laser printers, hardware and software. M
comp.lsi	Large scale integrated circuits.
comp.lsi.testing	Testing of electronic circuits.
comp.mail.elm	Discussion and fixes for the ELM mail system.
comp.mail.headers	Gatewayed from the Internet header-people list.
comp.mail.list-admin.policy	Policy issues in running mailing lists.
comp.mail.list-admin.software	Software used in the running of mailing lists.
comp.mail.maps	Various maps, including UUCP maps. M
comp.mail.mh	The UCI version of the Rand Message Handling system.
comp.mail.mime	Multipurpose Internet Mail Extensions of RFC 1341.
comp.mail.misc	General discussions about computer mail.
comp.mail.mush	The Mail User's Shell (MUInternet).
comp.mail.pine	The PINE mail user agent.
comp.mail.sendmail	Configuring and using the BSD sendmail agent.
comp.mail.smail	Administering and using the smail e-mail transport system.
comp.mail.uucp	Mail in the uucp network environment.
comp.mail.zmail	The various Z-Mail products and their configurability.
comp.misc	General topics about computers not covered elsewhere.
comp.multimedia	Interactive multimedia technologies of all kinds.
comp.newprod	Announcements of new products of interest. M
comp.object	Object-oriented programming and languages.
comp.object.logic	Integrating object-oriented and logic programming.
comp.org.acm	Topics about the Association for Computing Machinery.
comp.org.cpsr.announce	Computer Professionals for Social Responsibility.
comp.org.cpsr.talk	Issues of computing and social responsibility. M
comp.org.decus	Digital Equipment Computer Users' Society news group.
comp.org.eff.news	News from the Electronic Frontier Foundation. M
comp.org.eff.talk	Discussion of EFF goals, strategies, etc.
comp.org.fidonet	FidoNews digest, official news of FidoNet Assoc. M
comp.org.ieee	Issues and announcements about the IEEE and its members.
comp.org.issnnet	The International Student Society for Neural Networks.
comp.org.lisp-users	Association of Lisp Users related discussions.
comp.org.sug	Talk about/for the The Sun User's Group.
comp.org.uniforum	UniForum Association activities.
comp.org.usenix	USENIX Association events and announcements.
comp.org.usenix.roomshare	Finding lodging during Usenix conferences.
comp.os.chorus	CHORUS microkernel issues, research and developments.
comp.os.coherent	Discussion and support of the Coherent operating system.
comp.os.cpm	Discussion about the CP/M operating system.
comp.os.geos	The GEOS operating system by GeoWorks for PC clones.

comp.os.linux.advocacy	Benefits of Linux compared to other operating systems.
comp.os.linux.announce	Announcements important to the Linux community. M
comp.os.linux.answers	FAQs, How-To's, READMEs, etc. about Linux. M
comp.os.linux.development.apps	Writing Linux applications, porting to Linux.
comp.os.linux.development.system	Linux kernels, device drivers, modules.
comp.os.linux.hardware	Hardware compatibility with the Linux operating system.
comp.os.linux.misc	Linux-specific topics not covered by other groups.
comp.os.linux.networking	Networking and communications under Linux.
comp.os.linux.setup	Linux installation and system administration.
comp.os.linux.x	Linux X Window System servers, clients, libs and fonts.
comp.os.lynx	Discussion of LynxOS and Lynx Real-Time Systems.
comp.os.mach	The MACH OS from CMU and other places.
comp.os.magic-cap	Everything about General Magic's Magic Cap OS.
comp.os.minix	Discussion of Tanenbaum's MINIX system.
comp.os.misc	General OS-oriented discussion not carried elsewhere.
comp.os.ms-windows.advocacy	Speculation and debate about Microsoft Windows.
comp.os.ms-windows.announce	Announcements relating to Windows. M
comp.os.ms-windows.apps.comm	MS-Windows communication applications.
comp.os.ms-windows.apps.financial	MS-Windows financial and tax software.
comp.os.ms-windows.apps.misc	MS-Windows applications.
comp.os.ms-windows.apps.utilities	MS-Windows utilities.
comp.os.ms-windows.apps.winsock.mail	Winsock e-mail applications.
comp.os.ms-windows.apps.winsock.misc	Other Winsock applications.
comp.os.ms-windows.apps.winsock.news	Winsock news applications.
comp.os.ms-windows.apps.word-proc	MS-Windows word-processing applications.
comp.os.ms-windows.misc	General discussions about Windows issues.
comp.os.ms-windows.networking. misc	Windows and other networks.
comp.os.ms-windows.networking.ras	Windows RAS networking.
comp.os.ms-windows.networking. tcp-ip	Windows and TCP/IP networking.
comp.os.ms-windows.networking. windows	Windows' built-in networking.
comp.os.ms-windows.nt.admin.misc	Windows NT system administration.
comp.os.ms-windows.nt.admin. networking	Windows NT network administration.
comp.os.ms-windows.nt.advocacy	Windows NT advocacy arguments.
comp.os.ms-windows.nt.misc	General discussion about Windows NT.
comp.os.ms-windows.nt.pre-release	Unreleased and beta Windows NT versions.
comp.os.ms-windows.nt.setup	Configuring Windows NT systems.
comp.os.ms-windows.nt.setup. hardware	Windows NT hardware setup.
comp.os.ms-windows.nt.setup.misc	Windows NT software setup.
comp.os.ms-windows.nt.software. backoffice	Windows NT BackOffice.
comp.os.ms-windows.nt.software. compatibility	Win NT software compatibility.
comp.os.ms-windows.nt.software. services	Windows NT system services software.
comp.os.ms-windows.pre-release	Pre-release/beta versions of Windows.

comp.os.ms-windows.programmer.controls	Controls, dialogs and VBXs.
comp.os.ms-windows.programmer.drivers	Drivers and VxDs – no driver requests!
comp.os.ms-windows.programmer.graphics	GDI, graphics and printing.
comp.os.ms-windows.programmer.memory	Memory management issues.
comp.os.ms-windows.programmer.misc	Programming Microsoft Windows.
comp.os.ms-windows.programmer.multimedia	Multimedia programming.
comp.os.ms-windows.programmer.networks	Network programming.
comp.os.ms-windows.programmer.nt.kernel-mode	Windows NT driver development.
comp.os.ms-windows.programmer.ole	OLE2, COM and DDE programming.
comp.os.ms-windows.programmer.tools	Development tools in Windows.
comp.os.ms-windows.programmer.tools.mfc	MFC-based development for Windows.
comp.os.ms-windows.programmer.tools.misc	Windows Development tools.
comp.os.ms-windows.programmer.tools.owl	OWL-based development for Windows.
comp.os.ms-windows.programmer.tools.winsock	Winsock programming.
comp.os.ms-windows.programmer.vxd	Windows VxD and driver development.
comp.os.ms-windows.programmer.win32	32-bit Windows programming interfaces.
comp.os.ms-windows.programmer.winhelp	WinHelp/Multimedia Viewer development.
comp.os.ms-windows.setup	Installing and configuring Microsoft Windows.
comp.os.ms-windows.video	Video adapters and drivers for Windows.
comp.os.ms-windows.win95.misc	Miscellaneous Topics about Windows 95.
comp.os.ms-windows.win95.setup	Setup and Configuration of Windows 95.
comp.os.msdos.apps	Discussion of applications that run under MS-DOS.
comp.os.msdos.desqview	QuarterDeck's Desqview and related products.
comp.os.msdos.djgpp	DOS GNU C/C++ applications and programming environment.
comp.os.msdos.mail-news	Administering mail and network news systems under MS-DOS.
comp.os.msdos.misc	Miscellaneous topics about MS-DOS machines.
comp.os.msdos.pcgeos	GeoWorks PC/GEOS and PC/GEOS-based packages.
comp.os.msdos.programmer	Programming MS-DOS machines.
comp.os.msdos.programmer.turbovision	Borland's text application libraries.
comp.os.netware.announce	Netware announcements. M
comp.os.netware.connectivity	Connectivity products (TCP/IP, SAA, NFS, MAC).
comp.os.netware.misc	General Netware topics.
comp.os.netware.security	Netware Security issues.
comp.os.os2.advocacy	Supporting and flaming OS/2.
comp.os.os2.announce	Notable news and announcements related to OS/2. M
comp.os.os2.apps	Discussions of applications under OS/2.
comp.os.os2.beta	All aspects of beta releases of OS/2 systems software.
comp.os.os2.bugs	OS/2 system bug reports, fixes and work-arounds.

comp.os.os2.comm	Modem/Fax hardware/drivers/apps/utils under OS/2.
comp.os.os2.games	Running games under OS/2.
comp.os.os2.mail-news	Mail and news apps/utils (on- and off-line) under OS/2.
comp.os.os2.marketplace	For sale/wanted; shopping; commercial ads; job postings.
comp.os.os2.misc	Miscellaneous topics about the OS/2 system.
comp.os.os2.multimedia	Multi-media on OS/2 systems.
comp.os.os2.networking.misc	Miscellaneous networking issues of OS/2.
comp.os.os2.networking.tcp-ip	TCP/IP under OS/2.
comp.os.os2.networking.www	World wide web (WWW) apps/utils under OS/2.
comp.os.os2.programmer.misc	Programming OS/2 machines.
comp.os.os2.programmer.oop	Programming system objects (SOM, WPS, etc).
comp.os.os2.programmer.porting	Porting software to OS/2 machines.
comp.os.os2.programmer.tools	Compilers, assemblers, interpreters under OS/2.
comp.os.os2.setup.misc	Installing/configuring OS/2; misc. hardware/drivers.
comp.os.os2.setup.storage	Disk/tape/CD-ROM hardware/drivers under OS/2.
comp.os.os2.setup.video	Base video hardware/drivers under OS/2.
comp.os.os2.utilities	General purpose utils (shells/backup/compression/etc).
comp.os.os9	Discussions about the os9 operating system.
comp.os.parix	Forum for users of the parallel operating system PARIX.
comp.os.plan9	Plan 9 from Bell Labs. M
comp.os.qnx	Using and developing under the QNX operating system.
comp.os.research	Operating systems and related areas. M
comp.os.vms	DEC's VAX* line of computers and VMS.
comp.os.vxworks	The VxWorks real-time operating system.
comp.os.xinu	The XINU operating system from Purdue (D. Comer).
comp.parallel	Massively parallel hardware/software. M
comp.parallel.mpi	Message Passing Interface (MPI).
comp.parallel.pvm	The PVM system of multi-computer parallelization.
comp.patents	Discussing patents of computer technology. M
comp.periphs	Peripheral devices.
comp.periphs.scsi	Discussion of SCSI-based peripheral devices.
comp.programming	Programming issues that transcend languages and OSs.
comp.programming.contests	Announcements and results of programming contests.
comp.programming.literate	Knuth's 'literate programming' method and tools.
comp.protocols.appletalk	Applebus hardware and software.
comp.protocols.dicom	Digital Imaging and Communications in Medicine.
comp.protocols.ibm	Networking with IBM mainframes.
comp.protocols.iso	The ISO protocol stack.
comp.protocols.kerberos	The Kerberos authentication server.
comp.protocols.kermit.announce	Kermit announcements. M
comp.protocols.kermit.misc	Kermit protocol and software.
comp.protocols.misc	Various forms and types of protocol.
comp.protocols.nfs	Discussion about the Network File System protocol.

comp.protocols.ppp	Discussion of the Internet Point to Point Protocol.
comp.protocols.smb	SMB file sharing protocol and Samba SMB server/client.
comp.protocols.tcp-ip	TCP and IP network protocols.
comp.protocols.tcp-ip.ibmpc	TCP/IP for IBM(-like) personal computers.
comp.publish.cdrom.hardware	Hardware used in publishing with CD-ROM.
comp.publish.cdrom.multimedia	Software for multimedia authoring and publishing.
comp.publish.cdrom.software	Software used in publishing with CD-ROM.
comp.publish.electronic.developer	Electronic publishing developer tools.
comp.publish.electronic.end-user	Electronic publishing end-user tools.
comp.publish.electronic.misc	General electronic publishing issues.
comp.publish.prepress	Electronic prepress.
comp.realtime	Issues related to real-time computing.
comp.research.japan	The nature of research in Japan. M
comp.risks	Risks to the public from computers and users. M
comp.robotics.misc	All aspects of robots and their applications.
comp.robotics.research	Academic, government and industry research in robotics. M
comp.security.firewalls	Anything pertaining to network firewall security.
comp.security.misc	Security issues of computers and networks.
comp.security.unix	Discussion of Unix security.
comp.simulation	Simulation methods, problems, uses. M
comp.society	The impact of technology on society. M
comp.society.cu-digest	The Computer Underground Digest. M
comp.society.development	Computer technology in developing countries.
comp.society.folklore	Computer folklore and culture, past and present. M
comp.society.futures	Events in technology affecting future computing.
comp.society.privacy	Effects of technology on privacy. M
comp.soft-sys.app-builder.appware	Novell's visual development environment.
comp.soft-sys.app-builder.uniface	Uniface Client/Server App Development.
comp.soft-sys.dce	The Distributed Computing Environment (DCE).
comp.soft-sys.khoros	The Khoros X11 visualisation system.
comp.soft-sys.math.mathematica	Mathematical discussion group. M
comp.soft-sys.matlab	The MathWorks calculation and visualization package.
comp.soft-sys.powerbuilder	Application development tools from PowerSoft.
comp.soft-sys.ptolemy	The Ptolemy simulation/code generation environment.
comp.soft-sys.sas	The SAS statistics package.
comp.soft-sys.shazam	The InternetAZAM econometrics computer program.
comp.soft-sys.spss	The SPSS statistics package.
comp.software-eng	Software Engineering and related topics.
comp.software.config-mgmt	Configuration management, tools and procedures.
comp.software.international	Finding, using, and writing non-English software.
comp.software.licensing	Software licensing technology.
comp.software.testing	All aspects of testing computer systems.
comp.sources.3b1	Source code-only postings for the AT&T 3b1. M
comp.sources.acorn	Source code-only postings for the Acorn. M
comp.sources.amiga	Source code-only postings for the Amiga. M
comp.sources.apple2	Source code and discussion for the Apple2. M
comp.sources.atari.st	Source code-only postings for the Atari ST. M
comp.sources.bugs	Bug reports, fixes, discussion for posted sources.
comp.sources.d	For any discussion of source postings.

comp.sources.games	Postings of recreational software. M
comp.sources.games.bugs	Bug reports and fixes for posted game software.
comp.sources.hp48	Programs for the HP48 and HP28 calculators. M
comp.sources.mac	Software for the Apple Macintosh. M
comp.sources.misc	Posting of software. M
comp.sources.postscript	Source code for programs written in PostScript. M
comp.sources.reviewed	Source code evaluated by peer review. M
comp.sources.sun	Software for Sun workstations. M
comp.sources.testers	Finding people to test software.
comp.sources.unix	Postings of complete, UNIX-oriented sources. M
comp.sources.wanted	Requests for software and fixes.
comp.sources.x	Software for the X Window System. M
comp.specification.larch	Larch family of formal specification languages.
comp.specification.misc	Formal specification methods in general.
comp.specification.z	Discussion about the formal specification notation Z.
comp.speech	Research and applications in speech science and technology.
comp.std.c	Discussion about C language standards.
comp.std.c++	Discussion about C++ language, library, standards. M
comp.std.internat	Discussion about international standards.
comp.std.lisp	User group (ALU) supported standards. M
comp.std.misc	Discussion about various standards.
comp.std.mumps	Discussions about Mumps standards. M
comp.std.unix	Discussion for the P1003 committee on UNIX. M
comp.std.wireless	Examining standards for wireless network technology. M
comp.sw.components	Software components and related technology.
comp.sys.3b1	Discussion and support of ATandT 7300/3B1/UnixPC.
comp.sys.acorn.advocacy	Why Acorn computers and programs are better.
comp.sys.acorn.announce	Announcements for Acorn and ARM users. M
comp.sys.acorn.apps	Acorn software applications.
comp.sys.acorn.games	Discussion of games for Acorn machines.
comp.sys.acorn.hardware	Acorn hardware.
comp.sys.acorn.misc	Acorn computing in general.
comp.sys.acorn.networking	Networking of Acorn computers.
comp.sys.acorn.programmer	Programming of Acorn computers.
comp.sys.alliant	Info and discussion about Alliant computers.
comp.sys.amiga.advocacy	Why an Amiga is better than XYZ.
comp.sys.amiga.announce	Announcements about the Amiga. M
comp.sys.amiga.applications	Miscellaneous applications.
comp.sys.amiga.audio	Music, MIDI, speech synthesis, other sounds.
comp.sys.amiga.cd32	Technical and computing talk for Commodore Amiga CD32.
comp.sys.amiga.datacomm	Methods of getting bytes in and out.
comp.sys.amiga.emulations	Various hardware and software emulators.
comp.sys.amiga.games	Discussion of games for the Commodore Amiga.
comp.sys.amiga.graphics	Charts, graphs, pictures, etc.
comp.sys.amiga.hardware	Amiga computer hardware, Q and A, reviews, etc.
comp.sys.amiga.introduction	Group for newcomers to Amigas.
comp.sys.amiga.marketplace	Where to find it, prices, etc.
comp.sys.amiga.misc	Discussions not falling in another Amiga group.
comp.sys.amiga.multimedia	Animations, video, and multimedia.
comp.sys.amiga.networking	Amiga networking software/hardware.
comp.sys.amiga.programmer	Developers and hobbyists discuss code.
comp.sys.amiga.reviews	Reviews of Amiga software, hardware. M

comp.sys.amiga.uucp	Amiga UUCP packages.
comp.sys.amstrad.8bit	Amstrad CPC/PcW/GX4000 software/hardware.
comp.sys.apollo	Apollo computer systems.
comp.sys.apple2	Discussion about Apple II micros.
comp.sys.apple2.comm	Apple II data communications.
comp.sys.apple2.gno	The AppleIIgs GNO multitasking environment.
comp.sys.apple2.marketplace	Buying, selling and trading Apple II equipment.
comp.sys.apple2.programmer	Programming on the Apple II.
comp.sys.apple2.usergroups	All about Apple II user groups.
comp.sys.arm	The ARM processor architecture and support chips.
comp.sys.atari.8bit	Discussion about 8 bit Atari micros.
comp.sys.atari.advocacy	Attacking and defending Atari computers.
comp.sys.atari.announce	Atari related hard/software announcements. M
comp.sys.atari.programmer	Programming on the Atari computer.
comp.sys.atari.st	Discussion about 16 bit Atari micros.
comp.sys.atari.st.tech	Technical discussions of Atari ST hard/software.
comp.sys.att	Discussions about ATandT microcomputers.
comp.sys.cbm	Discussion about Commodore micros.
comp.sys.concurrent	The Concurrent/Masscomp line of computers. M
comp.sys.convex	Convex computer systems hardware and software.
comp.sys.dec	Discussions about DEC computer systems.
comp.sys.dec.micro	DEC Micros (Rainbow, Professional 350/380).
comp.sys.encore	Encore's MultiMax computers.
comp.sys.harris	Harris computer systems, especially real-time systems.
comp.sys.hp.apps	Discussion of software and apps on all HP platforms.
comp.sys.hp.hardware	Discussion of Hewlett Packard system hardware.
comp.sys.hp.hpux	Issues pertaining to HP-UX and 9000 series computers.
comp.sys.hp.misc	Issues not covered in any other comp.sys.hp.* group.
comp.sys.hp.mpe	Issues pertaining to MPE and 3000 series computers.
comp.sys.hp48	Hewlett-Packard's HP48 and HP28 calculators.
comp.sys.ibm.pc.demos	Demonstration programs which showcase programmer skill.
comp.sys.ibm.pc.digest	The IBM PC, PC-XT, and PC-AT. M
comp.sys.ibm.pc.games.action	Arcade-style games on PCs.
comp.sys.ibm.pc.games.adventure	Adventure (non-rpg) games on PCs.
comp.sys.ibm.pc.games.announce	Announcements for all PC gamers. M
comp.sys.ibm.pc.games.flight-sim	Flight simulators on PCs.
comp.sys.ibm.pc.games.marketplace	PC clone games wanted and for sale.
comp.sys.ibm.pc.games.misc	Games not covered by other PC groups.
comp.sys.ibm.pc.games.rpg	Role-playing games on the PC.
comp.sys.ibm.pc.games.strategic	Strategy/planning games on PCs.
comp.sys.ibm.pc.hardware.cd-rom	CD-ROM drives and interfaces for the PC.
comp.sys.ibm.pc.hardware.chips	Processor, cache, memory chips, etc.
comp.sys.ibm.pc.hardware.comm	Modems and communication cards for the PC.
comp.sys.ibm.pc.hardware.misc	Miscellaneous PC hardware topics.
comp.sys.ibm.pc.hardware.networking	Network hardware and equipment for the PC.
comp.sys.ibm.pc.hardware.storage	Hard drives and other PC storage devices.
comp.sys.ibm.pc.hardware.systems	Whole IBM PC computer and clone systems.
comp.sys.ibm.pc.hardware.video	Video cards and monitors for the PC.
comp.sys.ibm.pc.misc	Discussion about IBM personal computers.
comp.sys.ibm.pc.rt	Topics related to IBM's RT computer.
comp.sys.ibm.pc.soundcard.advocacy	Advocacy for a particular soundcard.

comp.sys.ibm.pc.soundcard.games	Questions about using soundcards with games.
comp.sys.ibm.pc.soundcard.misc	Soundcards in general.
comp.sys.ibm.pc.soundcard.music	Music and sound questions using soundcards.
comp.sys.ibm.pc.soundcard.tech	Technical questions about PC soundcards.
comp.sys.ibm.ps2.hardware	Microchannel hardware, any vendor.
comp.sys.intel	Discussions about Intel systems and parts.
comp.sys.isis	The ISIS distributed system from Cornell.
comp.sys.laptops	Laptop (portable) computers.
comp.sys.m6809	Discussion about 6809s.
comp.sys.m68k	Discussion about 68ks.
comp.sys.m68k.pc	Discussion about 68k-based PCs. M
comp.sys.m88k	Discussion about 88k-based computers.
comp.sys.mac.advocacy	The Macintosh computer family compared to others.
comp.sys.mac.announce	Important notices for Macintosh users. M
comp.sys.mac.apps	Discussions of Macintosh applications.
comp.sys.mac.comm	Discussion of Macintosh communications.
comp.sys.mac.databases	Database systems for the Apple Macintosh.
comp.sys.mac.digest	Apple Macintosh: info and uses, but no programs.
comp.sys.mac.games.action	Action games for the Macintosh.
comp.sys.mac.games.adventure	Adventure games for the Macintosh.
comp.sys.mac.games.announce	Announcements for Mac gamers. M
comp.sys.mac.games.flight-sim	Flight simulator gameplay on the Mac.
comp.sys.mac.games.marketplace	Macintosh games for sale and trade.
comp.sys.mac.games.misc	Macintosh games not covered in other groups.
comp.sys.mac.games.strategic	Strategy/planning games on the Macintosh.
comp.sys.mac.graphics	Macintosh graphics: paint, draw, 3D, CAD, animation.
comp.sys.mac.hardware.misc	General Mac hardware topics not already covered.
comp.sys.mac.hardware.storage	All forms of Mac storage hardware and media.
comp.sys.mac.hardware.video	Video input and output hardware on the Mac.
comp.sys.mac.hypercard	The Macintosh Hypercard: info and uses.
comp.sys.mac.misc	General discussions about the Apple Macintosh.
comp.sys.mac.oop.macapp3	Version 3 of the MacApp object oriented system.
comp.sys.mac.oop.misc	Object oriented programming issues on the Mac.
comp.sys.mac.oop.tcl	Symantec's THINK Class Library for object programming.
comp.sys.mac.portables	Discussion particular to laptop Macintoshes.
comp.sys.mac.printing	All about printing hardware and software on the Mac.
comp.sys.mac.programmer.codewarrior	Macintosh programming using CodeWarrior.
comp.sys.mac.programmer.help	Help with Macintosh programming.
comp.sys.mac.programmer.info	Frequently requested information. M
comp.sys.mac.programmer.misc	Other issues of Macintosh programming.
comp.sys.mac.programmer.tools	Macintosh programming tools.
comp.sys.mac.scitech	Using the Macintosh in scientific and technological work.
comp.sys.mac.system	Discussions of Macintosh system software.
comp.sys.mac.wanted	Postings of 'I want XYZ for my Mac.'
comp.sys.mentor	Mentor Graphics products and the Silicon Compiler System.
comp.sys.mips	Systems based on MIPS chips.
comp.sys.misc	Discussion about computers of all kinds.
comp.sys.msx	The MSX home computer system.
comp.sys.ncr	Discussion about NCR computers.
comp.sys.newton.announce	Newton information posts. M
comp.sys.newton.misc	Miscellaneous discussion about Newton systems.

comp.sys.newton.programmer	Discussion of Newton software development.
comp.sys.next.advocacy	The NeXT religion.
comp.sys.next.announce	Announcements related to the NeXT computer system. M
comp.sys.next.bugs	Discussion and solutions for known NeXT bugs.
comp.sys.next.hardware	Discussing the physical aspects of NeXT computers.
comp.sys.next.marketplace	NeXT hardware, software and jobs.
comp.sys.next.misc	General discussion about the NeXT computer system.
comp.sys.next.programmer	NeXT related programming issues.
comp.sys.next.software	Function, use and availability of NeXT programs.
comp.sys.next.sysadmin	Discussions related to NeXT system administration.
comp.sys.nsc.32k	National Semiconductor 32000 series chips.
comp.sys.palmtops	Super-powered calculators in the palm of your hand.
comp.sys.pen	Interacting with computers through pen gestures.
comp.sys.powerpc	General PowerPC Discussion.
comp.sys.prime	Prime Computer products.
comp.sys.proteon	Proteon gateway products.
comp.sys.psion	Discussion about PSION Personal Computers and Organisers.
comp.sys.pyramid	Pyramid 90x computers.
comp.sys.ridge	Ridge 32 computers and ROS.
comp.sys.sequent	Sequent systems (Balance and Symmetry).
comp.sys.sgi.admin	System administration on Silicon Graphics' Irises.
comp.sys.sgi.announce	Announcements for the SGI community. M
comp.sys.sgi.apps	Applications which run on the Iris.
comp.sys.sgi.audio	Audio on SGI systems.
comp.sys.sgi.bugs	Bugs found in the IRIX operating system.
comp.sys.sgi.graphics	Graphics packages and issues on SGI machines.
comp.sys.sgi.hardware	Base systems and peripherals for Iris computers.
comp.sys.sgi.misc	General discussion about Silicon Graphics's machines.
comp.sys.sinclair	Sinclair computers, eg. the ZX81, Spectrum and QL.
comp.sys.stratus	Stratus products, incl. System/88, CPS-32, VOS and FTX.
comp.sys.sun.admin	Sun system administration issues and questions.
comp.sys.sun.announce	Sun announcements and Sunergy mailings. M
comp.sys.sun.apps	Software applications for Sun computer systems.
comp.sys.sun.hardware	Sun Microsystems hardware.
comp.sys.sun.misc	Miscellaneous discussions about Sun products.
comp.sys.sun.wanted	People looking for Sun products and support.
comp.sys.tahoe	CCI 6/32, Harris HCX/7, and Sperry 7000 computers.
comp.sys.tandy	Discussion about Tandy computers: new and old.
comp.sys.ti	Discussion about Texas Instruments.
comp.sys.transputer	The Transputer computer and OCCAM language.
comp.sys.unisys	Sperry, Burroughs, Convergent and Unisys* systems.
comp.sys.xerox	Xerox 1100 workstations and protocols.
comp.sys.zenith.z100	The Zenith Z-100 (Heath H-100) family of computers.
comp.terminals	All sorts of terminals.
comp.text	Text processing issues and methods.

comp.text.desktop	Technology and techniques of desktop publishing.
comp.text.frame	Desktop publishing with FrameMaker.
comp.text.interleaf	Applications and use of Interleaf software.
comp.text.pdf	Adobe Acrobat and Portable Document Format technology.
comp.text.sgml	ISO 8879 SGML, structured documents, markup languages.
comp.text.tex	Discussion about the TeX and LaTeX systems and macros.
comp.theory.info-retrieval	Information Retrieval topics. M
comp.unix.admin	Administering a Unix-based system.
comp.unix.advocacy	Arguments for and against Unix and Unix versions.
comp.unix.aix	IBM's version of UNIX.
comp.unix.amiga	Minix, SYSV4 and other *nix on an Amiga.
comp.unix.aux	The version of UNIX for Apple Macintosh II computers.
comp.unix.bsd.386bsd.announce	Announcements pertaining to 386BSD. M
comp.unix.bsd.386bsd.misc	386BSD operating system.
comp.unix.bsd.bsdi.announce	Announcements pertaining to BSD/OS. M
comp.unix.bsd.bsdi.misc	BSD/OS operating system.
comp.unix.bsd.freebsd.announce	Announcements pertaining to FreeBSD. M
comp.unix.bsd.freebsd.misc	FreeBSD operating system.
comp.unix.bsd.misc	BSD operating systems.
comp.unix.bsd.netbsd.announce	Announcements pertaining to NetBSD. M
comp.unix.bsd.netbsd.misc	NetBSD operating system.
comp.unix.dos-under-unix	MS-DOS running under UNIX by whatever means.
comp.unix.internals	Discussions on hacking UNIX internals.
comp.unix.large	UNIX on mainframes and in large networks.
comp.unix.machten	The MachTen operating system and related issues.
comp.unix.misc	Various topics that don't fit other groups.
comp.unix.osf.misc	Various aspects of Open Software Foundation products.
comp.unix.osf.osf1	The Open Software Foundation's OSF/1.
comp.unix.pc-clone.16bit	UNIX on 286 architectures.
comp.unix.pc-clone.32bit	UNIX on 386 and 486 architectures.
comp.unix.programmer	QandA for people programming under Unix.
comp.unix.questions	UNIX neophytes group.
comp.unix.sco.announce	SCO and related product announcements. M
comp.unix.sco.misc	SCO Unix, Systems, and Environments.
comp.unix.sco.programmer	Programming in and for SCO Environments.
comp.unix.shell	Using and programming the Unix shell.
comp.unix.sys3	System III UNIX discussions.
comp.unix.sys5.misc	Versions of System V which predate Release 3.
comp.unix.sys5.r3	Discussing System V Release 3.
comp.unix.sys5.r4	Discussing System V Release 4.
comp.unix.ultrix	Discussions about DEC's Ultrix.
comp.unix.unixware.announce	Announcements related to UnixWare. M
comp.unix.unixware.misc	Products of Novell's Unix Systems Group.
comp.unix.user-friendly	Discussion of UNIX user-friendliness.
comp.unix.wizards	For only true Unix wizards. M
comp.unix.xenix.misc	General discussions regarding XENIX (except SCO).
comp.unix.xenix.sco	XENIX versions from the Santa Cruz Operation.
comp.virus	Computer viruses and security. M
comp.windows.garnet	The Garnet user interface development environment.

comp.windows.interviews	The InterViews object-oriented windowing system.
comp.windows.misc	Various issues about windowing systems.
comp.windows.news	Sun Microsystems' NeWS window system.
comp.windows.open-look	Discussion about the Open Look GUI.
comp.windows.suit	The SUIT user-interface toolkit.
comp.windows.ui-builders.teleuse	Using/augmenting the TeleUSE UI Builder.
comp.windows.ui-builders.uimx	Using and augmenting the UIM/X UI Builder.
comp.windows.x	Discussion about the X Window System.
comp.windows.x.announce	X Window System announcements. M
comp.windows.x.apps	Getting and using, not programming, applications for X.
comp.windows.x.i386unix	The XFree86 window system and others.
comp.windows.x.intrinsics	Discussion of the X toolkit.
humanities.answers	Repository for periodic USENET articles. M
humanities.lit.authors.shakespeare	Poetry, plays, history of Shakespeare.
humanities.misc	General topics in the arts and humanities.
misc.activism.militia	Citizens bearing arms for the common defence. M
misc.activism.progressive	Information for Progressive activists. M
misc.answers	Repository for periodic USENET articles. M
misc.books.technical	Discussion of books about technical topics.
misc.business.consulting	The business of consulting. M
misc.business.facilitators	Discussions for all types of facilitators.
misc.business.records-mgmt	All aspects of professional records management.
misc.consumers	Consumer interests, product reviews, etc.
misc.consumers.house	Discussion about owning and maintaining a house.
misc.creativity	Promoting the use of creativity in all human endeavours.
misc.education	Discussion of the educational system.
misc.education.adult	Adult education and adult literacy practice/research.
misc.education.home-school.christian	Christian home-schooling.
misc.education.home-school.misc	Almost anything about home-schooling.
misc.education.language.english	Teaching English to speakers of other languages.
misc.education.medical	Issues related to medical education.
misc.education.multimedia	Multimedia for education. M
misc.education.science	Issues related to science education.
misc.emerg-services	Forum for paramedics and other first responders.
misc.entrepreneurs	Discussion on operating a business.
misc.entrepreneurs.moderated	Entrepreneur/business topics. M
misc.fitness.aerobic	All forms of aerobic activity.
misc.fitness.misc	All other general fitness topics.
misc.fitness.weights	Bodybuilding, weightlifting, resistance.
misc.forsale.computers.discussion	Discussions only about items for sale.
misc.forsale.computers.mac-specific.cards.misc	Macintosh expansion cards.
misc.forsale.computers.mac-specific.cards.video	Macintosh video cards.
misc.forsale.computers.mac-specific.misc	Other Macintosh equipment.
misc.forsale.computers.mac-specific.portables	Portable Macintosh systems.
misc.forsale.computers.mac-specific.software	Macintosh software.
misc.forsale.computers.mac-specific.systems	Complete Macintosh systems.
misc.forsale.computers.memory	Memory chips and modules for sale and wanted.

misc.forsale.computers.modems	Modems for sale and wanted.
misc.forsale.computers.monitors	Monitors and displays for sale and wanted.
misc.forsale.computers.net-hardware	Networking hardware for sale and wanted.
misc.forsale.computers.other.misc	Miscellaneous other equipment.
misc.forsale.computers.other.software	Software for other systems.
misc.forsale.computers.other.systems	Complete other types of systems.
misc.forsale.computers.pc-specific.audio	PC audio equipment.
misc.forsale.computers.pc-specific.cards.misc	PC expansion cards.
misc.forsale.computers.pc-specific.cards.video	PC video cards.
misc.forsale.computers.pc-specific.misc	Other PC-specific equipment.
misc.forsale.computers.pc-specific.motherboards	PC motherboards.
misc.forsale.computers.pc-specific.portables	Portable PC systems.
misc.forsale.computers.pc-specific.software	PC software.
misc.forsale.computers.pc-specific.systems	Complete PC systems.
misc.forsale.computers.printers	Printers and plotters for sale and wanted.
misc.forsale.computers.storage	Disk, CDROM and tape drives for sale and wanted.
misc.forsale.computers.workstation	Workstation related computer items.
misc.forsale.non-computer	Non-computer items for sale and wanted.
misc.handicap	Items of interest for/about the handicapped. M
misc.headlines	Current interest: drug testing, terrorism, etc.
misc.health.aids	AIDS issues and support.
misc.health.alternative	Alternative, complementary and holistic health care.
misc.health.arthritis	Arthritis and related disorders.
misc.health.diabetes	Discussion of diabetes management in day to day life.
misc.immigration.canada	Canada immigration issues.
misc.immigration.misc	Miscellaneous countries immigration issues.
misc.immigration.usa	USA immigration issues.
misc.industry.pulp-and-paper	Technical topics in the pulp and paper industry.
misc.industry.quality	Quality standards and other issues.
misc.industry.utilities.electric	The electric utility industry.
misc.int-property	Discussion of intellectual property rights.
misc.invest	Investments and the handling of money.
misc.invest.canada	Investing in Canadian financial markets.
misc.invest.funds	Sharing info about bond, stock, real estate funds.
misc.invest.futures	Physical commodity and financial futures markets.
misc.invest.real-estate	Property investments.
misc.invest.stocks	Forum for sharing info about stocks and options.
misc.invest.technical	Analysing market trends with technical methods.
misc.jobs.contract	Discussions about contract labour.
misc.jobs.misc	Discussion about employment, workplaces, careers.
misc.jobs.offered	Announcements of positions available.
misc.jobs.offered.entry	Job listings only for entry-level positions.
misc.jobs.resumes	Postings of resumes and 'situation wanted' articles.
misc.kids	Children, their behaviour and activities.
misc.kids.computer	The use of computers by children.
misc.kids.consumers	Products related to kids.

misc.kids.health	Children's health.
misc.kids.info	Informational posts related to misc.kids hierarchy. M
misc.kids.pregnancy	Pre-pregnancy planning, pregnancy, childbirth.
misc.kids.vacation	Discussion on all forms of family-oriented vacationing.
misc.legal	Legalities and the ethics of law.
misc.legal.computing	Discussing the legal climate of the computing world.
misc.legal.moderated	All aspects of law. M
misc.misc	Various discussions not fitting in any other group.
misc.news.bosnia	News, articles, reports and information on Bosnia.
misc.news.east-europe.rferl	Radio Free Europe/Radio Liberty Daily Report. M
misc.news.southasia	News from Bangladesh, India, Nepal, etc. M
misc.rural	Devoted to issues concerning rural living.
misc.survivalism	Disaster and long-term survival techniques and theory.
misc.taxes	Tax laws and advice.
misc.test	For testing of network software. Very boring.
misc.test.moderated	Testing of posting to moderated groups. M
misc.transport.air-industry	Airlines, airports, commercial aircraft. M
misc.transport.rail.americas	Railroads and railways in North and South America.
misc.transport.rail.australia-nz	Railways in Australia and New Zealand.
misc.transport.rail.europe	Railroads and railways in all of Europe.
misc.transport.rail.misc	Miscellaneous rail issues and discussions.
misc.transport.trucking	Commercial trucking related issues.
misc.transport.urban-transit	Metropolitan public transportation systems.
misc.wanted	Requests for things that are needed (not software).
misc.writing	Discussion of writing in all of its forms.
misc.writing.screenplays	Aspects of writing and selling screenplays.
news.admin.hierarchies	Network news hierarchies.
news.admin.misc	General topics of network news administration.
news.admin.net-abuse.announce	Information regarding network resource abuse. M
news.admin.net-abuse.misc	Network facility abuse, including spamming.
news.admin.technical	Technical aspects of maintaining network news. M
news.announce.conferences	Calls for papers and conference announcements. M
news.announce.important	General announcements of interest to all. M
news.announce.newgroups	Calls for newgroups and announcements of same.
news.announce.newusers	Explanatory postings for new users. M
news.answers	Repository for periodic USENET articles. M
news.groups	Discussions and lists of news groups.
news.groups.questions	Where can I find talk about topic X?
news.groups.reviews	What is going on in group or mailing list named X? M
news.lists	News-related statistics and lists. M
news.lists.ps-maps	Maps relating to USENET traffic flows. M
news.misc	Discussions of USENET itself.
news.newusers.questions	Q and A for users new to the Usenet.
news.software.anu-news	VMS B-news software from Australian National Univ.

news.software.b	Discussion about B-news-compatible software.
news.software.nn	Discussion about the 'nn' news reader package.
news.software.nntp	The Network News Transfer Protocol.
news.software.readers	Discussion of software used to read network news.
rec.animals.wildlife	Wildlife related discussions/information.
rec.answers	Repository for periodic USENET articles. M
rec.antiques	Discussing antiques and vintage items.
rec.antiques.marketplace	Buying/selling/trading antiques.
rec.antiques.radio+phono	Audio devices and materials of yesteryear.
rec.aquaria	Keeping fish and aquaria as a hobby.
rec.arts.animation	Discussion of various kinds of animation.
rec.arts.anime	Japanese animation fen discussion.
rec.arts.anime.info	Announcements about Japanese animation. M
rec.arts.anime.marketplace	Things for sale in the Japanese animation world.
rec.arts.anime.stories	All about Japanese comic fanzines. M
rec.arts.ascii	ASCII art, info on archives, art, and artists. M
rec.arts.bodyart	Tattoos and body decoration discussions.
rec.arts.bonsai	Dwarfish trees and shrubbery.
rec.arts.books	Books of all genres, and the publishing industry.
rec.arts.books.childrens	All aspects of children's literature.
rec.arts.books.hist-fiction	Historical fictions (novels) in general.
rec.arts.books.marketplace	Buying and selling of books.
rec.arts.books.reviews	Book reviews. M
rec.arts.books.tolkien	The works of J.R.R. Tolkien.
rec.arts.comics.alternative	Alternative (non-mainstream) comic books.
rec.arts.comics.creative	Encouraging good superhero-style writing.
rec.arts.comics.dc.lsh	The Legion of Super-Heroes and related characters.
rec.arts.comics.dc.universe	DC Comics' shared universe and characters.
rec.arts.comics.dc.vertigo	Comics from the Vertigo imprint.
rec.arts.comics.elfquest	The Elfquest universe and characters.
rec.arts.comics.info	Reviews, convention information and other comics news. M
rec.arts.comics.marketplace	The exchange of comics and comic related items.
rec.arts.comics.marvel.universe	Marvel Comics' shared universe and characters.
rec.arts.comics.marvel.xbooks	The Mutant Universe of Marvel Comics.
rec.arts.comics.misc	Comic books, graphic novels, sequential art.
rec.arts.comics.other-media	Comic book spinoffs in other media.
rec.arts.comics.strips	Discussion of short-form comics.
rec.arts.dance	Any aspects of dance not covered in another news group.
rec.arts.disney.animation	Animated features, cartoons, short subjects.
rec.arts.disney.announce	FAQs, lists, info, announcements. M
rec.arts.disney.merchandise	Toys, videos, music, books, art, collectibles.
rec.arts.disney.misc	General topics pertinent to the Disney Company.
rec.arts.disney.parks	Parks, resorts, dining, attractions, vacations.
rec.arts.drwho	Discussion about Dr Who.
rec.arts.erotica	Erotic fiction and verse. M
rec.arts.fine	Fine arts and artists.
rec.arts.int-fiction	Discussions about interactive fiction.
rec.arts.manga	All aspects of the Japanese storytelling art form.
rec.arts.marching.band.college	College marching bands.
rec.arts.marching.band.high-school	High school marching bands.
rec.arts.marching.colorguard	Competitive colour guard activity.
rec.arts.marching.drumcorps	Drum and bugle corps.
rec.arts.marching.misc	Marching-related performance activities.
rec.arts.misc	Discussions about the arts not in other groups.
rec.arts.movies.announce	Newsworthy events in the movie business. M

rec.arts.movies.current-films	The latest movie releases.
rec.arts.movies.lists+surveys	Top-N lists and general surveys.
rec.arts.movies.local.indian	Indian movies and the Indian film industry.
rec.arts.movies.misc	General aspects of movies not covered by other groups.
rec.arts.movies.movie-going	Going-to-movies experiences.
rec.arts.movies.past-films	Past movies.
rec.arts.movies.people	People in the movie business.
rec.arts.movies.production	Filmmaking, amateur and professional.
rec.arts.movies.reviews	Reviews of movies. M
rec.arts.movies.tech	Technical aspects of movies.
rec.arts.mystery	Mystery and crime books, plays and films.
rec.arts.poems	For the posting of poems.
rec.arts.prose	Short works of prose fiction and follow-up discussion.
rec.arts.puppetry	For discussion of puppets in any form or venue.
rec.arts.sf.announce	Major announcements of the SF world. M
rec.arts.sf.fandom	Discussions of SF fan activities.
rec.arts.sf.marketplace	Personal for sale notices of SF materials.
rec.arts.sf.misc	Science fiction lovers' news group.
rec.arts.sf.movies	Discussing SF motion pictures.
rec.arts.sf.reviews	Reviews of science fiction/fantasy/horror works.
rec.arts.sf.science	Real and speculative aspects of SF science.
rec.arts.sf.starwars.collecting	Topics relating to Star Wars collecting.
rec.arts.sf.starwars.games	Star Wars games: RPG, computer, card, etc.
rec.arts.sf.starwars.info	General information pertaining to Star Wars. M
rec.arts.sf.starwars.misc	Miscellaneous topics pertaining to Star Wars.
rec.arts.sf.tv	Discussing general television SF.
rec.arts.sf.tv.babylon5	Babylon 5 creators meet Babylon 5 fans.
rec.arts.sf.tv.quantum-leap	Quantum Leap TV, comics, cons, etc.
rec.arts.sf.written	Discussion of written science fiction and fantasy.
rec.arts.sf.written.robert-jordan	Books by author Robert Jordan.
rec.arts.startrek.current	New Star Trek shows, movies and books.
rec.arts.startrek.fandom	Star Trek conventions and memorabilia.
rec.arts.startrek.info	Information about the universe of Star Trek. M
rec.arts.startrek.misc	General discussions of Star Trek.
rec.arts.startrek.reviews	Reviews of Star Trek books, episodes, films, etc.
rec.arts.startrek.tech	Star Trek's depiction of future technologies.
rec.arts.theatre.misc	Miscellaneous topics and issues in theatre.
rec.arts.theatre.musicals	Musical theatre around the world.
rec.arts.theatre.plays	Dramaturgy and discussion of plays.
rec.arts.theatre.stagecraft	Issues in stagecraft and production.
rec.arts.tv	The boob tube, its history, and past and current shows.
rec.arts.tv.interactive	Developments in interactive television.
rec.arts.tv.mst3k.announce	Mystery Science Theatre 3000 announcements. M
rec.arts.tv.mst3k.misc	For fans of Mystery Science Theatre 3000.
rec.arts.tv.soaps.abc	Soap operas produced by or for the ABC network.
rec.arts.tv.soaps.cbs	Soap operas produced by or for the CBS network.
rec.arts.tv.soaps.misc	Postings of interest to all soap opera viewers.
rec.arts.tv.uk.comedy	Regarding UK-based comedy shows.
rec.arts.tv.uk.coronation-st	Regarding the UK based show Coronation Street.
rec.arts.tv.uk.eastenders	Regarding the UK based show Eastenders.
rec.arts.tv.uk.misc	Miscellaneous topics about UK-based television.
rec.arts.wobegon	'A Prairie Home Companion' radio show discussion.
rec.audio.car	Discussions of automobile audio systems.

rec.audio.high-end	High-end audio systems. M
rec.audio.marketplace	Buying and selling of home audio equipment.
rec.audio.misc	Post about audio here if you can't post anywhere else.
rec.audio.opinion	Everybody's two bits on audio in your home.
rec.audio.pro	Professional audio recording and studio engineering.
rec.audio.tech	Theoretical, factual, and DIY topics in home audio.
rec.audio.tubes	Electronic audio circuits which use vacuum tubes.
rec.autos.4x4	The on and off-road four-wheel drive vehicle.
rec.autos.antique	Discussing all aspects of automobiles over 25 years old.
rec.autos.driving	Driving automobiles.
rec.autos.makers.chrysler	Dodge, Plymouth, Jeep, Eagle, etc. info/talk.
rec.autos.makers.ford.mustang	Ford Mustangs in all their flavours.
rec.autos.makers.saturn	All about Saturn cars, fans and company.
rec.autos.makers.vw.aircooled	Bug, Bus, Ghia, Squareback, Thing, etc.
rec.autos.makers.vw.watercooled	Golf, Jetta, Corrado, Vanagon, new models, etc.
rec.autos.marketplace	Buy/Sell/Trade automobiles, parts, tools, accessories.
rec.autos.misc	Miscellaneous discussion about automobiles.
rec.autos.rod-n-custom	High performance automobiles.
rec.autos.simulators	Discussion of automotive simulators.
rec.autos.sport.f1	Formula 1 motor racing.
rec.autos.sport.indy	Indy Car motor racing.
rec.autos.sport.info	Auto racing news, results, announcements. M
rec.autos.sport.misc	Organized, legal auto competitions.
rec.autos.sport.nascar	NASCAR and other professional stock car racing.
rec.autos.sport.tech	Technical aspects and technology of auto racing.
rec.autos.tech	Technical aspects of automobiles, etc.
rec.autos.vw	Issues pertaining to Volkswagen products.
rec.aviation.announce	Events of interest to the aviation community. M
rec.aviation.answers	Frequently asked questions about aviation. M
rec.aviation.hang-gliding	Hang-gliding, paragliding, foot-launched flight.
rec.aviation.homebuilt	Selecting, designing, building, and restoring aircraft.
rec.aviation.ifr	Flying under Instrument Flight Rules.
rec.aviation.marketplace	Aviation classifieds.
rec.aviation.military	Military aircraft of the past, present and future.
rec.aviation.misc	Miscellaneous topics in aviation.
rec.aviation.owning	Information on owning airplanes.
rec.aviation.piloting	General discussion for aviators.
rec.aviation.products	Reviews and discussion of products useful to pilots.
rec.aviation.questions	Aviation questions and answers. M
rec.aviation.rotorcraft	Helicopters and other rotary wing aircraft.
rec.aviation.simulators	Flight simulation on all levels.
rec.aviation.soaring	All aspects of sailplanes and hang-gliders.
rec.aviation.stories	Anecdotes of flight experiences. M
rec.aviation.student	Learning to fly.
rec.aviation.ultralight	Light aircraft in general, all topics.
rec.backcountry	Activities in the great outdoors.
rec.bicycles.marketplace	Buying, selling and reviewing items for cycling.
rec.bicycles.misc	General discussion of bicycling.
rec.bicycles.off-road	All aspects of off-road bicycling.
rec.bicycles.racing	Bicycle racing techniques, rules and results.
rec.bicycles.rides	Discussions of tours and training or commuting routes.

rec.bicycles.soc	Societal issues of bicycling.
rec.bicycles.tech	Cycling product design, construction, maintenance, etc.
rec.birds	Hobbyists interested in bird watching.
rec.boats	Hobbyists interested in boating.
rec.boats.building	Boat building, design, restoration, and repair.
rec.boats.cruising	Cruising in boats.
rec.boats.marketplace	Boating products for sale and wanted. M
rec.boats.paddle	Talk about any boats with oars, paddles, etc.
rec.boats.racing	Boat racing.
rec.climbing	Climbing techniques, competition announcements, etc.
rec.collecting	Discussion among collectors of many things.
rec.collecting.cards.discuss	Discussion of sports and non-sports cards.
rec.collecting.cards.non-sports	Non-sports cards.
rec.collecting.coins	Coin, currency, medal, etc. collecting forum.
rec.collecting.dolls	Doll and bear collecting and crafting.
rec.collecting.phonecards	Info and Marketplace group for phonecards.
rec.collecting.sport.baseball	Baseball memorabilia (cards, photos, etc).
rec.collecting.sport.basketball	Basketball memorabilia (cards, photos, etc).
rec.collecting.sport.football	Football memorabilia (cards, photos, etc).
rec.collecting.sport.hockey	Hockey memorabilia (cards, photos, etc).
rec.collecting.sport.misc	Sports memorabilia not in any other group.
rec.collecting.stamps	Discussion of all things related to philately.
rec.crafts.beads	Making, collecting, and using beads.
rec.crafts.brewing	The art of making beers and meads.
rec.crafts.glass	All aspects of glassworking and glass.
rec.crafts.jewelry	All aspects of jewellery making and lapidary work.
rec.crafts.marketplace	Small-scale ads for craft products of all kinds.
rec.crafts.metalworking	All aspects of working with metal.
rec.crafts.misc	Handiwork arts not covered elsewhere.
rec.crafts.polymer-clay	Techniques and resources relating to polymer clay.
rec.crafts.pottery	The ancient art of making clay pots.
rec.crafts.textiles.misc	Fibre and textile crafts not covered elsewhere.
rec.crafts.textiles.needlework	Any form of decorative stitching done by hand.
rec.crafts.textiles.quilting	All about quilts and other quilted items.
rec.crafts.textiles.sewing	Sewing: clothes, furnishings, costumes, etc.
rec.crafts.textiles.yarn	Yarn making and use: spin, dye, knit, weave etc.
rec.crafts.winemaking	The tasteful art of making wine.
rec.drugs.cannabis	The drug cannabis (marijuana).
rec.drugs.misc	Stimulants, sedatives, smart drugs, etc.
rec.drugs.psychedelic	LSD, Ecstasy, magic mushrooms and the like.
rec.equestrian	Discussion of things equestrian.
rec.folk-dancing	Folk dances, dancers, and dancing.
rec.food.chocolate	Chocolate.
rec.food.cooking	Food, cooking, cookbooks, and recipes.
rec.food.drink	Wines and spirits.
rec.food.drink.beer	All things beer.
rec.food.drink.coffee	The making and drinking of coffee.
rec.food.drink.tea	Tea as beverage and culture.
rec.food.historic	The history of food making arts.
rec.food.preserving	Preserving foodstuffs, herbs, and medicinals.
rec.food.recipes	Recipes for interesting food and drink. M
rec.food.restaurants	Discussion of dining out.
rec.food.sourdough	Making and baking with sourdough.
rec.food.veg	Vegetarians.
rec.food.veg.cooking	Vegetarian recipes, cooking, nutrition. M

rec.gambling.blackjack	Analysis of and strategy for blackjack, aka 21.
rec.gambling.craps	Analysis of and strategy for the dice game craps.
rec.gambling.lottery	Strategy and news of lotteries and sweepstakes.
rec.gambling.misc	All other gambling topics including travel.
rec.gambling.other-games	Gambling games not covered elsewhere.
rec.gambling.poker	Analysis and strategy of live poker games.
rec.gambling.racing	Wagering on animal races.
rec.gambling.sports	Wagering on human sporting events.
rec.games.abstract	Perfect information, pure strategy games.
rec.games.backgammon	Discussion of the game of backgammon.
rec.games.board	Discussion and hints on board games.
rec.games.board.ce	The Cosmic Encounter board game.
rec.games.board.marketplace	Trading and selling of board games.
rec.games.bolo	The networked strategy war game Bolo.
rec.games.bridge	Hobbyists interested in bridge.
rec.games.chess.analysis	Analysis of openings/middlegames/endgames.
rec.games.chess.computer	Reports on game servers, databases, software.
rec.games.chess.misc	Forum for news/discussion related to chess.
rec.games.chess.play-by-email	Reports/discussions regarding e-mail chess.
rec.games.chess.politics	News of nat'l/international chess organizations.
rec.games.chinese-chess	Discussion of the game of Chinese chess, Xiangqi.
rec.games.computer.doom.announce	Info/FAQs/reviews about DOOM. M
rec.games.computer.doom.editing	Editing and hacking DOOM-related files.
rec.games.computer.doom.help	DOOM Help Service (new players welcome).
rec.games.computer.doom.misc	Talking about DOOM and ID Software.
rec.games.computer.doom.playing	Playing DOOM and user-created levels.
rec.games.computer.puzzle	Puzzle-solving computer games.
rec.games.computer.xpilot	About the X11 game XPilot.
rec.games.corewar	The Core War computer challenge.
rec.games.design	Discussion of game design related issues.
rec.games.diplomacy	The conquest game Diplomacy.
rec.games.empire	Discussion and hints about Empire.
rec.games.frp.advocacy	Flames and rebuttals about various role-playing systems.
rec.games.frp.announce	Announcements of happenings in the role-playing world. M
rec.games.frp.archives	Archivable fantasy stories and other projects. M
rec.games.frp.cyber	Discussions of cyberpunk related roleplaying games.
rec.games.frp.dnd	Fantasy role-playing with TSR's Dungeons and Dragons.
rec.games.frp.gurps	The GURPS role playing game.
rec.games.frp.live-action	Live-action role playing games.
rec.games.frp.marketplace	Role-playing game materials wanted and for sale.
rec.games.frp.misc	General discussions of role-playing games.
rec.games.frp.storyteller	World of Darkness and StoryTeller games.
rec.games.go	Discussion about Go.
rec.games.int-fiction	All aspects of interactive fiction games.
rec.games.mecha	Giant robot games.
rec.games.miniatures.historical	Historical and modern tabletop wargaming.
rec.games.miniatures.misc	Miniatures and various tabletop wargames.
rec.games.miniatures.warhammer	Wargaming in the Warhammer Universe.
rec.games.misc	Games and computer games.
rec.games.mud.admin	Administrative issues of multiuser dungeons.
rec.games.mud.announce	Informational articles about multiuser dungeons. M
rec.games.mud.diku	All about DikuMuds.

rec.games.mud.lp	Discussions of the LPMUD computer role playing game.
rec.games.mud.misc	Various aspects of multiuser computer games.
rec.games.mud.tiny	Discussion about Tiny Muds, like MUInternet, MUSE and MOO.
rec.games.netrek	Discussion of the X window system game Netrek (XtrekII).
rec.games.pbm	Discussion about Play by Mail games.
rec.games.pinball	Discussing pinball-related issues.
rec.games.playing-cards	Recreational (non-gambling) card playing.
rec.games.programmer	Discussion of adventure game programming.
rec.games.roguelike.angband	The computer game Angband.
rec.games.roguelike.announce	Major info about rogue-styled games. M
rec.games.roguelike.misc	Rogue-style dungeon games without other groups.
rec.games.roguelike.moria	The computer game Moria.
rec.games.roguelike.nethack	The computer game Nethack.
rec.games.roguelike.rogue	The computer game Rogue.
rec.games.trading-cards.announce	Important news about trading card games. M
rec.games.trading-cards.jyhad	Jyhad trading card game discussions.
rec.games.trading-cards.magic.misc	General 'Magic: the Gathering' postings.
rec.games.trading-cards.magic.rules	'Magic: the Gathering' rules Q and A.
rec.games.trading-cards.magic.strategy	'Magic: the Gathering' strategy.
rec.games.trading-cards.marketplace	Sales, auctions, trades of game cards.
rec.games.trading-cards.misc	Other trading card game discussions.
rec.games.trivia	Discussion about trivia.
rec.games.video.3do	Discussion of 3DO video game systems.
rec.games.video.advocacy	Debate on merits of various video game systems.
rec.games.video.arcade	Discussions about coin-operated video games.
rec.games.video.arcade.collecting	Collecting, converting, repairing etc.
rec.games.video.atari	Discussion of Atari's video game systems.
rec.games.video.cd-i	CD-i topics with emphasis on games.
rec.games.video.cd32	Gaming talk, info and help for the Amiga CD32.
rec.games.video.classic	Older home video entertainment systems.
rec.games.video.marketplace	Home video game stuff for sale or trade.
rec.games.video.misc	General discussion about home video games.
rec.games.video.nintendo	All Nintendo video game systems and software.
rec.games.video.sega	All Sega video game systems and software.
rec.games.video.sony	Sony games hardware and software.
rec.games.xtank.play	Strategy and tactics for the distributed game Xtank.
rec.games.xtank.programmer	Coding the Xtank game and its robots.
rec.gardens	Gardening, methods and results.
rec.gardens.orchids	Growing, hybridizing, and general care of orchids.
rec.gardens.roses	Gardening information related to roses.
rec.guns	Discussions about firearms. M
rec.heraldry	Discussion of coats of arms.
rec.humor	Jokes and the like. May be somewhat offensive.
rec.humor.d	Discussions on the content of recent humour articles.
rec.humor.funny	Jokes that are funny (in the moderator's opinion). M
rec.humor.oracle	Sagacious advice from the USENET Oracle. M
rec.humor.oracle.d	Comments about the USENET Oracle's comments.
rec.hunting	Discussions about hunting. M
rec.hunting.dogs	Hunting topics specifically related to using dogs. M

rec.juggling	Juggling techniques, equipment and events.
rec.kites	Talk about kites and kiting.
rec.mag	Magazine summaries, tables of contents, etc.
rec.mag.dargon	DargonZine fantasy fiction emag issues and discussion.
rec.martial-arts	Discussion of the various martial art forms.
rec.misc	General topics about recreational/participant sports.
rec.models.railroad	Model railroads of all scales.
rec.models.rc	Radio-controlled models for hobbyists.
rec.models.rc.air	Radio-controlled air models.
rec.models.rc.land	Radio-controlled land models.
rec.models.rc.misc	Radio-controlled miscellaneous items.
rec.models.rc.water	Radio-controlled water models.
rec.models.rockets	Model rockets for hobbyists.
rec.models.scale	Construction of models.
rec.motorcycles	Motorcycles and related products and laws.
rec.motorcycles.dirt	Riding motorcycles and ATVs off-road.
rec.motorcycles.harley	All aspects of Harley-Davidson motorcycles.
rec.motorcycles.racing	Discussion of all aspects of racing motorcycles.
rec.music.a-cappella	Vocal music without instrumental accompaniment.
rec.music.afro-latin	Music with Afro-Latin, African and Latin influences.
rec.music.ambient	Ambient music and artists.
rec.music.artists.beach-boys	The Beach Boys' music and the effect they've had.
rec.music.artists.bruce-hornsby	The music of Bruce Hornsby.
rec.music.artists.queensryche	The Thinking Mind's Metal Band.
rec.music.artists.springsteen	Forum for fans of Bruce Springsteen's music.
rec.music.beatles	Postings about the Fab Four and their music.
rec.music.bluenote	Discussion of jazz, blues, and related types of music.
rec.music.bluenote.blues	The Blues in all forms and all aspects.
rec.music.cd	CDs – availability and other discussions.
rec.music.celtic	Traditional and modern music with a Celtic flavour.
rec.music.christian	Christian music, both contemporary and traditional.
rec.music.classical	Discussion about classical music.
rec.music.classical.guitar	Classical music performed on guitar.
rec.music.classical.performing	Performing classical (including early) music.
rec.music.classical.recordings	Classical music on CD, vinyl, cassette, etc.
rec.music.collecting.cd	Compact discs of collector value.
rec.music.collecting.misc	Music collecting other than vinyl or CD.
rec.music.collecting.vinyl	Collecting vinyl records.
rec.music.compose	Creating musical and lyrical works.
rec.music.country.old-time	Southern fiddle/banjo music and beyond.
rec.music.country.western	C and W music, performers, performances, etc.
rec.music.dementia	Discussion of comedy and novelty music.
rec.music.dylan	Discussion of Bob's works and music.
rec.music.early	Discussion of pre-classical European music.
rec.music.filipino	All types and forms of Filipino music.
rec.music.folk	Folks discussing folk music of various sorts.
rec.music.funky	Funk, soul, rhythm and blues and related.
rec.music.gaffa	Discussion of Kate Bush and other alternative music. M
rec.music.gdead	A group for (Grateful) Dead-heads.
rec.music.hip-hop	Hip-hop music and culture in general.

rec.music.indian.classical	Hindustani and Carnatic Indian classical music.
rec.music.indian.misc	Discussing Indian music in general.
rec.music.industrial	Discussion of all industrial-related music styles.
rec.music.info	News and announcements on musical topics. M
rec.music.makers	For performers and their discussions.
rec.music.makers.bagpipe	Music and playing of all types of bagpipes.
rec.music.makers.bands	For musicians who play in groups with others.
rec.music.makers.bass	Upright bass and bass guitar techniques and equipment.
rec.music.makers.bowed-strings	Violin family (current and old) performance.
rec.music.makers.builders	Design, building, repair of musical instruments.
rec.music.makers.dulcimer	Dulcimers and related instruments.
rec.music.makers.french-horn	About horn players and playing.
rec.music.makers.guitar	Electric and acoustic guitar techniques and equipment.
rec.music.makers.guitar.acoustic	Discussion of acoustic guitar playing.
rec.music.makers.guitar.tablature	Guitar tablature/chords.
rec.music.makers.marketplace	Buying and selling used music-making equipment.
rec.music.makers.percussion	Drum and other percussion techniques and equipment.
rec.music.makers.piano	Piano music, performing, composing, learning, styles.
rec.music.makers.songwriting	All about songwriting.
rec.music.makers.synth	Synthesizers and computer music.
rec.music.makers.trumpet	The exchange of trumpet related information.
rec.music.marketplace	Records, tapes, and CDs: wanted, for sale, etc.
rec.music.marketplace.cd	Buying and selling collectable compact discs.
rec.music.marketplace.misc	Buying and selling non-vinyl/CD music.
rec.music.marketplace.vinyl	Buying and selling collectable vinyl records.
rec.music.misc	Music lovers' group.
rec.music.movies	Music for movies and television.
rec.music.newage	'New Age' music discussions.
rec.music.opera	All aspects of opera.
rec.music.phish	Discussing the musical group Phish.
rec.music.progressive	Symphonic rock, art rock, fusion, Canterbury, RIO, etc.
rec.music.promotional	Information and promo materials from record companies. M
rec.music.ragtime	Ragtime and related music styles.
rec.music.reggae	Roots, Rockers, Dancehall Reggae.
rec.music.rem	The musical group REM.
rec.music.reviews	Reviews of music of all genres and mediums. M
rec.music.tori-amos	Discussion of the female singer/songwriter Tori Amos.
rec.music.video	Discussion of music videos and music video software.
rec.nude	Hobbyists interested in naturist/nudist activities.
rec.org.mensa	Talking with members of the high IQ society Mensa.
rec.org.sca	Society for Creative Anachronism.
rec.outdoors.fishing	All aspects of sport and commercial fishing.
rec.outdoors.fishing.fly	Fly fishing in general.
rec.outdoors.fishing.saltwater	Saltwater fishing, methods, gear, Q and A.
rec.outdoors.national-parks	Activities and politics in national parks.
rec.outdoors.rv-travel	Discussions related to recreational vehicles.
rec.parks.theme	Entertainment theme parks.
rec.pets	Pets, pet care, and household animals in general.
rec.pets.birds	The culture and care of indoor birds.

rec.pets.cats	Discussion about domestic cats.
rec.pets.dogs.activities	Dog events: showing, obedience, agility, etc.
rec.pets.dogs.behavior	Behaviours and problems: housetraining, chewing, etc.
rec.pets.dogs.breeds	Breed specific – breed traits, finding breeders, etc.
rec.pets.dogs.health	Info about health problems and how to care for dogs.
rec.pets.dogs.info	General information and FAQs posted here. M
rec.pets.dogs.misc	All other topics, chat, humour, etc.
rec.pets.dogs.rescue	Information about breed rescue, placing and adopting.
rec.pets.herp	Reptiles, amphibians and other exotic vivarium pets.
rec.photo.advanced	Advanced topics (equipment and technique).
rec.photo.darkroom	Developing, printing and other darkroom issues.
rec.photo.help	Beginners' questions about photography (and answers).
rec.photo.marketplace	Trading of personal photographic equipment.
rec.photo.misc	General issues related to photography.
rec.photo.moderated	The art and science of photography. M
rec.ponds	Pond issues: plants, fish, design, maintenance.
rec.puzzles	Puzzles, problems, and quizzes.
rec.puzzles.crosswords	Making and playing gridded word puzzles.
rec.pyrotechnics	Fireworks, rocketry, safety, and other topics.
rec.radio.amateur.antenna	Antennas: theory, techniques and construction.
rec.radio.amateur.digital.misc	Packet radio and other digital radio modes.
rec.radio.amateur.equipment	All about production amateur radio hardware.
rec.radio.amateur.homebrew	Amateur radio construction and experimentation.
rec.radio.amateur.misc	Amateur radio practices, contests, events, rules, etc.
rec.radio.amateur.policy	Radio use and regulation policy.
rec.radio.amateur.space	Amateur radio transmissions through space.
rec.radio.broadcasting	Discussion of global domestic broadcast radio. M
rec.radio.cb	Citizen-band radio.
rec.radio.info	Informational postings related to radio. M
rec.radio.noncomm	Topics relating to noncommercial radio.
rec.radio.scanner	'Utility' broadcasting traffic above 30 MHz.
rec.radio.shortwave	Shortwave radio enthusiasts.
rec.radio.swap	Offers to trade and swap radio equipment.
rec.roller-coaster	Roller coasters and other amusement park rides.
rec.running	Running for enjoyment, sport, exercise, etc.
rec.scouting	Scouting youth organizations worldwide.
rec.scuba	Hobbyists interested in SCUBA diving.
rec.skiing.alpine	Downhill skiing technique, equipment, etc.
rec.skiing.announce	FAQ, competition results, automated snow reports. M
rec.skiing.backcountry	Backcountry skiing.
rec.skiing.marketplace	Items for sale/wanted.
rec.skiing.nordic	Cross-country skiing technique, equipment, etc.
rec.skiing.resorts.europe	Skiing in Europe.
rec.skiing.resorts.misc	Skiing in other than Europe and North America.
rec.skiing.resorts.north-america	Skiing in North America.
rec.skiing.snowboard	Snowboarding technique, equipment, etc.
rec.skydiving	Hobbyists interested in skydiving.
rec.sport.archery	All aspects of archery for archers of any skill level.
rec.sport.baseball	Discussion about baseball.
rec.sport.baseball.analysis	Analysis and discussion of baseball. M

rec.sport.baseball.college	Baseball on the collegiate level.
rec.sport.baseball.data	Raw baseball data (stats, birthdays, scheds).
rec.sport.baseball.fantasy	Rotisserie (fantasy) baseball play.
rec.sport.basketball.college	Hoops on the collegiate level.
rec.sport.basketball.europe	A European basketball forum.
rec.sport.basketball.misc	Discussion about basketball.
rec.sport.basketball.pro	Talk of professional basketball.
rec.sport.basketball.women	Women's basketball at all levels.
rec.sport.billiard	Billiard sports, including pool, snooker, carom games.
rec.sport.boxing	Boxing in all its pugilistic facets and forms.
rec.sport.cricket	Discussion about the sport of cricket.
rec.sport.cricket.info	News, scores and info related to cricket. M
rec.sport.disc	Discussion of flying disc based sports.
rec.sport.fencing	All aspects of swordplay.
rec.sport.football.australian	Discussion of Australian rules football.
rec.sport.football.canadian	All about Canadian rules football.
rec.sport.football.college	US-style college football.
rec.sport.football.fantasy	Rotisserie (fantasy) football play.
rec.sport.football.misc	Discussion about American-style football.
rec.sport.football.pro	US-style professional football.
rec.sport.golf	Discussion about all aspects of golfing.
rec.sport.hockey	Discussion about ice hockey.
rec.sport.hockey.field	Discussion of the sport of field hockey.
rec.sport.misc	Spectator sports.
rec.sport.olympics	All aspects of the Olympic Games.
rec.sport.orienteering	All matters related to the sport of orienteering.
rec.sport.paintball	Discussing all aspects of the survival game paintball.
rec.sport.pro-wrestling	Discussion about professional wrestling.
rec.sport.pro-wrestling.fantasy	Rotisserie league professional wrestling.
rec.sport.rowing	Crew for competition or fitness.
rec.sport.rugby	Discussion about the game of rugby.
rec.sport.rugby.league	Everything related to playing/supporting Rugby League.
rec.sport.rugby.union	Everything related to playing/supporting Rugby Union.
rec.sport.skating.ice.figure	Figure/artistic skating.
rec.sport.skating.ice.recreational	Recreational ice skating.
rec.sport.skating.inline	Inline skating, aka rollerblading.
rec.sport.skating.misc	Miscellaneous skating topics.
rec.sport.skating.racing	Racing and speed skating.
rec.sport.skating.roller	Conventional (quad) roller skating.
rec.sport.soccer	Discussion about soccer (Association Football).
rec.sport.squash	Forum for all aspects of squash.
rec.sport.swimming	Training for and competing in swimming events.
rec.sport.table-soccer	Table-soccer of all types: football and Subbuteo.
rec.sport.table-tennis	Things related to table tennis (aka ping pong).
rec.sport.tennis	Things related to the sport of tennis.
rec.sport.triathlon	Discussing all aspects of multi-event sports.
rec.sport.unicycling	All sorts of fun on one wheel.
rec.sport.volleyball	Discussion about volleyball.
rec.sport.water-polo	Discussion of water polo.
rec.sport.waterski	Waterskiing and other boat-towed activities.
rec.toys.cars	Toy car collecting.
rec.toys.lego	Discussion of Lego, Duplo (and compatible) toys.
rec.toys.misc	Discussion of toys that lack a specific news group.
rec.travel.air	Airline travel around the world.

rec.travel.asia	Travel in Asia.
rec.travel.cruises	Travel by cruise ship.
rec.travel.europe	Travel in Europe.
rec.travel.latin-america	Travel in Caribbean, Central and South America.
rec.travel.marketplace	Tickets and accommodations wanted and for sale.
rec.travel.misc	Everything and anything about travel.
rec.travel.usa-canada	Travel in the United States and Canada.
rec.video	Video and video components.
rec.video.cable-tv	Technical and regulatory issues of cable television.
rec.video.desktop	Amateur, computer-based video editing and production.
rec.video.production	Making professional quality video productions.
rec.video.professional	Professional video, technical and artistic. M
rec.video.releases	Pre-recorded video releases on laserdisc and videotape.
rec.video.satellite.dbs	DBS systems and technologies.
rec.video.satellite.europe	European satellite broadcasting.
rec.video.satellite.misc	Non-TVRO and non-DBS satellite information.
rec.video.satellite.tvro	'Large Dish' ('BUD') systems and technologies.
rec.windsurfing	Riding the waves as a hobby.
rec.woodworking	Hobbyists interested in woodworking.
sci.aeronautics	The science of aeronautics and related technology.
sci.aeronautics.airliners	Airliner technology. M
sci.aeronautics.simulation	Aerospace simulation technology. M
sci.agriculture	Farming, agriculture and related topics.
sci.agriculture.beekeeping	Beekeeping, bee-culture and hive products.
sci.answers	Repository for periodic USENET articles. M
sci.anthropology	All aspects of studying humankind.
sci.anthropology.paleo	Evolution of man and other primates.
sci.aquaria	Only scientifically-oriented postings about aquaria.
sci.archaeology	Studying antiquities of the world.
sci.archaeology.mesoamerican	The field of mesoamerican archaeology.
sci.astro	Astronomy discussions and information.
sci.astro.amateur	Amateur astronomy equipment, techniques, info, etc.
sci.astro.fits	Issues related to the Flexible Image Transport System.
sci.astro.hubble	Processing Hubble Space Telescope data. M
sci.astro.planetarium	Discussion of planetariums.
sci.astro.research	Forum in astronomy/astrophysics research. M
sci.bio.botany	The scientific study of plants.
sci.bio.conservation	Conservation biology research. M
sci.bio.ecology	Ecological research.
sci.bio.entomology.lepidoptera	Lepidoptera: butterflies and moths.
sci.bio.entomology.misc	General insect study and related issues.
sci.bio.ethology	Animal behaviour and behavioural ecology.
sci.bio.evolution	Discussions of evolutionary biology. M
sci.bio.fisheries	All aspects of fisheries science and fish biology.
sci.bio.food-science	Topics related to food science and technology.
sci.bio.herp	Biology of amphibians and reptiles.
sci.bio.microbiology	Protists, fungi, algae, other microscopic organisms.
sci.bio.misc	Biology and related sciences.
sci.bio.paleontology	Life of the past (but no creation vs evolution!).
sci.bio.phytopathology	All aspects of plant diseases and pests. M

sci.bio.systematics	Systematics, taxonomy, and the tree of life.
sci.chem	Chemistry and related sciences.
sci.chem.analytical	Analytical chemistry.
sci.chem.electrochem	The field of electrochemistry.
sci.chem.labware	Chemical laboratory equipment.
sci.chem.organomet	Organometallic chemistry.
sci.classics	Studying classical history, languages, art and more.
sci.cognitive	Perception, memory, judgement and reasoning.
sci.comp-aided	The use of computers as tools in scientific research.
sci.cryonics	Theory and practice of biostasis, suspended animation.
sci.crypt	Different methods of data en/decryption.
sci.crypt.research	Cryptography, cryptanalysis, and related issues. M
sci.data.formats	Modelling, storage and retrieval of scientific data.
sci.econ	The science of economics.
sci.econ.research	Research in all fields of economics. M
sci.edu	The science of education.
sci.electronics	Circuits, theory, electrons and discussions.
sci.electronics.cad	Schematic drafting, printed circuit layout, simulation.
sci.electronics.repair	Fixing electronic equipment.
sci.energy	Discussions about energy, science and technology.
sci.energy.hydrogen	All about hydrogen as an alternative fuel.
sci.engr	Technical discussions about engineering tasks.
sci.engr.biomed	Discussing the field of biomedical engineering.
sci.engr.chem	All aspects of chemical engineering.
sci.engr.civil	Topics related to civil engineering.
sci.engr.control	The engineering of control systems.
sci.engr.geomechanics	Geomechanics issues and related topics.
sci.engr.heat-vent-ac	Heating, ventilating, air conditioning and refrigeration.
sci.engr.lighting	Light, vision and colour in architecture, media, etc.
sci.engr.manufacturing	Manufacturing technology.
sci.engr.marine.hydrodynamics	Marine hydrodynamics.
sci.engr.mech	The field of mechanical engineering.
sci.engr.metallurgy	Metallurgical engineering.
sci.engr.safety	All aspects of the safety of engineered systems.
sci.engr.semiconductors	Semiconductor devices, processes, materials, physics.
sci.engr.surveying	Measurement and mapping of the earth's surface.
sci.engr.television.advanced	HDTV/DATV standards, equipment, practices, etc.
sci.engr.television.broadcast	Broadcast facility equipment and practices.
sci.environment	Discussions about the environment and ecology.
sci.fractals	Objects of non-integral dimension and other chaos.
sci.geo.earthquakes	For discussion of earthquakes and related matters.
sci.geo.eos	NASA's Earth Observation System (EOS).
sci.geo.fluids	Discussion of geophysical fluid dynamics.
sci.geo.geology	Discussion of solid earth sciences.
sci.geo.hydrology	Surface and groundwater hydrology.

sci.geo.meteorology	Discussion of meteorology and related topics.
sci.geo.oceanography	Oceanography, oceanology and marine science.
sci.geo.petroleum	All aspects of petroleum and the petroleum industry.
sci.geo.satellite-nav	Satellite navigation systems, especially GPS.
sci.image.processing	Scientific image processing and analysis.
sci.lang	Natural languages, communication, etc.
sci.lang.japan	The Japanese language, both spoken and written.
sci.lang.translation	Problems and concerns of translators/interpreters.
sci.life-extension	Slowing, stopping or reversing the ageing process.
sci.logic	Logic – math, philosophy and computational aspects.
sci.materials	All aspects of materials engineering.
sci.materials.ceramics	Ceramic science.
sci.math	Mathematical discussions and pursuits.
sci.math.research	Discussion of current mathematical research. M
sci.math.symbolic	Symbolic algebra discussion.
sci.mech.fluids	All aspects of fluid mechanics.
sci.med	Medicine and its related products and regulations.
sci.med.aids	AIDS: treatment, pathology/biology of HIV, prevention. M
sci.med.cardiology	All aspects of cardiovascular diseases.
sci.med.dentistry	Dentally related topics; all about teeth.
sci.med.diseases.cancer	Diagnosis, treatment, and prevention of cancer.
sci.med.diseases.hepatitis	Hepatitis diseases.
sci.med.diseases.lyme	Lyme Disease: patient support, research and information.
sci.med.immunology	Medical/scientific aspects of immune illness.
sci.med.informatics	Computer applications in medical care.
sci.med.nursing	Nursing questions and discussion.
sci.med.nutrition	Physiological impacts of diet.
sci.med.occupational	Repetitive Strain Injuries (RSI) and job injury issues.
sci.med.orthopedics	Orthopedic Surgery, related issues and management. M
sci.med.pathology	Pathology and laboratory medicine.
sci.med.pharmacy	The teaching and practice of pharmacy.
sci.med.physics	Issues of physics in medical testing/care.
sci.med.psychobiology	Dialog and news in psychiatry and psychobiology.
sci.med.radiology	All aspects of radiology.
sci.med.telemedicine	Hospital/physician networks. No diagnosis questions.
sci.med.transcription	Information for and about medical transcriptionists.
sci.med.vision	Human vision, visual correction, and visual science.
sci.military.moderated	Military technology. M
sci.military.naval	Navies of the world, past, present and future.
sci.misc	Short-lived discussions on subjects in the sciences.
sci.nanotech	Self-reproducing molecular-scale machines. M
sci.nonlinear	Chaotic systems and other nonlinear scientific study.
sci.op-research	Research, teaching and application of operations research.
sci.optics	Discussion relating to the science of optics.

sci.philosophy.tech	Technical philosophy: math, science, logic, etc.
sci.physics	Physical laws, properties, etc.
sci.physics.accelerators	Particle accelerators and the physics of beams.
sci.physics.computational.fluid-dynamics	Computational fluid dynamics.
sci.physics.cond-matter	Condensed matter physics, theory and experiment.
sci.physics.electromag	Electromagnetic theory and applications.
sci.physics.fusion	Info on fusion, esp. 'cold' fusion.
sci.physics.particle	Particle physics discussions.
sci.physics.plasma	Plasma Science and Technology community exchange. M
sci.physics.research	Current physics research. M
sci.polymers	All aspects of polymer science.
sci.psychology.announce	Psychology-related announcements. M
sci.psychology.consciousness	On the nature of consciousness. M
sci.psychology.journals.psyche	E-journal on consciousness. M
sci.psychology.journals.psycoloquy	E-journal on psychology. M
sci.psychology.misc	General discussion of psychology.
sci.psychology.personality	All personality systems and measurement.
sci.psychology.psychotherapy	Practice of psychotherapy.
sci.psychology.research	Research issues in psychology. M
sci.psychology.theory	Theories of psychology and behaviour.
sci.research	Research methods, funding, ethics, and whatever.
sci.research.careers	Issues relevant to careers in scientific research.
sci.research.postdoc	Anything about postdoctoral studies, including offers.
sci.skeptic	Sceptics discussing pseudo-science.
sci.space.news	Announcements of space-related news items. M
sci.space.policy	Discussions about space policy.
sci.space.science	Space and planetary science and related technical work. M
sci.space.shuttle	The space shuttle and the STS programme.
sci.space.tech	Technical and general issues related to space flight. M
sci.stat.consult	Statistical consulting.
sci.stat.edu	Statistics education.
sci.stat.math	Statistics from a strictly mathematical viewpoint.
sci.systems	The theory and application of systems science.
sci.techniques.mag-resonance	Magnetic resonance imaging and spectroscopy.
sci.techniques.mass-spec	All areas of mass spectrometry. M
sci.techniques.microscopy	The field of microscopy.
sci.techniques.spectroscopy	Spectrum analysis.
sci.techniques.testing.misc	General testing techniques in science.
sci.techniques.testing.nondestructive	Nondestructive tests in science.
sci.techniques.xtallography	The field of crystallography.
sci.virtual-worlds	Virtual reality – technology and culture. M
sci.virtual-worlds.apps	Current and future uses of virtual-worlds technology. M
soc.answers	Repository for periodic USENET articles. M
soc.bi	Discussions of bisexuality.
soc.college	College, college activities, campus life, etc.
soc.college.admissions	The university admissions process.
soc.college.financial-aid	Financial aid issues, college and beyond.
soc.college.grad	General issues related to graduate schools.
soc.college.gradinfo	Information about graduate schools.
soc.college.org.aiesec	The Int'l Assoc. of Business and Commerce Students.

soc.college.teaching-asst	Issues affecting collegiate teaching assistants.
soc.couples	Discussions for couples (cf. soc.singles).
soc.couples.intercultural	Inter-cultural and inter-racial relationships.
soc.couples.wedding	Wedding planning.
soc.culture.afghanistan	Discussion of Afghan society.
soc.culture.african	Discussions about Africa and things African.
soc.culture.african.american	Discussions about Afro-American issues.
soc.culture.albanian	Albania and Albanians around the world.
soc.culture.algeria	From A to Z about Algeria.
soc.culture.arabic	Technological and cultural issues, not politics.
soc.culture.argentina	All about life in Argentina.
soc.culture.asean	Countries of the Assoc. of SE Asian Nations.
soc.culture.asian.american	Issues and discussion about Asian-Americans.
soc.culture.assyrian	Assyrian culture, history, language, current diaspora.
soc.culture.australian	Australian culture and society.
soc.culture.austria	Austria and its people.
soc.culture.baltics	People of the Baltic states.
soc.culture.bangladesh	Issues and discussion about Bangladesh.
soc.culture.belgium	Belgian society, culture(s) and people.
soc.culture.bengali	Sociocultural identity of worldwide Bengali population.
soc.culture.berber	The Berber language, history, and culture.
soc.culture.bolivia	Bolivian people and culture.
soc.culture.bosna-herzgvna	The independent state of Bosnia and Herzegovina.
soc.culture.brazil	Talking about the people and country of Brazil.
soc.culture.british	Issues about Britain and those of British descent.
soc.culture.bulgaria	Discussing Bulgarian society.
soc.culture.burma	Politics, culture, news, discussion about Burma.
soc.culture.cambodia	Cambodia and its people.
soc.culture.canada	Discussions of Canada and its people.
soc.culture.caribbean	Life in the Caribbean.
soc.culture.celtic	Irish, Scottish, Breton, Cornish, Manx and Welsh.
soc.culture.chile	All about Chile and its people.
soc.culture.china	About China and Chinese culture.
soc.culture.colombia	Colombian talk, social, politics, science.
soc.culture.croatia	The lives of people of Croatia.
soc.culture.cuba	Cuban culture, society and politics.
soc.culture.czecho-slovak	Bohemian, Slovak, Moravian and Silesian life.
soc.culture.dominican-rep	The life and people of the Dominican Republic.
soc.culture.ecuador	The culture and people of Ecuador.
soc.culture.egyptian	Egypt, and its society, culture, heritage, etc.
soc.culture.estonia	Estonian culture, language, news, politics. M
soc.culture.europe	Discussing all aspects of all-European society.
soc.culture.filipino	Group about the Filipino culture.
soc.culture.french	French culture, history, and related discussions.
soc.culture.german	Discussions about German culture and history.
soc.culture.greek	Group about Greeks.
soc.culture.haiti	Haiti specific development and cultural issues.
soc.culture.hongkong	Discussions pertaining to Hong Kong.
soc.culture.hongkong.entertainment	Entertainment in Hong Kong.
soc.culture.indian	Group for discussion about India and things Indian.
soc.culture.indian.delhi	Information related to Delhi, capital of India.
soc.culture.indian.info	Info group for soc.culture.indian, etc. M
soc.culture.indian.kerala	Culture of the people of Keralite origin.
soc.culture.indian.marathi	Discussion related to Marathi Culture.
soc.culture.indian.telugu	The culture of the Telugu people of India.

soc.culture.indonesia	All about the Indonesian nation.
soc.culture.iranian	Discussions about Iran and things Iranian/Persian.
soc.culture.iraq	Iraq, its society, culture and heritage.
soc.culture.irish	Ireland and Irish culture.
soc.culture.israel	Israel and Israelis.
soc.culture.italian	The Italian people and their culture.
soc.culture.japan	Everything Japanese, except the Japanese language.
soc.culture.jewish	Jewish culture and religion (cf. talk.politics.mideast).
soc.culture.jewish.holocaust	The Shoah. M
soc.culture.jordan	All topics concerning The Hashemite Kingdom of Jordan.
soc.culture.korean	Discussions about Korea and things Korean.
soc.culture.kurdish	People from Kurdistan and Kurds around the world.
soc.culture.kuwait	Kuwaiti culture, society, and history.
soc.culture.laos	Cultural and social aspects of Laos.
soc.culture.latin-america	Topics about Latin-America.
soc.culture.lebanon	Discussion about things Lebanese.
soc.culture.maghreb	North African society and culture.
soc.culture.magyar	The Hungarian people and their culture.
soc.culture.malagasy	Madagascar and the Malagasy culture.
soc.culture.malaysia	All about Malaysian society.
soc.culture.mexican	Discussion of Mexico's society.
soc.culture.mexican.american	Mexican-American/Chicano culture and issues.
soc.culture.misc	Group for discussion about other cultures.
soc.culture.mongolian	Everything related to Mongols and Mongolia.
soc.culture.native	Aboriginal people around the world.
soc.culture.nepal	Discussion of people and things in and from Nepal.
soc.culture.netherlands	People from the Netherlands and Belgium.
soc.culture.new-zealand	Discussion of topics related to New Zealand.
soc.culture.nigeria	Nigerian affairs, society, cultures, and peoples.
soc.culture.nordic	Discussion about culture up north.
soc.culture.pakistan	Topics of discussion about Pakistan.
soc.culture.palestine	Palestinian people, culture and politics.
soc.culture.peru	All about the people of Peru.
soc.culture.polish	Polish culture, Polish past, and Polish politics.
soc.culture.portuguese	Discussion of the people of Portugal.
soc.culture.puerto-rico	Puerto Rican culture, society and politics.
soc.culture.punjab	Punjab and Punjabi culture.
soc.culture.quebec	Quebec society and culture.
soc.culture.romanian	Discussion of Romanian and Moldavian people.
soc.culture.russian	All things Russian in the broadest sense.
soc.culture.scientists	Cultural issues about scientists and scientific projects.
soc.culture.scottish	Anything regarding Scotland or things Scots.
soc.culture.sierra-leone	The culture of Sierra Leone.
soc.culture.singapore	The past, present and future of Singapore.
soc.culture.slovenia	Slovenia and Slovenian people.
soc.culture.somalia	Somalian affairs, society, and culture.
soc.culture.south-africa	South African society, culture, and politics.
soc.culture.soviet	Topics relating to Russian or Soviet culture.
soc.culture.spain	Spain and the Spanish.
soc.culture.sri-lanka	Things and people from Sri Lanka.
soc.culture.swiss	Swiss culture.
soc.culture.syria	Syrian cultural matters and affairs.

soc.culture.taiwan	Discussion about things Taiwanese.
soc.culture.tamil	Tamil language, history and culture.
soc.culture.thai	Thai people and their culture.
soc.culture.turkish	Discussion about things Turkish.
soc.culture.ukrainian	The lives and times of the Ukrainian people.
soc.culture.uruguay	Discussions of Uruguay for those at home and abroad.
soc.culture.usa	The culture of the United States of America.
soc.culture.venezuela	Discussion of topics related to Venezuela.
soc.culture.vietnamese	Issues and discussions of Vietnamese culture.
soc.culture.welsh	The people, language and history of Wales.
soc.culture.yugoslavia	Discussions of Yugoslavia and its people.
soc.culture.zimbabwe	Culture and other issues pertaining to Zimbabwe.
soc.feminism	Discussion of feminism and feminist issues. M
soc.genealogy.australia+nz	Australia, New Zealand, and their territories.
soc.genealogy.benelux	Genealogy in Belgium, the Netherlands and Luxembourg.
soc.genealogy.computing	Genealogical computing and net resources.
soc.genealogy.french	Francophone genealogy.
soc.genealogy.german	Family history including a German background.
soc.genealogy.hispanic	Genealogy relating to Hispanics.
soc.genealogy.jewish	Jewish genealogy group. M
soc.genealogy.marketplace	Genealogy services and products.
soc.genealogy.medieval	Genealogy in the period from roughly AD500 to AD1600.
soc.genealogy.methods	Genealogical methods and resources. M
soc.genealogy.misc	General genealogical discussions.
soc.genealogy.nordic	Genealogy in the Scandinavian countries.
soc.genealogy.surnames	Surname queries and tafels. M
soc.genealogy.uk+ireland	Genealogy of Britain, Ireland and offshore isles.
soc.history	Discussions of things historical.
soc.history.living	Living history and reenactment, issues and info.
soc.history.moderated	All aspects of history. M
soc.history.science	History of science and related areas.
soc.history.war.misc	History and events of wars in general.
soc.history.war.us-civil-war	Aspects of the US Civil War. M
soc.history.war.vietnam	The Vietnam War. M
soc.history.war.world-war-ii	History and events of World War Two. M
soc.history.what-if	Alternate history.
soc.libraries.talk	Discussing all aspects of libraries.
soc.men	Issues related to men, their problems and relationships.
soc.misc	Socially-oriented topics not in other groups.
soc.motss	Issues pertaining to homosexuality.
soc.net-people	Announcements, requests, etc. about people on the net.
soc.org.nonprofit	Nonprofit organizations.
soc.org.service-clubs.misc	General info on all service topics.
soc.penpals	In search of net.friendships.
soc.politics	Political problems, systems, solutions. M
soc.politics.arms-d	Arms discussion digest. M
soc.religion.bahai	Discussion of the Baha'i Faith. M
soc.religion.christian	Christianity and related topics. M
soc.religion.christian.bible-study	Examining the Holy Bible. M
soc.religion.christian.youth-work	Christians working with young people. M
soc.religion.eastern	Discussions of Eastern religions. M
soc.religion.gnosis	Gnosis, marifat, jnana and direct sacred experience. M

soc.religion.hindu	Discussion about the Hindu dharma, philosophy, culture. M
soc.religion.islam	Discussions of the Islamic faith. M
soc.religion.quaker	The Religious Society of Friends.
soc.religion.shamanism	Discussion of the full range of shamanic experience. M
soc.religion.sikhism	Sikh religion and Sikhs all over the world. M
soc.religion.unitarian-univ	Unitarian-Universalism and non-creedal religions.
soc.rights.human	Human rights and activism (e.g. Amnesty International).
soc.singles	News group for single people, their activities, etc.
soc.support.fat-acceptance	Self-acceptance for fat people. No diet talk.
soc.support.transgendered	Transgendered and intersexed persons.
soc.support.youth.gay-lesbian-bi	Gay youths helping each other. M
soc.veterans	Social issues relating to military veterans.
soc.women	Issues related to women, their problems and relationships.
soc.women.lesbian-and-bi	Lives of lesbian and bisexual women. M
talk.abortion	All sorts of discussions and arguments on abortion.
talk.answers	Repository for periodic USENET articles. M
talk.bizarre	The unusual, bizarre, curious, and often interesting.
talk.environment	Discussion the state of the environment and what to do.
talk.euthanasia	All aspects of euthanasia.
talk.origins	Evolution versus creationism (sometimes hot!).
talk.philosophy.humanism	Humanism in the modern world.
talk.philosophy.misc	Philosophical musings on all topics.
talk.politics.animals	The use and/or abuse of animals.
talk.politics.china	Discussion of political issues related to China.
talk.politics.crypto	The relation between cryptography and government.
talk.politics.drugs	The politics of drug issues.
talk.politics.european-union	The EU and political integration in Europe.
talk.politics.guns	The politics of firearm ownership and (mis)use.
talk.politics.libertarian	Libertarian politics and political philosophy.
talk.politics.medicine	The politics and ethics involved with health care.
talk.politics.mideast	Discussion and debate over Middle Eastern events.
talk.politics.misc	Political discussions and ravings of all kinds.
talk.politics.soviet	Discussion of Soviet politics, domestic and foreign.
talk.politics.theory	Theory of politics and political systems.
talk.politics.tibet	The politics of Tibet and the Tibetan people.
talk.rape	Discussions on stopping rape; not to be crossposted.
talk.religion.buddhism	All aspects of Buddhism as religion and philosophy.
talk.religion.misc	Religious, ethical, and moral implications.
talk.religion.newage	Esoteric and minority religions and philosophies.
talk.rumors	For the posting of rumours.

Index